SLOW WINTER

ALEX HICKMAN

Published by TravellersEye Ltd

Slow Winter
1st Edition
Published by TravellersEye
July 2000

Head Office:
60B High Street
Bridgnorth
Shropshire
WV16 4DX
United Kingdom
tel: (0044) 1746 766447
fax: (0044) 1746 766665
email: books@travellerseye.com
website: www.travellerseye.com

Set in Times
ISBN: 0953057585
Copyright 2000 Alex Hickman

Printed and bound in Great Britain by Creative Print & Design.

TO JOHN AND ROGER

ABOUT THE AUTHOR

Alex trained as a management consultant in London. He left the City to work for Student Partnership Worldwide, a youth development charity. Based between Zimbabwe, Tanzania and Uganda he spent his time persuading the private sector to engage in rural development. His experience convinced him that the future of the global economy depends upon its ability to integrate the world's poorest countries.

He is now campaign manager for Business for Sterling, the UK's leading pro-European, anti-euro campaign. While Alex believes that joining the euro would be a disaster for the UK, he also feels that the European Union has a moral obligation to assimilate the new democracies of central and eastern Europe. "The euro looks set to create a rich man's club with stringent entry criteria that developing countries like Albania can never hope to meet."

Business for Sterling is a non-party political campaign which represents the 73% of UK businesses (according to the latest ICM opinion poll) who want Britain to keep the pound. Alex argues that "joining the euro would mean higher taxes, more regulation and the loss of economic control." He also believes that e-commerce and the internet make the euro, and the whole concept of regional currency blocks, irrelevant.

Three boys and a tall man are marching along a moonlit cliff top. Their hair is being tugged by a cool breeze that brings with it the smell of the sea. Torches swing from the boys' hands, skating messages of white light around their feet. Up on the turf path their footsteps thud like rain drops.

In a concrete pill box, hidden among gorse bushes, we strain our eyes out to sea. U-boats have been sighted. There is a danger of enemy landings and the patrol is on red alert. Then we move on. Tom has filled his haversack with fir-cone grenades. James has fitted a bayonet to the end of his rifle. I am out in front, machine gun at the ready.

Just by the old Roman fort we come across a landing party of German marines. James charges their position with a bloodcurdling yell and I pick them off, one-by-one, with the machine gun. The skirmish over, we turn for home across the marshes, towards the lights of the village. Running ahead I tumble into a dyke, face first, falling through the silky bulrushes and into the black water below. The breath has been knocked out of me by the cold water, now I swallow it in salty mouthfuls. Something long and slimy slicks against my thigh. My boots fill up with water. I can't stand - my waterlogged boots weigh me down towards the bottom of the dyke. Choking and clawing at the wet feet of the rushes, I wonder whether I am drowning and begin to scream.

A great force plunges near me in the water, and then a heavy hand hooks under my arm, heaving me so hard that my feet drag out of my boots. Lying on the bank, in a pool of torchlight, I begin to cry.

"It's alright, I'm here," says my father.

Acknowledgements

Many people made this book possible – too many for me to mention them all. But I must name a few whose particular input or intervention has been vital: Xandra Bingley, Jim Cogan, Jessica Douglas-Home, Olivia Fraser, my Grandparents, Dan Hiscocks, Jill Ibberson, Charlotte Metcalfe and Charles Monck.

I must also thank all of those who appear (in some form) in Slow Winter, for providing the friendship, curiosity, tension, hilarity and hardship that made my time in the Balkans so memorable. I have changed their names, because very few of them know about this book's existence, and because what I have written is very much my own tale.

But three people deserve special thanks. Firstly, Susan Inkin, to whom I am already indebted for providing me with a best friend (her son Edmund); and who, in the summer of 1997, let me stay in her beautiful corner of Wales and provided me with the companionship and enthusiasm without which this book would never have got off the ground. And infinitely, my mother and Mark, to whom I owe everything and without whose love, wisdom and care ...

Contents

Glossary

AGO	'Albanian Geographic Outline'. Communist guide book published in Tirana, 1981.
AlbPetrol	State-owned oil company.
AlbTelecom	State-owned telephone utility.
AWP	Albanian Workers Party. State communist party formed by Enver Hoxha after World War II. Disbanded in 1992.
DP	Democratic Party. Established in 1992, it formed Albania's first post-communist government.
EBRD	European Bank of Reconstruction and Development, set up by the European Union to fund the redevelopment of post-communist economies in central and eastern Europe.
Enver Hoxha	As leader of the communist partisans Hoxha led Albanian resistance to occupying Axis forces in World War II. Ruled communist Albania from 1945 to 1985.
Ghegs	Major ethnic group, based in northern Albania.
KESH	State-owned electricity utility.
KLA	Kosovo Liberation Army – guerrilla organisation fighting for Kosovan independence from Serbia.
Leka	Son of Zog I – claimant to Albanian throne.
ODA	Overseas Development Agency – British Government department responsible for implementing aid programme in Sarajevo.
Oslobodjenje	Bosnia's leading newspaper. Published every day of the siege despite being targeted by Serb artillery.
Ratko Mladic	Former officer in Yugoslavian National Army (JNA), military leader of Bosnian Serbs during siege of Sarajevo. Indicted for war crimes.
ShIK	Albanian Intelligence Service – loyal to the President.
Slobodan Milosevic	President of Serbia (1991-). Architect of Yugoslavian conflict.
SP	Socialist Party. Formed in 1992 out of discredited AWP. Major opposition party to DP in 1995.
Tosqs	Largest ethnic group based in southern Albania.
Unprofor	United Nations Protection Force – international military coalition set up to monitor the war in Bosnia, and to protect the rights of the civilian population.
Zog I	King of Albania – 1926 to 1945.

THE BALKANS

There were seven of us, our bodies scattered about the beach like flotsam from last night's storm. Around us lay cricket bats, empty wine bottles, lunch, sandy life jackets and wet towels; a sailing boat rested on its side in the shallow water, its sail drumming softly. A peewit snatched overhead.

Finals were over - a lot was over. We had left Edinburgh. Now we were leaving each other for foreign countries, law school, the lonely avenues of the City. We lay there, seven browning bodies, the salt water drying in our hair. All of us squinting up at the sky and it felt like a homecoming and a departure all at once.

"What about you, Alex? What are you going to do?"

"I'm not sure. I've got this overwhelming urge to run away. I need to have an adventure. I need to decide what happens next."

Running away had been inevitable for most of my life. Ever since my brilliant father died, leaving my mother alone with three boys in a large London house. Throughout my childhood I wanted to be like my father. First of all emulating my father meant becoming a doctor. But I was hopeless at physics and chemistry, so by the age of sixteen medicine was out. Being like my father immediately became more complex, more of a challenge. Instead of following him into his consulting rooms I would have to match him for pace, for success.

And when I looked into the future there was always this great premium on speed, on getting somewhere as quickly as possible. Because I knew that life ended at thirty-eight, I had this chilling, childish logic, that mine would be a short life, colourful and swift, just like my father's. All through university I wondered what on earth I would do at the other end. And when I got there, escape seemed the logical solution. I needed time to resolve everything once and for all, to sort myself out.

As a bloodthirsty schoolboy I had this thing about the Balkans -

they seemed wild, cruel and refreshingly unaccomplished. They made my Europe feel plain and old, distracted by factory disputes and trade agreements. The Balkans had wolves and eagles, we had bird baths... I was thoroughly jealous. While I was at Edinburgh old tempers and hatreds broke out in the Balkans. War and disorder cast a curious spell. In a crude way they reflected my own sense of turmoil. I was drawn to their flame, to their promise of drama and catharsis. Hardship seemed attractive. So, secretly, I began to prepare to go.

A few of us used to visit a seedy casino after the pubs closed. Inside we would order whisky and sandwiches and hold onto the blackjack table, squinting at the cards as the croupier spun them onto the green baize table. There was always a Chinese at the table, his fingers stained yellow with nicotine, and in the corner a group of footballers from Hearts or Hibs, out on the piss in cashmere coats and bouncy gold hair. It was a pretty terrible place and it was always a pleasure to walk away from the mirrors and striped wallpaper and the doormen who hated you for being English *and* a student and out into the fizzy ozone and the night sky paling over Carlton Hill. I won several thousand pounds during those dawn raids. My sock drawer became choked with red Scottish £100 notes. Which was OK because all my socks were on the floor, along with the rest of my clothes. I opened a special bank account and told myself I would spend it on an adventure.

NOVEMBER

Roma and I share a desk in one cold corner of Oslobodjenje's newsroom. Sanda is at university. They are cousins. Their apartment is about twenty minutes walk from Oslobodjenje, along cobbled streets lined with stalls and groups gathered around small fires and people walking fast along the pavement. This is not squalor. Not quite.

Roma and Sanda live high up in a modern towerblock, one of several gathered around a concrete square littered with burnt-out cars and rubble. Most of the block's windows are broken. The others are boarded shut. Where there are not bullet holes, the concrete walls are covered in graffiti - some in Bosnian, some in English. 'There are no devils left in hell. They are all in Bosnia'. 'Fuck Karadzic'. That sort of thing. On the far side of the square one block has been gutted by fire, its shell now black and punched with holes. Nearby stands the ragged Holiday Inn. Four hundred metres away are the Serb lines.

Outside the flat sleeps an old drunk. The front door is reinforced with planks of wood, its sheet of reinforced glass shattered milky grey. Inside it is snug and well furnished and I could be anywhere. Tonight Roma is cooking. He is tall and thin, he looks sick. We eat fried potatoes and cabbage and talk about university and the war. Afterwards I go to bed, high up in the damaged old tower. Outside the night is busy - machine gun fire crackles across the valley and there is the odd whump of artillery. I lie there listening to the guns. They seem harmless and oddly comforting, like the background ticking of a clock.

SATURDAY 8TH NOVEMBER
R & R

Sarajevo's main street is rutted with an old tram-line, smooth and still shiny even though the trams were stopped some time ago. They used to run down the main road by the river, but they were easy targets for the snipers. Across the street is a market. Stalls sell vegetables, Bosnian cigarettes, cooking oil and sheep brains split and sealed like half a cabbage. They are set out under blue plastic tarpaulins.

It begins to rain, quite hard, the clouds tipping their spare water onto this sad city. Some of the tarpaulins are bulging with rain. Others are running small streams onto the ground. The ground is concrete and pitted. This is where a mortar fell last February, looping over Oslobodjenje's office building and thumping down among the stalls. The market was busy, there were plenty of people about. Sixty-nine died and the shrapnel that splashed about this small market square, cutting them down, has left its scars on the ground. The locals call the scars 'Sarajevo roses'.

Following the tram lines I walk down the high street, past the Roman Catholic church. There is some fine (though filthy) old Austro-Hungarian architecture here, much chipped and chocolate brown, and the street is broad and a little ponderous, like a rich old man. Most of the shops are boarded up, there is little life except for the pedestrians and they aren't stopping. But there is a bookshop open, and a single old lady behind a tall counter. There is a great deal of dust and a few piles of silly old books on Soviet armaments and lives of Yugoslav politicians - books from the past. Yugoslavia doesn't exist anymore and nor does the Soviet Union. Armaments, however, and politicians endure.

It is dark. Sanda, Roma and I eat some of the soup I have brought with me from Venice. Afterwards we walk into the centre of town. She wants to show me Sarajevo's night-life. In front of the mayor's office, where there is a small park and trees, we meet up with two of their friends. Mata is twenty-two, a wan philosophy student, her round face quite white, her lips and eyes quite black with make-up. She is a ghoulish sight. Jim is her boyfriend, with a beard and a sailor's cap on his head. He is a brilliant physicist. Both are dressed in grunge-dark colours. They are an angry, cynical pair. Uncomfortable to be with.

Sitting among the trees we pass around an acid bottle of brandy and get drunk. There is little talk - this is escape, not entertainment. When the brandy is finished we walk towards a club off the main road. There are quite a few people about, it is two hours before the curfew. The club's front door is protected by the wreckage of an old bus. The Serb lines are across the river, a couple of hundred yards away.

"It is safe when it's dark" explains Sanda and we walk quickly through the door. Downstairs a band is playing thrash metal, very loud. The atmosphere is tense. As if everyone in there just wanted the chance to land a punch, or kick someone. Everyone looks very young and very drunk. We sit in a corner, drinking beer and shouting at one another.

A friend of Sanda's walks over. He is my age, pasty and so drunk he can't speak. He lunges at Sanda and puts his arm around her. He has big hands, there is dirt under the finger nails. Mata tells me that he has been in a trench for a week. Now he has two days leave and he can lose himself in this cellar. Three years ago, Sanda and he were in the same class. Now he is a drunk soldier. When he tries to kiss Sanda she slaps him and he falls to the ground. Sanda bends to help him up and they hug each other, swaying a little, both crying.

MONDAY 20TH NOVEMBER
SANDA

Sanda and I walk into the centre of town. I have discarded my bulletproof vest, none of the locals have one. It is just before eight, the late autumn air smokes our breath. Sanda wears gloves and carries an umbrella. She tells me that Roma is sick, she's worried he's got hepatitis. A JCB, watched by French soldiers, is pushing a container across a street which runs down towards the Serb lines, giving their snipers a clear line of fire at pedestrians like us. There was shooting earlier this morning. An old man was hit. Sarajevo's cease-fire is coming apart.

Wherever the Serbs have a clear line of fire, people are running. We do the same, sprinting across the mouths of streets and along an exposed stretch of road. It is an odd feeling. I wonder if there is an etiquette to this sort of thing, positioning myself on her Serb-side as she runs beside me. I don't for a moment expect to be hit but then I've never done it before. I wonder when you begin to fancy your luck might run out? After two months, four, six?

In the centre we stand staring at each other, a little out of breath. She has brown eyes and freckles on her neck.

"Goodbye Alexi" she says, touching my hand, "be careful" and walks off up the hill to meet a friend.

TUESDAY 21ˢᵀ NOVEMBER
THE AMBASSADOR

The Holiday Inn, yolk yellow, has taken one hell of a battering. Most of its windows have been smashed, the upper floors are bombed out. Inside the lobby a few lights are running off a loud generator. Tables and chairs are spread about, much like any other hotel. A waiter approaches and sells me a beer out of a cardboard box. I read a book.

In one gloomy corner I find the loos. They are in a state of disarray. I cannot turn off the taps in the basin. The plug-hole is blocked and water begins to run over the basin and splatter onto the floor. I try to unplug the hole. I try to turn off the taps. But they won't budge and I give the thing up for a bad job and walk back into the lobby. The British Ambassador is waiting for me. He is a kind-looking man, in his late thirties, in an open-necked shirt and glasses. I have a letter of introduction from a friend who works in the Foreign Office. He reads it, sitting down in the gloom.

"How the hell did you get here?" he asks, putting the letter in his pocket.

"I flew in last week, with the Luftwaffe. I'm working as a sub-editor at Oslobodjenje."

"Sarajevo's best selling daily, eh! What persuaded them to give you a job?"

"I'm on loan from the Kent Messenger," I explain. "I'm their foreign correspondent."

"The Kent what?"

"Messenger... here's my letter of accreditation." I hand him a scruffy piece of paper.

To whom it may concern: The bearer of this letter requires UN accreditation to fulfil his activities as a correspondent for this newspaper in Sarajevo. The Kent Messenger has carried a story about his plans to work in Yugoslavia and he will be submitting regular reports to us on his progress and experiences.

Editor, Kent Messenger

The Ambassador is shaking his head. "And where on earth are you living?"

I describe Roma and Sanda's apartment.

"Just off the main road..."

He watches me for a few seconds, thinking.

"You know you shouldn't really be here. I should put you on the next plane to Italy. All the other foreigners here are accounted for – they're with Unprofor or the army or some other organisation that has vehicles, radios, evacuation strategies. You're on your own and, to be honest, you're out of your depth. OK, you've got a job to do but the paper can't really look after you, let alone the Kent bloody Messenger."

The waiter brings us another beer.

"But I admire your pluck and I'm willing to let you stay. For the time being. But a few ground rules. One: be very careful. This place is safe if you're careful, dangerous if you're not. It's not Tunbridge Wells. There are roads that you shouldn't go down. Others that you must run across. You'll learn soon enough but if in doubt, copy the locals. Two: you will not leave this city. The hills are very dangerous. Up there no one can help you. You could easily get killed. Three: you're to report to me if the situation deteriorates or if you get into any serious trouble. Four: if and when I say go, you go. Agreed?"

I nod.

"Right. I'm throwing a party tonight. Why don't you come along?"

Walking with him across the lobby he points out a long line of water spreading slowly from beneath the door of the loos.

"Bloody city's coming apart at the edges."

About twenty people are drinking and talking in a candlelit restaurant. The BBC's Sarajevo correspondent is talking to a group of soldiers at the bar. There are aid workers, people attached to Unprofor, a few diplomats from other Embassies. At dinner I sit next to a cavalry officer, who is responsible for evacuating the British community in the event of trouble.

"You're registered with us I suppose," he clips. "If not you'll need to be. It's 'invitation only' if the place goes up, I'm afraid."

"What's the plan?"

"Depends on what's up. If the airport's open, then we'll fly everyone out. Call in a few Harriers to give us some cover. Otherwise it's a night march, over the hills and far away. Neither option's very pretty - anything could happen: angry locals wanting us to stay, old women lying in front of the trucks; Serbs having a crack at us while we leave. Not something any of us look forward to. You're registered with us I suppose. If not you'll need to be. It's 'invitation only' if the place goes up, I'm afraid."

"I'll be on the list," I reply grimly, taking a sip of the Ambassador's tepid white wine.

Helen works at the American Embassy. She was an exchange student here in the sixties.

"This was the most fantastic city to live in. Beautiful and green and so cosmopolitan. I just have these fantastic memories of being here - I was a flower power kid, and the university was a real exciting place to live. We used to talk forever in the evenings, drinking wine and just like ... talking, playing guitar. It felt like this was the happiest, most sorted place."

Before I leave she invites me to a Hemingway evening that she is organising in town. A look-alike is flying in specially.

The cavalry officer gives me a lift home in his armoured Land Rover. We drive down the river road and he points up to the invisible hills.

"That's the Jewish cemetery," he points out, and we both stare at a piece of jet black hill. "Crawling with snipers. Had a go at me before. Got the holes to prove it" he laughs, slapping the door of the Land Rover. Moments later we turn into the square of wasteland in front of the tower block. It is blanched in the moonlight. By the stairwell we stop and I hop out.

"You sure this is the place?"

I nod. "Recognise it anywhere."

"Well, good night. And good luck" and I slam shut the door and walk into the darkness.

At the office everyone is already busy. Black rain clouds are squatting along the valley and outside the city looks dark grey. The strobe lights on the ceiling are bright.

It is another slow morning, until the reports begin to come in off the printers and I crawl through them with a red felt tip. I had imagined long days of busy work, reaching into the evening, with shell blasts and power cuts and deadlines met against all odds. Well, I am a foolish romantic and nothing could be further from the truth. I spend most of my time irritating a lot of fragile tempers and fiddling about constructing sentences about UN debates and small arms fire.

One reporter is particularly difficult. She has a face like a pretty doll, wears bright colours and her hair tight back under an alice band. Pretty in a neat sort of way, she has a high voice like a little bird and is spoilt as anything. Just hint at criticism and she lets out a brittle laugh and shakes her head.

"... but we are always writing it this way."

Finally she agrees to change her report, a little flushed and as her head leans over the keyboard I stare at her smooth brown neck with its black down and think how much I would like to squeeze it between both hands.

Just outside the editor's office the charging figure of a tall man nearly knocks me down. He is wearing a heavy leather jerkin over a blue turtleneck sweater. Moleskin trousers are tucked into long boots and he carries an umbrella, hanging horizontal to the ground as a bushman carries his spear. He marches past me, his white-blond head bent forward. I have met him before.

"Jolly good of you," he mutters.

Oslobodjenje's editor, a modest little man in a moustache and brown suit, is standing in the doorway, looking after him.

"That was a very strange man, Alex. An Englishman like yourself, but very cold. He has come here from Albania, overland he tells me, through Kosovo. If that is possible, and he is telling the truth, he is a brave man. Perhaps he did, perhaps he did not. He is certainly a little crazy. When he came into my office, he did so with great ceremony, bowing and sweeping his umbrella like a sword. 'I bring greetings from a neighbouring power' he announced like a general 'I bring with me the prayers of a nation'."

The editor shakes his head. "Crazy."

FRIDAY 24TH NOVEMBER
OSLOBODJENJE

Another difficult day in the newsroom. I read through yesterday's reports. A fair amount of my corrections have been ignored and the reports have gone out in a kind of polyglot Americana. It is raining again and I sit at a desk reading *Lady Chatterley's Lover*.

The journalists eat their lunch at their desks - sandwiches, an orange, glucose biscuits, that sort of thing. I have a Mars bar in my bag, my last one. It is too small to share so I tiptoe upstairs to eat it, lest the sight of chocolate has a dampening affect on morale.

SATURDAY 25TH NOVEMBER
HEMINGWAY

It is Hemingway's opening night. Hemingway is as good as it gets here and the evening has been much trailed on the local radio station. It even gets a mention in today's Oslobodjenje. In a candlelit basement, the old man, in a Spanish blouse and white beard, remembers bull fights and trout fishing, shoots a Kudu and drinks a good cold beer after tuna fishing. The audience sits spellbound and, after the interval the rattle of gunfire splices the silences.

The Ambassador is there and afterwards calls me over to a round table where Hemingway is easing his thirst and chatting to Helen.

"... and I woke up the next morning and said to myself in the mirror, Ernest, old man, you gotta get your butt down to Sarajevo and give those good people your support..."

I walk home with the Ambassador, full of bull fights and Spanish sun, his torch picking out the pot-holes in the road.

"Do you know someone called Pace?"

The Ambassador's torch kicks forward up the road.

"You mean Maurice Pace! He used to be in the service. I was stationed with him in Prague during the Velvet revolution."

"What's he up to now?"

"I dread to think."

SUNDAY 26TH NOVEMBER
SUNDAY BLUES

Roma is quiet during supper and afterwards goes off to bed. Before the war Sanda spent a summer in Italy restoring damaged frescos. She shows me pictures of her work. In a church in Tuscany she and a friend discovered a medieval fresco hidden for hundreds of years. It took them two months to uncover it, carefully brushing away the layers of white paint and dust.

"And one day we discover the face of God," she says quietly, pointing to a man's face, framed by a radiant halo of gold.

The man's face was drawn in pure sorrow and tears fell from his blue eyes.

"You see, He is crying for his children."

The Pope is coming to Sarajevo. There are posters everywhere advertising his visit, his hands outstretched, a great white dove overhead.

I saw him a few weeks ago – while I was in Zagreb picking up my press card and bulletproof jacket. I watched his arrival one morning on telly. I was having breakfast in bed, pampering myself in the knowledge that Sarajevo's water queues and shortages were just around the corner. At Zagreb airport President Tudjman, a rascal, stood on the tarmac ready to embrace the Pope. When in public, (and for all I knew, about his state palace) Tudjman liked to wear a uniform of his own design. It was white and and gold and very busy around the shoulders. He had awarded himself a large number of medals and a peaked cap and he looked like a traffic policeman.

Later that afternoon there was a buoyant sense of festival in the city. Special trams rattled in from the suburbs, full of faces, hooting in the holiday. The square in front of the cathedral was packed. Happy parents worried over their children, sailor suited, hands full of flags and ice cream. Flocks of white nuns pushed in groups towards the cathedral. The Pope was arriving any minute, on his way to celebrate mass. I had found myself a good spot in the Grand Hotel. From the balcony off the first floor bar I could see more people pouring into the square. A waiter in dark green livery brought me a cup of coffee. The noise was deafening.

"Papa, Papa!" chanted the crowd. The maitre d'hotel, in a lemon blazer, dipped about, straightening the bow ties of his waiters and sending out bottles of cold mineral water to the policeman lining the route.

The afternoon light was fading, enough to blur the headlights of the white Popemobile, which moved slowly through the crowd, escorted by outriders. The sky was beige. Swallows tumbled overhead, disturbed by the shouting. I got a clear view of the Pope, standing up in his bulletproof container. A bent figure in a white gown, waving his fragile hand high above his head, lit by a single strobe light. The crowd was hysterical. Fathers lifted up their children to give them a better view, thrusting them in sight of the Pope.

"Papa! Papa! Papa!" The policemen lining the street drew their truncheons. Slowly the procession moved up the cobbled hill towards the cathedral, rust coloured in the evening light. The crowd moved after it, walking in step like soldiers.

WEDNESDAY 29TH NOVEMBER
SIEGE LIFE

Lunch at the embassy. Liver and tomato salad. I hate liver, even in a siege, but manage to swallow most of it and leave the rest in a chopped up pile under my knife, something that I haven't done since prep school. At lunch are two old boys from the ODA, cheerful engineers from the West Midlands, both in their sixties, and I learn a great deal about Land Rover spares and Sarajevo's water supply, which they seem to be in charge of.

I have been here three weeks and already I feel cramped, confined by this city. The hills look so close, lapping at the walls of the city - the beginning of a soft, green landscape, full of rivers and woodland and small villages. What a pleasure to take off, up the slope and climb out of this ugly city. But the villages are on fire and there are soldiers and forced labour camps among the trees. It's strange how landscapes can look beautiful in war.

DECEMBER

This morning there is a stiff white envelope lying on my desk.

Dear Alex. How rude you must have felt me the other day, when I failed to recognise you outside the editor's office. Please accept my apologies. I was tired after a long journey and had much on my mind. However, I am now recovered and anxious to resume our acquaintance.

I am staying in the Holiday Inn. For diplomatic reasons I am registered under the name of (Colonel) Rosemary, Albanian Army. Please do stop by for a drink this evening. I am keeping an excellent bottle of whisky in my room. Yours ever, Maurice

Before I found my job with Oslobodjenje, I spent most of the summer in London pestering friends, contacts, newspapers and anyone else I could think of, asking them to help me find me something to do in the Balkans, and in particular Albania.

I had had a thing about Albania since I was nine, and I spent Easter with my grandparents. They lived in a pretty village in Kent, in an old house by the churchyard, full of damp green shadow and the mouldy tint of yew hedges.

"Here," said my grandmother one day, handing me a book. "You'll enjoy this. It was your father's - he left it here years ago, and I never remembered to give it back to him. It's a real adventure, about a brave man called Aubrey Herbert who nearly became King of Albania."

"Where's Albania?" I asked her.

"It's in the Balkans, which is a rough sort of place north of Greece, full of people fighting and calling each other names."

"It sounds like my playground at school."

Aubrey was a soldier, politician and adventurer who spent much of his life in the Balkans, where he fell in love with Albania. The tiny, impoverished country played to his sense of justice and his weakness for banditry and wild things. When he was elected to Parliament he became Albania's champion. He helped the country win sovereignty in 1921 and worked hard to secure stable government across the country. Twice he was offered Albania's throne. He visited the country as often as he was allowed and his diaries describe a roguish, romantic place - full of hide-outs in caves, night rides through mountain passes, raki, revolvers and scimitar moons. Aubrey loved Albania and its bandit people and, galloping beside him, I loved it too.

The other compelling thing about the book was that inside the front cover my father had written his name and a date - May 1971. It was the month I was born. And below he had scribbled some notes in blue ink. Even then I thought them wonderful:

> *If my few years have taught me anything it is that life is made up of an endless sequence of borders, stretching far away from one's immediate self. In the beginning we are all small uncluttered islands, closely defined by the love and dependence we feel for our immediate family and location - concentrated gene pools, bearing instinctive traits, inherent temperaments inherited from our parents.*
>
> *As such we are mostly not ourselves. True, we have certain traits – 'John always was keen on yellow' or 'Jill's never lost her quick temper' - but they tend to be simple, hot-blooded things. It is not until we mature and begin to take on life alone that we define our complex selves and emerge as interesting men and women with*

subtle humours, a preference for certain landscapes and political parties, a feel for the rhythm of language.

Thus we spread ourselves through the acquisition of experience. The small uncluttered island becomes creased with highland and lowland, inland waterways form, cities and villages are built in strategic places and crops are grown variously. If our experience is significant and successful we gain other islands as colonies, claim a buffer of ocean as our own. Very occasionally we become a great continent.

Aubrey died aged forty-three but he outlived most of his friends, many of whom were killed in the Great War. John Buchan, who based his character Sandy Arbuthnot on Aubrey, was horrified when he died. In a letter to Aubrey's widow he described Aubrey as a 'delightful and brilliant survivor of the age of chivalry...he was the most extraordinary combination of tenderness and gentleness with the most insane gallantry I have ever known.' No surprise I wanted to follow him to Albania.

"Of course you must go to Albania," said a well-placed friend just in time (I was about to give it all up and take up my place at law school) "but first of all you must speak to Maurice. He's there all the time. Knows everyone between Belgrade and Istanbul. Bloody rogue. God knows what he does in Albania, but he's the man to talk to."

Maurice, I was told, had a right-hand man, a sort of gentleman valet called Spencer. I got hold of Spencer's number in Knightsbridge and asked whether it might be possible to meet Maurice.

"Oh, yes, you must meet Maurice," gushed Spencer. "He so enjoys meeting the young – we both do."

"I understand he has a lot to do with Albania."

"Well he's quite a cause célèbre across the Balkans. He served there, you see, when he was with the Diplomatic Service. Made a tremendous number of friends. Now he's a businessman, and – shall we say – a champion of worthy causes. Albania is one of his *favourite* places."

"What exactly does he do there?"

"All sorts. Albania's a complicated place at the moment – transition from communism, green shoots of capitalism and all that. I'm afraid Maurice has rather fallen out with its President and taken up with someone called the Professor. Opposition leader and public enemy number one. Maurice is convinced he'll take power some day - and people are already saying the Professor'll want Maurice in his cabinet. Whether Maurice will have time for all that ... well, we'll have to see."

One September night I met Maurice and Spencer in a restaurant in the City. A squall was blowing in from the river and, as Maurice marched in under an enormous black umbrella, the door snapped shut behind him with a crash. He wore a navy suit and striped tie. He looked like a prosperous banker, tall and well groomed. Late thirties, big shoulders, pale blond hair and long, careful hands. I was disappointed; he seemed an indoor smooth. Spencer followed him in, brushing raindrops off a cashmere coat. He was tiny and wore a neat RAF moustache. The inside of his gloves were lined with rabbit fur and he made a great thing of ordering Champagne cocktails 'quick as you can'.

Maurice was a banker of sorts, he claimed, though he preferred to call himself a 'fixer' and spread his narrow lips in a pale imitation grin.

"Odd job man, jack of all trades – that's me. Help out old friends, trade a bit, buy a few things, sell others. Eastern Europe's the place. Got space you see. Not too many people looking over ya shoulder." At that moment his mobile rang and turning from the table, he began a conversation with someone in Tiblisi about oil pipelines in Bulgaria.

"Off to Sofia tomorrow" he explained afterwards, nodding at Spencer, "Government's pissing me about. Opening a little bank there but the Finance Minister's stalling my application. Still, we know a thing or two about our friend the Minister, don't we Spence? He'll come round soon enough."

He looked at me with eyes that would, I had no doubt, shortly terrify the Finance Minister. Maurice no longer disappointed. He was, as they say, the real thing.

"Still, haven't got time to bang on about Bulgaria. What the hell do you want to do in Albania?"

I spread my hands rather feebly.

"I'm looking for a bit of adventure."

"In my day one joined the FO if you were that way inclined - still room for people with ideas. Not now - bloody place is full of clerks and politicos – wouldn't know the national interest if it walked up and kicked them in the fucking balls. Well, never mind. My friend the Professor could do with a hand. Especially from someone like you. A bit of research, a bit of speech writing - someone to carry his bags. Tighten up his image - what he bloody needs. He's had a hard time since the revolution. He led the charge then, you know, along with El Presidente. He was a bloody hero: took his students over the top - had them hunger striking and smearing their shit all over the walls. Terrified the communists into submission. Got into government after the first elections but the President was as scared of him as the commies and kicked him out. Still, we'll get him back there, won't we Spence?"

He stared at me, tipping an oyster down his throat.

"Yep, you could do a lot worse than the Professor. God knows what you want from the thing but he'd keep you entertained."

After supper Maurice smoked a cigar, which Spencer lit for him with his quick little fingers. Then he sat back, crossed his legs and talked about Albania. He told ghoulish tales about a dark, sinister little country worked by secret policemen and smugglers and ruled by a moody and cruel man. About vendettas and grenade attacks, political persecution, anonymous thuggery, mishaps at garden parties, heirs to Balkan thrones biding their time in anonymity, lorry loads of fake Scotch crossing the mountains bound for Serbia. Outside the rain poured down.

"Give him my Albanian card, will you Spence."

Maurice stubbed his cigar out in the butter dish, which gave out a bitter smell as it slipped around the stub. It was a stiff card, with an address in Moorgate and Tirana. Maurice was staring at me again, his eyes a cool blue like antifreeze. Then, with startling rapidity, he was on his feet and Spencer had snatched out of his chair and was standing beside him.

"Well, you know where to get me. I'll set you up with the Professor, if that's what you want. Delighted."

Unnerved, I watched them out of the restaurant - Maurice snapping open his umbrella with vicious hands, Spencer pulling on his gloves. Behind them the room blurred back into focus. A couple of weeks later I finally persuaded my local paper that it needed a Balkan correspondent and set off for Sarajevo. It sounded much safer than Albania.

The lobby of the Holiday Inn lies under a foot of water. Upturned beer crates, lined up like stepping stones across the flat black pool, lead me to the reception desk. Behind it a man is standing carefully on a small step-ladder. "Colonel Rosemary please."

Maurice has taken a suite on the eighth floor. It is a long way by the stairs and before I knock on the door I have to catch my breath, staring through a boarded window onto the Serb lines. It is quite dark and tracer is flitting about below, like bright fish at the bottom of a pool.

Maurice's suite is full of fluttering orange colour, thrown by candles scattered about the room.

"Well, well. You've come a long way Alex." He holds a cigar in his long fingers, looking at me, his long face half in shadow.

"Where are you staying in this fine city?"

"I'll show you," I reply, walking to the window, but his suite looks away from the Serb lines and anyway, it is impossible to make out any buildings.

"Having fun? Must be all sorts of things a young chap could get up to here" The full stop is dropped deliberately, leaving the sentence hanging there, snapping backwards and forwards over a realm of shady possibilities, like the broken half of a worm. I wonder what exactly Maurice would be doing in my position - running blood plasma or hand grenades, or selling girls to the bored Unprofor squaddies.

I tell him about Oslobodjenje, Sanda and Roma, the Ambassador. It sounds reassuringly dull. By the time I have finished he has walked over to the window and is standing there with his back to me, staring into the darkness, the end of his cigar reflecting a crimson splash, like a blood stain, in the window.

"I know the Ambassador quite well. Stationed together once, pretty wife if I remember. Never very close."

"Have a whisky." He seems agitated. He pours me a glass of single malt, and one for himself.

"Reason I've called you up here Alex, is I've got a job for you. Not here of course, not my manor. Albania. What do you think?"

My heart sinks, I do not know how to play this man, or his shoving questions.

"As I mentioned, my job with Oslobodjenje lasts until February.

I haven't decided what I'm going to do after that..."

He waves his hand. My own plans are of no interest to him.

"Listen, deal's this. Last time I saw you I told you that our hero Professor could do with a hand. Well the thing is I was right. He's bloody desperate. He's having a difficult time at the minute, Albania's a tricky play for the best of us, and he's got pretty low. You'd do him the power of good."

"But..."

"You're just the ticket – bright, presentable, good for morale. You could write his speeches, bit of research, bit of PR, carry his bags, hold his hand, that sort of thing. Bloody fascinating. You'll earn peanuts but you'll learn, you'll be at the heart of the whole thing, Tirana in your hand. The Professor will be President one day, if a few of us have anything to do with it. He might not be the toast of Tirana at the moment, but he's got some powerful friends outside the country. He's a good man the Professor. You could help put him where he belongs. What do ya think?"

I could feel myself being squeezed into place, a piece in Maurice's jigsaw. Why did he really want me in Albania? How would I fit in to his plans? Standing in his candlelit eyrie, with artillery going off down below, it was a bizarre location for a job offer.

"Look Maurice. I appreciate the offer, but I've told Oslobodjenje that I'll stay until February and I can't just go running off. After February I could be very interested. But not before."

He pours himself some more whisky, baring his teeth in a cross sort of smile.

"Point taken. No can do until Oslobodjenje throws you out." He is clearly irritated. "Well, the job's there if you want it. For the time being mind. And between you and me, you may well want it sooner then you think. This place is going up in smoke any minute," and his blond eyebrows rise impressively in the half light.

SATURDAY 9TH DECEMBER
SIEGE LIFE

In a bar I drink a cup of Turkish coffee. It is lunch-time and I am hiding
from the dark rain, which has the ominous chill of snow about it. The
bar is called *New York.* So-named by the pilgrim fathers, religious
haters to a man, building their Utopia in the new world. A couple of
boys are watching me from the corner of the room. I wave them over,
asking them if they want coffee. They are both dark, their hair is cropped.
One is wearing a purple shell suit. He must be freezing. Both are
soldiers, back to the front tomorrow. They are seventeen.

"We kill Cetniks. Now we fuck girls. Tomorrow we kill more
Cetniks. We are Muslims."

Back home by three. The apartment is deserted. It is still light
but there is nothing to do. I couldn't walk anywhere if I wanted to and
I don't – it's cold, my shoes are wet and I'm tired of walking. And I've
got nowhere to go. There is no television. My radio's World Service
reception is poor. I'd love a bath but there's no water at the moment. I
suppose I could read, but I've been reading all day. This, I realise is
what a siege feels like. An hour later I am fatigued, aching with ennui.
At last Roma comes home and I brew up coffee and we sit eating stale
bread and talking about Africa.

SUNDAY 10TH DECEMBER
MICE

Roma and I march down the hill to fetch water from a tap. It is a low,
dull day and the queue is long. We stand in line, smoking cigarettes.
This is a humbling procedure, irksome and cold and these people do it
every day. Roma shrugs. The queue grumbles. There is a crack and a

few metres down the hill a woman falls, her plastic drum rolling down the hill. Someone screams and only then do I realise that she has been shot. In a moment everything slows and I remember the terror of running Hemingway's bulls on a July morning in Pamplona, the looks in people's eyes as hooves skid round the bend and everyone begins to move for themselves, scattering like minnows. Roma pulls me by the arm and we run sliding on the oily cobbles for cover. The woman lies still, her drum rolling down the hill.

There is a violet twilight this evening. And a great deal of shooting. Roma and I stand out on the balcony and watch green tracer drift lazily across the shadows on the hillside. The tracer is a pretty thing to watch, better than fireworks. We are talking about the shooting we saw, and the dead woman. And then we stop talking about her, because neither of us has anything more to say. The woman is dead. Neither of us knew her, we can do nothing about it. Sanda has cooked us a feast - bacon and eggs and a few tomatoes. Even some bread. It is the first meat that I have eaten here, save for the liver which doesn't count.

An hour later the three of us are crouching in the larder. It is dark. I wave my torchlight over the bare shelves.

"Are you not afraid?" asks Sanda. "I am afraid and so is Roma."

"No, I'm not afraid," I reply, feeling pleased with my sangfroid. I wave my torch around the larder, trying to reassure them.

"Look, there's nothing here."

Sanda has seen a mouse.

MONDAY 11TH DECEMBER
MAYHEM

The psychology of this city is fractured. Boredom, fear, resentment, exhaustion, hardship, death, imprisonment have brought on a communal psychosis. It is visible only to visitors and, I suspect, only for a bit. There is powerful juju here and it takes hold pretty fast. You can see it in the sour sense of humour, the heavy smoking, the thin white faces of the girls and the constant, tactile affection that people show each other. There is a great deal of touching here, hand-holding and kissing. As if communication is incomplete without physical contact, as if it is the only thing that can really break their isolation.

Round the table we eat supper (the last of the bacon) and talk, three figures cast in candlelight. Afterwards we slump in the big chairs in the sitting room, drinking coffee and smoking cigarettes. The gunfire escalates. The chattering small arms fire is now constant, and the 'tuk tuk tuk' of heavy machine guns. Artillery crumps nearby. We sit there talking, pretending that everything is normal. Then there is a startling crash, just outside the window, and everything is not normal. The bulb swings from the ceiling. And then there is another crash and in a moment the night has become mayhem.

Roma and I sit there in silence. Sanda is in the kitchen. She runs in shaking, holding onto the door.

"We must go into the cellar. This is how it was before. We must hide!" She is terrified. Another crash, the loudest yet and I feel the crunch of the shell's impact and the squeaky sounds of shrapnel. The large balcony window rattles. Sanda screams.

"I am going to the cellar. You two are crazy."

I am sitting in an armchair, with my back to the window, sunk down into my seat, mechanically plotting the flight of broken glass and shrapnel. It is a strange feeling, sitting there in the dark, hanging on to myself, making small talk to Roma while the night shatters itself against the glass windows. How absurd that they haven't broken. Roma and I sit there, he stubborn, refusing to be cowed by these guns, me curious, never having been shelled before and thinking it would be a shame to

41

miss it. The waiting is the really frightening part - knowing there will be another shell, but not when it will come. It is an irresponsible fear, that of the weak in the face of omnipotent strength: one cannot fight back, only wait.

And wait we do, sitting there finishing off the brandy, and I find myself enjoying the terror, the sensation of nakedness, feeling the softness of my skin, my own liquidity in the midst of all this sharp, killing steel. It is like being on a bizarre fairground ride. Terrifying but somehow bound to end happily; white-faced but alive. And so, legs crossed, a glass of brandy in my hand, my head sunk low in the armchair lest it be chopped off by a slither of hot steel, I endure what Sanda and Roma have endured night after night. There are German 'tourists' who pay to spend a weekend on the Croat lines, the ultimate in adventure holidaying. And sitting there, terrified and exhilarated in equal measure, I wonder whether I am really any different. Opposite me Roma is quiet, tears running down his cheeks.

Around midnight the shelling falls away, like a great storm blowing itself out. Leaving the crackle of small arms fire and the rain swelling so gently against the glass. I go to bed and in my dreams I am back in that black dike, choking on its salt water, shouting for help.

"It's all right, I'm here," says a once familiar voice in my ear and I wake up, gasping for air. It is dawn and very cold and I stand shivering on the balcony, fetching 'V' signs at the hills.

TUESDAY 12TH DECEMBER
THE MORNING AFTER

The next day people are sweeping broken glass and shrapnel off the wet streets, as if they were clearing paths in the snow. There are new dents in the pavement where shells have fallen. They are filling up with rainwater. I walk to work. The ambassador drives past in his Land

Rover, a union flag fluttering from the bonnet. His driver slows as he passes me and the ambassador shouts through the window "come and see me when you've got a moment".

The newsroom is subdued. The events of last night have drawn the journalists together, into some silent unity. Private grief and I do not know what to say, or how to say it.

"That was quite a shelling last night" sounds too much like, "...nice to see Spurs can still put a few in the back of the net." So I stay quiet.

I have never felt a part of the newsroom. Any interest in me has been erratic and shallow: "how are you finding Sarajevo?" or "how is the weather in England?"

I ask one of the girls if there is anything that I can do.

"No, Alex. Nothing." For once her clumsy English was as good as gold.

WEDNESDAY 13TH DECEMBER
DANCING TO MAURICE'S TUNE

On the fifth floor of the Holiday Inn 'Colonel Rosemary' is preparing to leave. He is back in his leather jerkin, moleskin trousers tucked into boots. A Bosnian officer is with him. They are talking in what sounds like Turkish. The Bosnian hands Maurice some papers. At the door he turns and salutes. Maurice waves back at him. Then he walks over to a table and pours us both a glass of whisky.

"Might as well polish it off, eh. Bottoms up!"

I drain the glass and the whisky fires the back of my throat. I feel like getting drunk.

"I suppose you're off eh? Bet the Ambassador's given you the shove. You'd better make it snappy - ceasefire's broke". He is grinning like the school know-all, a step ahead as usual.

"I'm flying out tomorrow."

"Brave man. Let's hope the Serbs don't have a go at your plane. I hear General Mladic has just taken delivery of some ground-to-air whizzbangs. He'll be itching to try them out. I'm off overland, got a pack of Mujahedin as an escort - much safer."

"I'm thinking of going to Albania," I say between set teeth, the whisky sinking into my stomach. I have no choice - it is Albania or home. And it's not yet time to go home.

"Smashing idea. I'll give the Professor a ring."

There's a knock on the door.

"That'll be the Afghans. Toodlepip old man. See you in Tirana" and he tucks his umbrella under one arm and marches out of the room.

SUNDAY 17TH DECEMBER
BRINDISI - ATHENS

The Poseidon is crossing a glassy sea, between brown islands. The sun is yellow, even in December, the sky blue and the brown islands flecked with green clusters of pine and the white villages. Everything is clean and bright and, I like to think, smells of wild thyme. I stand out on the bow and warm my hands around a cup of syrupy coffee. Below me a couple of dolphin move alongside the bow, bending like whippets through the clear water.

MONDAY 18TH DECEMBER
ATHENS

It's strange to be alone and anonymous in this indifferent place, after the urgency of Sarajevo. I don't like Athens; it is a loud and dirty sprawl, with its vulgarised ruins and its angry people.

In a bookshop off Omonia Square I buy a *Blue Guide to Albania* and an old communist guidebook called *Albania - a Geographic Outline* (or AGO). On the AGO's cover is a photograph of a chalky blue river, snaking along a gravel bed between wooded banks. Green mountains run across the horizon. The book is a glimpse into the inclinations of Albania's late dictator, Enver Hoxha, and his Albanian Workers Party (AWP). There is an abundance of statistics, mostly foolish; but photographs - of the workers' holiday home in Durres, Tirana's italiante Shanderberg Square with its fountains, a wire factory in the northern city of Shkodra and young men building a sunlit railway - make it bearable.

There has been savage fighting in Sarajevo today. Mladic has let off one of his new whizzbangs and the UN authorities have closed the airport.

WEDNESDAY 20TH DECEMBER
GLOOM

My despondency continues, I feel wary and unsure of myself. Just crossing the road seems dangerous and I linger suspiciously by the pavement, waiting for a gap in the traffic. As if I've already used up enough lives in the chaos of that bombardment in Sarajevo, as if my spoiled Balkan adventure has now well and truly lost its way.

I buy a walking stick from a dusty shop full of nurses' uniforms, artificial limbs and stainless steel spittoons for dentists. I will look like an invalid and have something with which to hit aggressive dogs or people. Out in the sunlight I practise limping down the street. The stick, which has a fake horn handle and a rubber tip, doesn't look quite right.

Back in my hotel room I remove the rubber tip and scratch off the varnish with my knife. It no longer looks brand new and I feel slightly less ridiculous. I slash it about, lunging at imaginary bandits.

After lunch I walk to the Albanian Embassy for a chat and some expert advice. Like where to stay, how much to pay for a bus, the Albanian word for 'thank you', that sort of thing. But a sign on the door says the Embassy is closed. No one answers the doorbell. It cannot be closed at 3.00 pm on a Wednesday afternoon. Angrily I rap on its door with my stick. A surprised-looking child watches me from across the street. A head, dark and male, appears out of an upstairs window.

"I am going to Albania tomorrow," I shout at him, as slowly as I can. "I want to ask questions."

He looks cross. "No go to Albania. Albania not good. Albania closed."

THURSDAY 21ST DECEMBER
ATHENS - ALBANIAN BORDER

Buses for Albania leave from a dilapidated warehouse in the suburbs. It is full of blue and white buses. Conductors and drivers lounge around them, smoking and laughing. Families, led by frantic looking women in dark clothes, scurry about in a subterranean light. I buy *souvlaki* at a café full of men playing backgammon and ask one of the backgammon players "bus to Albania?"

"Eh?"

"Albania," I repeat, raising my eyebrows suggestively.

He scowls and points to the end of the warehouse.

"Kakavia," he says, "bus to Kakavia". Before I go he asks "why Albania? - why not Greece? Greece good. Albania very bad."

At the very end of the warehouse, quite on its own, stands the bus for Albania. It is surrounded by a subdued group of people. Some lean against the bus, some squat on the floor. A few have grabbed seats onboard. The scene is bound with a kind of gentle, lowly energy. Mouths unbend to chew bits of old meat held in a battered steel bowl, showing broken teeth. Juices run onto chins. A young girl changes a baby's nappy. It lies in a suitcase opened to act as a bed. In fact it is a double bed: another baby sleeps in the next compartment. A bald man repacks a cheap-looking stereo into its box. The gossips smoke and laugh. One, a little drunk, playfully slaps the other. They both have long black hair and wear denim jackets and cowboy boots. As I approach the diners look up from their food. The nappy is forgotten for a second, the gossips fall silent. They see a young man carrying a large rucksack. He is limping and supports his weight on a peculiar-looking stick. The young man looks upon his first Albanians and smiles grimly.

At last the driver arrives, wiping the coffee from his moustache, and we climb aboard. The engine throbs into life, the grey-green on-board lights dim, cigarettes are lit. The bus swings out of the warehouse and we climb through the suburbs and onto a motorway which hugs the hooked coastline. Out in the bay tankers lie still at their moorings, oil-black shadows against the water. We pass several refineries smoking in the warm evening air. The alien forms come to life around me. The momentum towards the north and Albania seems to reassure them. The anxiety and the subdued faces fade into conversations and sleep.

A few hours later, in hilly country through which the bus grinds its gears, we stop at a roadside restaurant for supper. The Albanians pile out, laughing and talking, and spread themselves across the restaurant. I follow them, practising my limp and feeling left out. But in the queue for macaroni and meat stew my isolation is broken. A young man walks up to me and introduces himself, landing a heavy arm across my shoulders. He is 'John', with thick blue-black hair and bright blue eyes, six foot and heavily built. His face is sharp and intelligent, cast with creases running like scratches across his forehead.

John insists on paying for my food and tugs me out onto a pretty terrace that looks over the road. There are floodlit trees and concrete pools full of fish. John wants to make friends. He points at my stick and I describe a bad car crash in England - making a great cracking sound while pointing to my femur and feeling very foolish.

He is genuinely upset. Then "blood brothers" he says, cheering up. "John, Alexi - blood brothers" and he slides the forefinger of one huge hand across his wrist.

John is thirty-one, married and with a son. He has left his wife and child in Athens where he works at a petrol station. He is an illegal immigrant, having crossed the border at night in 1990, walking for eight days to the Greek capital. For two of them he had nothing to eat, he drank water from streams and finally stole a shepherd's picnic of bread and cheese to keep himself going. His first job was cleaning public lavatories for fifty Dr a day. John is on his way to the southern town of Fier to spend the Christmas holiday with his family. In the hold of the bus are several cardboard boxes full of presents.

Back onboard we admire his new suit, a shiny petrol-blue affair. The tailor's label is still on the sleeve. John points it out with pride. He also wears a little black hat like a trilby, a white shirt, a black leather tie, white socks and fake leather shoes. We exchange vocabulary - John is learning English and wrestles with each word until is made safe and filed away somewhere under his hat. Then he asks to see my passport and in exchange reveals a filofax, mirror sunglasses in a plastic case, a Parker ball-point which doesn't work and a flick knife, which he carries in a cardboard box in the inside pocket of his jacket. He weighs the knife lovingly in his hand, working the mechanism over and over again.

"For Albanians," he explains, grinning and waving furtively at the bus. "Albanians very bad - Albanians animals."

John invites me to spend Christmas with his family. I'm not sure whether he's being serious but thank him all the same. He grins - it is settled. Slowly we grow bored of our language lessons and I return to staring out of the window until somehow I fall asleep, John's heavy head resting on my shoulder.

FRIDAY 22ND DECEMBER
ALBANIAN BORDER — FIER

It is dawn. Just inside the Greek border, among olive groves, the bus is stopped by a Greek unit with parachute badges on their epaulettes. A captain in a pale blue beret and sun glasses climbs into the bus, bringing with him the sharp cold of dawn. His armed men begin to check passports. They are looking for 'illegals'. The bus stiffens like a wild animal in the presence of its pursuer. I stiffen too, my sense of solidarity surprising me. One, two, then three men are ordered off the bus. A middle-aged man sitting near me is slapped around the head by the captain and pulled him off the bus by his hair. When it is my turn I look up into the hateful sunglasses and give the captain my passport and my best Roger Moore smile. He tosses it back with a sneer. At last we move off and there is a great outpouring of tension. Young men resume nonchalant expressions and light cigarettes. John shakes his head and smiles at me. He is terrified.

The road ends at a barrier, guarded by a concrete customs house flying the Greek flag. There is rubbish everywhere. Beyond the barrier a muddy road leads into Albania. Out in the cold morning, we add to the crush in the compound. John, increasingly proprietorial, pulls me by the sleeve to the side of the bus. He has straightened his tie and combed his thick hair and is being terribly business-like. We gather his cardboard boxes in a pile, to which we add my rucksack. Seizing my passport he urges me to stay with the things, pointing at the crowds and

49

whispering "Albanians - very bad!"

He walks off into the throng, leaving me his knife just in case. It is still in its cardboard box. I am beginning to tire of his theatricals and put it uselessly in my pocket.

John is some time. I watch a fat Greek customs officer emerge from his office, stretch and do nothing. His fat breath oozes smoke in the cold air. John remains busily away. I catch an occasional glimpse of his shiny suit through the crowd, or his little hat, cocked back on his head. He seems to spend most of his time chatting to strange men. Meanwhile I collect a gang of young spectators in holey jerseys and dribbling noses. I practice my golf swing, fag in mouth and calculate my value to the ne'er-do-wells around me. The crowd moves sulkily about.

Somehow the Balkan inefficiency runs itself out and the cars and trucks are let through the barrier and drive across no-mans land to another queue waiting to enter Albania. The sulky crowd follows. John returns with my passport and we grab the boxes and join the march across the border. By now the sun has climbed into a pale sky. Border guards watch us from behind the thick collars of their overcoats. One calls me over. John has disappeared into the crowd. Reluctantly I put down my rucksack and limp across. He is a timid conscript, younger than me. His face is covered in weeping acne. It turns out he just wants to practice his English, putting down his gun to enunciate 'goodbye' with relish.

After a sham inspection of our luggage we walk towards the passport office. Beside it flies the Albanian flag, a double headed eagle (black) against a blood-red background. Its line snaps on its aluminium pole. Against the walls of the brick building press a group of shouting men with passports in their hands. There is a new energy about the crowd now that they are back home. Heads are held higher, there are more smiles and more aggression. John is ahead, worming his way into the throng like a spaniel into gorse. I watch him, leaning on my stick. The men are shouting because there is no one to stamp our passports. John looks back to me, shrugs and smiles. An elbow catches him on the cheek and he glares at a thick set man whose mouth is full of something. John gives him a push and for a moment I wonder whether he will go for his knife. Then I remember it is still in my pocket, in its cardboard box.

Suddenly one of the crowd (I recognise him from the bus) pushes his way up to the low window of the passport office and climbs in. Sitting down in the chair he searches through the drawers of the desk and produces a stamp. Wetting it emphatically in an ink pad, he waves forward the crowd with a sweep of his hand. Arms stretch through the window, waving plastic passports, and with great chutzpah he stamps them, one-by-one. We are all impressed by this display, especially the man himself. When all are stamped he lets himself out by the office door and walks away, puffed up like a cockerel. The border guards look on. The sunlight is now piercing. Through it emerges John, energetic as ever, dragging his cardboard boxes.

"Albania," he smiles, as if he is giving me a present.

John has found a truck going to Fier. He knows the driver – he seems to know everyone. Underneath a bulging tarpaulin sit several men. We climb on board and the truck crunches forward down the rough road. The others make room for us, staring at me as I stare out at the landscape sliding past. John explains who I am and they ask him questions. Gradually they ask them direct to me, prodding a shy, bright-looking boy to practice his English.

"You English?", "…why are you in Albania?", "…where is your wife?" I reply patiently and ask them questions back but there is little meaningful communication. The boy has a downy moustache and wears faded, Oxfam clothes. We look at each other across an infinity. Out in a field a man is crouching with his trousers round his ankles. He waves as we drive past and everyone smiles.

The road moves across the flat Drinos valley. On each side mountains rise like walls, their shoulders white with snow. They have a wild, cold air - clean against a huge blue sky. I can see a large bird hanging on a thermal. The scale of this place is exciting. But the valley floor is scruffy, poor fields scattered with concrete bunkers.

Ever fearful of invasion, Hoxha ordered millions of these round bunkers to be cast across his tiny country. And there they lie today; in hedgerows, orchards, behind the dunes at Durres, above the mighty Vjosa river north of Gjirokaster. They seem to have been constructed quite randomly - without much consideration for military science. Some are on their own, some in groups, some in a neat row, with another row and then another spread out like mini-maginot lines across a valley floor. The majority smell, like their cousins along the Norfolk coast, of shit.

Bunkers weren't the end of Hoxha's national defences. Fruit orchards became death-traps by the simple addition of metal spikes designed to skewer enemy parachutists. Roads were tweaked with unnecessary bends in order to deny enemy aircraft an ad hoc runway. On the weekends the countryside sang with the voices of local militias performing bayonet practice in the fields. At Himara, north of Saranda, there was a submarine nest. At an airbase south of Tirana antique jet fighters waited ready on the tarmac.

The road passes peculiar, unfinished villages. The Albanians call them towns. They are depressing places, a cluster of post-war apartment blocks which look derelict but crawl with crammed-in families. Their silhouette is broken by the blur from scores of television aerials. Washing hangs from square balconies, flapping in the icy breeze. Mangy dogs bark and, in the muddy square below the blocks, children play football. There is a post-apocalypse feel to these places - it is how I imagine life would recreate itself in Croydon or Southport in the slipstream of nuclear war. Man's genius for order and civilisation evaporated, authority gone, Sunday newspapers and milk on the doorstep forgotten. The centre-piece of the town – a white and grey marble esplanade, its steps leading to a fountain flanked by a monument to WWII partisan heroes – is littered with broken glass. The fountain doesn't work, the marble is chipped. A donkey grazes in the tiny park, where every night a family of gypsies sleep by a purple fire. The few people on the streets aren't doing much more than walking about. A few stand by a stall drinking brandy. By the side of the road a gang of boys leave alone a smoking tyre to throw stones at our truck.

We beat on down the valley, caught between the wide flood plain of the Drinos and the steep haunches of the hills. There is an invigorating sense of theatre about this natural funnel into southern Albania, weaving its way between the tall mountains. It is a route well-trodden by invaders from Ottoman horsemen to Italian armoured cars. And now me, underneath a dusty tarpaulin.

The road reaches Gjirokaster, famous for being the birthplace of Enver Hoxha, for its great citadel, which looms above us, black against the sea-blue sky, its snowy Ottoman houses and for producing great quantities of snuff. Past Gjirokaster, the valley floor narrows and the river becomes deeper and more dramatic. Above a narrow gorge we pull off the road and park by an old bus. Below us woods fall sharply to the rushing river. It is a lovely spot, congested with the sound of rushing water. A stream chutes under the road and down to the river, filling a large square drinking trough on its way with shining water. Another stream has been tamed into a number of runnels and ornamental ponds with statues of herons and small figures. There is an Oriental quality to the place. I follow John, the driver and his mute son out of the sunlight and down into the dank of the wood, where a path weaves its way between the watercourses to a small restaurant overlooking the river.

The boy is terrified of the water. He points towards the Vjosa and screams. John puts an arm around his shoulders, whispering to him as he coaxes him down to the door of the restaurant. Inside it is deathly cold, like an English church. Groups sit at tables eating silently. An unsmiling old man in a filthy tweed jacket takes our order, nods and disappears. The driver has ordered raki, which arrives oily like the Victory Gin in *Nineteen Eighty Four*. They all watch me try it. It tastes of cow dung but is smooth and warming in the cold restaurant. We eat a soup full of tiny bits of pasta. It is starchy and tastes of old lemons and a whisper of chicken. There is bread which we dip in rich olive oil, scattered with damp brown salt from a bowl. Outside the river slips past in winter sunlight towards Vlora and the Adriatic. After a bit I can no longer feel my toes.

Afterwards they will not let me pay. The driver invites John and me into the cab. It is fuggy and warm inside and smells of damp wool. We set off, docile and sleepy after the raki and John tells me the story of the driver's son. During the anarchy that followed the collapse of communism, when industry stopped and food was hard to find, many Albanians tried to escape their country, across the mountains into Greece or over the sea to Italy in a scruffy, odds and ends armada. Families, friends, civil servants and agricultural engineers, thieves and loners in their thousands gathered at the ports, staring silently towards the horizon. The largest vessel to cross the Adriatic was an Italian merchant ship carrying sacks of flour and sugar. The ship was overrun while docking in Durres and its captain forced to take on board the hundreds gathered on the quay, including the driver, his wife and his young son.

In the middle of the Adriatic the boy's mother, jostled by the huge crowd, toppled into the water. She could not swim. The ship did not stop – the captain was terrified that the ship would capsize. Meanwhile the crowd closed around the screaming boy and someone filled his mother's place at the gunwale. I have seen television pictures of the vessel arriving in Brindisi harbour – its silhouette hidden by the writhing mass of people. They balance on the gunwales, up the rigging, on top of the bridge. They are waving and moving with all the long distance energy of maggots mouthing in the decay of a dead animal. As the ship creeps forward a couple dive into the water and start to swim towards shore. By now the boy's mother is dead. He has not spoken since.

I doze off. When I wake up we are at the top of a high pass where we stop to pee and drink from a spring. I put my head under the icy water which gives me a thumping headache - as if someone had kicked it smartly with a metalled toecap. Around me empty hills tumble away towards a brown horizon. I stumble back into the cab and we drive down the pass and through more hilly country. Occasionally we stop to drop someone off the back. Behind us they stand deserted, watching us out of sight, before turning to a dirt track that leads to a lone house or over the crest of a far hill.

At Patos, a grimy town gathered around a belching smokestack, the main road moves into a flat landscape of black fields, broken glass-houses and nodding-donkey oil wells. The thick smell of crude oil is everywhere. Irrigation channels glitter with its traces. By the side of the road lies an old locomotive engine, still and black with oil. We pass old Soviet trucks on the dirt tracks, their loads of young men watch us through eyes clenched against the dust sprays. As they pass us we hear the shouted words of a song they are singing. Their hair is long and thick like straw. Where they are going or coming from, what they have to do in this greasy, spent dustbowl I do not know. John does not understand my question and simply points ahead and shouts "familia, familia". I have a sudden fear that all this is an elaborate plot to lure me into a silent corner where I will be set upon and robbed by chanting automatons. I wrap my hands around the handle of my stick and picture my flight across the dirty fields.

An hour later we reach the outskirts of Fier: gutted buildings, stray dogs, smouldering heaps of rubbish smoke into the dying sunlight. At a petrol station outside the town we queue behind an old Mercedes. A diesel pump stands inside a heavy iron cage guarded by a chained dog and a man smoking a cigarette. The place reeks. Ten yards away lies the burnt-out shell of a car. Just inside the town the truck stops outside a row of small, dilapidated houses. Their neat gardens, crammed with vegetable beds, give them the air of suburban villas. Behind looms the concrete cooling tower of a power station. John tugs my arm and points to one of the houses, engulfed by the skeleton of a predatory vine. We are home.

Through the garden gate stream John's family, down tumble his boxes and my rucksack and off puffs the truck with a cowboy blare of the horn. I am pulled through the gate. On a terrace the family assembles in front of me, still and self conscious, like an old family photograph. John introduces me to his parents and his two sisters and a brother who is dumb. No wonder John was so gentle with the driver's son. His mother motions for me to sit down and begins to undo my shoe laces. A plastic bowl full of warm water is brought and she washes my feet, all the time speaking to John excitedly over her shoulder. He in the meantime is peeling off his socks. My feet are dried, I am given a pair of plastic flip flops and it is John's turn.

Later we eat a supper of fried chicken and bread in front of an enormous stove. John's father, whom everyone calls Baba, gets drunk and takes himself off somewhere when the women start teasing him.

He reels back a couple of hours later plastered and singing. After supper John and I lie about drinking coffee and smoking like a couple of pashas. John's dumb brother has an epileptic fit and the women look frightened and hold him quietly. The mother asks me what they can do for the boy and I mumble something hopelessly about doctors in Tirana. At last he goes limp their arms. The next day, Baba, looking cross, tells me that the boy is possessed by evil spirits, making his daughters cry.

I share a big double bed with John, who, a little drunk, stands above me in purple Y-fronts showing off his muscles. The room smells strongly of yeast, which is drying on wooden boards in a corner.

SUNDAY 24TH DECEMBER
CHRISTMAS EVE

> *Fier is a completely new city built during the years of socialist construction. It is beyond any comparison with the pre-Liberation Fier, which was nothing but a small inhabited centre in a backward agricultural zone covered with marshland and a hotbed of malaria. Today, Fier has been turned into one of the more important industrial centres of the country: the biggest complex for the production of chemicals and electrical power has been built there. Fier turns out 10 per cent of the total industrial production of the country. The main branch of industry is energy production (the extraction and processing of oil and production of electrical power), the chemical, engineering and food-stuffs industries. Two other important industrial centres, Ballsh - an oil extracting and refining centre, and Patos - a centre of oil extraction and the engineering for the oil industry, have been built in Fier district.* (AGO, p.73)

At the post office, John makes a call. He is arranging a business meeting. The telephones and the post office staff, like the petrol pump, lie behind heavy bars. Otherwise the post office looks like a stables, the floor is filthy and the glass in the windows is broken. A young girl dials a number and waits patiently as it rings. She holds the telephone uneasily, as if she doubts its authenticity or can smell the breath of the last speaker on the mouthpiece. Suddenly her eyes light up in shock and then pleasure and she starts talking animatedly down the line.

This 'important industrial centre' is a wasteland. The roads are bad, the vehicles on them archaic, the settlements filthy and tumble-down. There is a background pong of crude oil. Mud is everywhere, and mangy dogs. There are no recognisable shops. What there is to buy is handed to you through iron bars, like the petrol and the phones. It seems nothing here is safe, no one can be trusted. And everywhere is a sense of fragile calm. People do not walk the streets on their own, they go in twos and threes. Cars drive too fast, as if they are keen to leave something behind. Dogs bark. Someone screams. A window smashes.

I have only been here a day but already it feels like a place where most people merely exist, survive. The erratic electricity supply disturbs study, most of the old industries have crashed, there are few jobs, pensions aren't paid, you can't buy nappies anywhere. If the bus isn't running to the next town, how can you meet the girl you might otherwise have fallen in love with and one day married. Your best friend's run away to Greece. Your uncle's washing car windscreens in Rome. Your sister's got rickets. And cinemas, outings, school sports, ice creams, holidays. One day.

That evening the whole family walks into the centre of the town. All of Fier is there, promenading up and down the main street. It is a touching sight, dignified and civilised against this backdrop of decay. Old men pace slowly along the dusty pavement, in black suits that are greasy with age, their hands sieving worry beads behind their backs. Beside them stroll their wives in cardigans looking like sensible school dinner ladies. Young men walk past, hand in hand. John is a great draw. He is cast in the role of young returning hero and makes the most of it.

MONDAY 25TH DECEMBER
CHRISTMAS DAY

In 1967, Hoxha officially banned all religious practice and declared Albania an atheist state. Borrowing the ghastly tactics of China's cultural revolution, imams and priests were disposed of, religious buildings destroyed or put to secular use (mosque as cattle-shed, cathedral as basketball court etc.) and religious texts burnt. It was a canine, wounding exercise – one of Hoxha's greatest crimes. Brave men and women, and isolated communities, did keep pockets of religious faith alive - Hoxha couldn't erode the private memories and devotions of all his people. But most conformed, adjusting once more to the new status quo. Pragmatism triumphed.

Which explains why John's family, like the rest of Fier, didn't much go in for Christmas, despite the fact that Baba and his wife grew up in the Greek Orthodox faith. The Christian function had been snipped out of their consciousnesses, like an unnecessary piece of flesh, a spiritual appendix. Their son John, trained as a communist, regards Christmas as a holiday, a break, like most Christian-trained, rat race Brits.

After lunch John's mother produces a small metal cross on a necklace. She had been given it by her grandmother, before the Second World War. She has never shown it to her family before. The necklace is passed around the table, held by her husband and her children, who have never known their mother's secret. Why not - had she been afraid to tell them? Hoxha's secret police, the Sigurimi, encouraged family members, especially children, to keep their relations under observation, and report any suspicious behaviour to the authorities.

John's mother has straight black hair with badger stripes of grey, blue-grey eyes and the aquiline features of a fifties' starlet. She is kneeling on the floor over the stove and when she stands up to fetch some water there is soot on her cheek, like a fat scar. It breaks the symmetry of her face, and when her attempts to remove it with the back of one hand smudge the soot across the side of her face she grins. At this moment, she is so beautiful.

Baba, who as man of the house is lord and master, seems oddly sidelined by all his women. The Albanian man is proud and nurses the aspect of a fighter, a man of action. Not for him soapsuds and bedtime stories. Like all Albanian men, Baba is treated like an honoured guest in his own home. But his natural authority seems to go no further than precedence at meal times and the best piece of meat. It is the women who seem to run things and make decisions and generally take charge. During the day Baba sits outside under a thick rug, smoking and smiling. Sipping coffee. In the afternoon he has his first glass of raki and his mood swings from joy and choking laughter to tears and despair. This evening the raki has made him maudlin and he stands out on the terrace, crying as he shakes his head from side to side. He tries to help his wife make coffee but he is so drunk he is clumsy and his wife gently sits him down.

THURSDAY 28TH DECEMBER
BLOCKADE AND ENCIRCLEMENT

John wants to build himself a house with the money he has saved in

60

Athens. This morning he has an appointment with a man who owns a vacant site. It might be what John is looking for. He wants me to come along. We walk into the centre of town. John has a roll of papers tucked under his arm. On our way down the street a group of boys playing football dribble their ball towards me and, in a rush of blood, I pass it back with my 'bad' foot. John looks at me out of the corner of his eye but says nothing.

At the taxi rank a man with a moustache rises from his Mercedes to greet us. We get into the car and drive to an area of wasteland on Fier's outskirts. Another man, fat and vulgar in sun glasses, is waiting for us. He is the owner of the site. John spreads his papers on the bonnet and kicks off this little piece of new capitalism. The papers are architect's plans. It looks a simple enough building - international suburbia with Mediterranean touches. The fat man takes us to a nearby building site where another house is already being built on similar lines to John's. By now the fat man has discovered I am English and is reeling off every football team in the first division. "Leevapool, Spurse, Lids." I make encouraging noises as he breaks off to show John a specimen of local brick. Materials are apparently difficult to find and therefore expensive. "Menchestur Unyted, Babby Moore, Geoff Hursse."

We move on to the site that the fat man has earmarked for John, pegged out on the ground. John takes us through his dream home. He opens an imaginary front door and carves a floor plan on the dirty grass. Kitchen: microwave, dishwasher; sitting room with television, sofas, video; loo... He has a television in his bedroom and a shower but no bath. The fat man puts a heavy arm over John's shoulder. "Meessiss Thachair, Weenstan Chursheel," he drawls at me over his shoulder.

John talks quietly with the fat man for a while, leaving the taxi driver to take up fatty's chant "Qween Lizbeth, Preence Charlss". I throw stones at a piece of hardboard and swing my stick and wonder how much all this will cost John.

"How much?" I ask him when the taxi driver has dropped us back on the main street. John looks at me for a moment as if sizing me up and says "many dollars" rather flatly. I drop the subject. Later, after supper of rice and mutton, we sit on the terrace, wrapped in thick rugs and drinking raki. It is a brilliant night and the purple black sky is frosted with stars. Far away we can hear Baba singing his way home.

Tomorrow, John says, he must make the deal. I have decided to leave for Tirana in the morning. This small place is becoming claustrophobic - I am weary of so much kind attention. And it's time to find the Professor. But when I broach this subject there is a great hoohah. John says 'no', the women say 'no', Baba, who stumbles suddenly onto the terrace, says 'no'. I say 'yes' until they accept it's all up.

SATURDAY 30ᵀᴴ DECEMBER
FIER - TIRANA

> *Tirana ('Hero City') is the capital and the biggest city of Albania, as well as the biggest political, economic, educational and cultural centre of the country. In Tirana the Communist Party of Albania was founded on 8th November 1941. Up till the liberation of the country Tirana remained a small commercial administrative city. During the years of socialist construction Tirana has undergone great changes both in its layout and its demographic and economic development. Now it has the appearance of a modern city. The value of its industrial production today makes up 17.8 per cent of the total industrial production of the country, having increased fivefold in comparison with 1960.*
>
> *The engineering industry, which has now set out on*

the course of machine building, contributes about 30
per cent of the total industrial production of the city.
The 'Enver Hoxha' automobile and tractor combine is
the most important productive centre of the engineering
industry. Light industry turns out 25.3 per cent of the
industrial production of the city. Its main centre is the
'Stalin' tekstile combine...   (AGO, pp. 66-67)

John's mother has prepared fried eggs for her wheeler-dealer son and his English blood brother. Before John sits down for breakfast he performs a fantastic number of press-ups in his Y-fronts. He then puts on his shiny suit and a shirt and tie that he has bought in Athens. They are still in their box, a ready to wear combination of pale blue shirt, red patterned tie and red handkerchief.

Out on the terrace the family wave me goodbye.

"Thank you" I say to John's mother and she kisses me on the cheek before turning away.

"Good bye Alexi. Good bye England" says John's sister carefully. She has been practising.

Baba insists on walking me to the bus. At the gate John kicks a fat cockerel, as if for luck and picks the mud off his shoes. In the street he shows me what is in his inside pocket - the flick knife in its cardboard box.

"Very strong. John Albanian business man number one!"

Baba, cackling with delight, grabs my hand and together the three of us walk into town.

A bullying conductor with blond hair marches up and down the aisle, shoving people out of the way and generally enjoying himself. His harassed passengers are quiet. Through the grimy window I notice scenes in isolation - a boy whipping the behind of a donkey, a large crowd of men standing still by the bus station of a town. I suppose that they were looking for work. All of them seem to have drooping moustaches. The bus is slow and every so often an old Mercedes or lorry toots it horn as it pulls out to overtake us. Each one belches treacle black smoke.

The warmth in the bus unleashes Albania's characteristic smell - a heady combination of cow dung, stale milk, damp wool, unwashed bodies, earth, mouldy fruit, paraffin, woodsmoke, cheap soap powder and greasy hair. In front of me a peasant in baggy trousers and puttees eats a lemon, starting with the peel. Watching him chew the flesh makes me wince. He spits the pips on the floor with relish. A number of women hold pieces of orange and lemon peel to their noses like nosegays. They too notice the smell.

Several hours later we pass a bullet-holed sign saying 'Tirana'. I can see brown hills in the distance. Tirana lies heroically in the plain, beneath grey, squatting cloud. I suppose this rotting landscape is Tirana's suburb, but not as Mr Betjeman would recognise: tidy villas and well kept gardens. Instead there are clusters of tenement blocks, like those I saw in the towns on my way to Fier, only larger. They lean here and there, casting crooked shadows across the scrub. Some look fit to fall down, little better than slums. Old factories stand smoking on either side of the road.

The bus hammers into a pothole, and then another. I can smell sewers. There are spare dogs licking filth off the pavement. A patch of dirty grass supports a gypsy - drunk, asleep or dead. A few people walk the streets, mainly women with scarves tied about their heads. There is a queue below a window that opens onto the pavement. Bundles are passed through it wrapped in newspaper. Loaves of bread, I suppose, but they could be unwanted babies, pink and perfect for spit roast.

The traffic gets thicker, slowing around the potholes. There are few vehicles but the few are all geriatric. Donkeys pull carts down the middle of the road. There do not seem to be any traffic lights. I remember the shiny photographs of Italianate squares in the AGO and Mr Hoxha's claim that Albania was the greatest country in the world. Well here I am at its capital and I have never seen anything so pitiful. If the countryside looks like it has been ravaged by an enemy army, Tirana feels like the army is camped at its gates and everywhere the city's inhabitants are in a state of weary siege. Out of the frying pan ...

The bus pulls off the road onto a patch of wasteland and the conductor chases us down the aisle.

"Skanderberg Square?" I ask an old man, picking at the dust with my stick. He looks at me suspiciously and mutters what sounds like 'piss off' and walks away. Life suddenly feels rather unfair. The other bus passengers have disappeared. Behind a metal fence a group of young boys watch me vacantly. I begin to walk up the road, hoping that it will take me into the centre and the familiar symmetry of a few fountains and a Square.

Behind me there is a man, long hair, gypsy features, black leather jacket, following me. He breaks into a run in order to catch me up.

"Where?" he asks smiling. He holds an arm out, softly pulling mine, as if to slow me down better to make conversation. But the mood of the man is malevolent, not friendly. He smiles at me stupidly. Nervously. It is the smile of someone who is nervous because he wants to rob me. He looks at my heavy rucksack. And my stick. I remember the head leaning out of the window at the Athens Embassy:

"No go to Albania. Albania not good." Too late.

"Ingleterra," I say in pigeon something.

"Embassadia Ingleterra" hoping he might think I am something to do with the Embassy. And then "very good" for want of something better. I shrug off his arm and walk faster, swinging my stick about.

The road is deserted. It is Sunday lunch time, the first Sunday after Christmas. My family will be eating lunch in the kitchen, an old clock ticking above the aga, green fields through the window. Thousands of miles away I can see damp scrub land, the chimneys of a factory, tenement blocks in the distance. No fountains. The gypsy stays alongside, looking about nervously. I know that I am about to be attacked. I cannot run in my rucksack, I cannot fight in my rucksack. I can only wait and hope that I am wrong. A car is coming towards us. Suddenly the gypsy runs into me with enough force to knock me down. The stick clatters away. My head hits the pavement.

Hands grab my rucksack and try to pull it off. Having no success, they pull me over, forcing me onto my back. The man has a gun in his hand and is pointing it at my nose.

"Dollars," he shouts nervously.

"Dollars, dollars. Give me!" He looks quite terrified. Which is terrifying. I point to a pouch hanging inside my shirt. He grabs it and rips it off, third time lucky. Inside are over one hundred dollars and a Young Person's Rail card. The man grunts and unzips the pockets of my rucksack. Woolf, Golding, Tolstoy. He shuffles them like a pack of cards.

"Piss off," I whisper. They suddenly seem very precious. The man drops them on my chest and gets into the car. I hear him slam the door and the engine revving.

My palms are badly grazed and one knee is cut, my trousers are ripped. I feel dizzy and very angry. I take off my rucksack and put the books back into the side pocket. An old woman runs out of a doorway followed by her husband. She picks up my rucksack and takes my arm, pulling me into a doorway. Her husband follows, clicking his teeth. I cannot understand why they are so upset until I remember my stick, which the old man has picked up. They think I am an invalid.

Inside the room is freezing. It is a kitchen with a long sofa made up as a bed. The old woman makes me lie down on it. The man brings me a glass of brandy, which I drink greedily, mainly to warm up. All the time they are talking and stroking my arm and shaking their heads. I am at once touched and irritated by their attentions. They do go on, and the woman is clumsy with my knee. I am no longer in the mood to be coerced. Since I arrived in Albania I have been at the mercy of crowds, John, John's family, the gypsy and now this kind pair. It is time to take over.

"Hotel, hotel!" Slowly they understand and after a few minutes we push off down the road, at the speed of the shuffling old man in his slippers. Me tapping my stick and walking into town between a silver haired bodyguard.

The lobby of the Dajti Hotel is cold and dark. There is no one about. A bovine looking women gazes at me from behind a reception desk. I'm not staying here. The kind old couple plant wet kisses on my cheeks, and patter out into the daylight. After a hauty tour of the lobby I follow them, swinging my stick and feeling like a bit of luxury. At the bottom of the Dajti's marble steps I stand, looking about and wondering what to do next. In front of the hotel is a garden of wet grass and empty flower beds. Tall pines stand between me and a busy road. A taxi driver shuffles up in a tight fitting sports jacket.

"Where you wanna go?" he asks, taking my rucksack.

"Take me to another hotel," I announce grandly "…take me to the best hotel in Tirana."

"I am Gzim," he announces as he helps me put my rucksack in the back of his old Volvo.

"Gzim drive Wolvo - best car in Tirana! I drive you best hotel." Gzim is a round little man with a bald head and face like an imp. We pull out of the Dajti and drive four hundred metres into Skanderberg

Square. It is a wide, cobbled plaza, built during the reign of King Zog. In the middle of the Square are four square pools with fountains, half-hearted plumes of water wobbling in a breeze. At last.

At the far end of Skanderberg Square stands the Tirana Hotel. Tall by Albanian standards, it is an awkward concrete block - a product of the 'Yugoslav school'. Inside, the decor is obscure: oranges and browns, cool pale marble, sculpture in white steel. In the lobby I count my dollars. Most of my cash is still in a money belt around my waist - I am good for a couple of nights at the Tirana. Then I will have to find the Professor. I order beer and some lunch and open a book.

"Hi there," says a soft American accent.

I look up into the eyes of a young man standing in front of me. He looks about eighteen, wearing a thick sweater, jeans, thick socks and sandals and clutches a sheaf of papers. He is handsome in a blond kind of way and has a wide smile full of clean teeth. He looks like he smiles all the time. But it is his eyes that catch me. They are bright blue and touched with a diamond thrill that signals some kind of genius, or fanaticism.

"My name is Daniel." His voice is soft, almost tender.

"Alex," I reply tersely.

"Can I sit down?"

Daniel sits down, staring at me intensely.

"What are you doing in Albania, Alex?"

"Just visiting."

"Oh yeah – how's it going?"

"I've just been mugged. What are you doing here?"

"I'm working for a mission over here – you know, preaching and spreading God's holy word."

"Oh, great." I turn back to my book, hoping that he'll go away.

"Yeah, it's great. We've got this day centre where kids come off the streets and play and sing and read scripture. We also do the best hamburgers in town." He laughs as if he has said something funny.

"I suppose that there are a lot of you around?"

"Quite a few. Country sure needs us. You know, Alex, it's so poor here. There's *real* poverty."

"Mmmm. I've noticed."

"And, Alex, there's a lot of, well, misunderstanding in this place. It used to be part of the Turkish empire and they're real vulnerable to dangerous ideas, you know, especially now when they're all so poor and stuff. You know, Alex, Iranians. Saudis. Islam. *Fundamentalists.*" He has stopped smiling.

"What does Jesus mean to you, Alex?" The eyes harden. Suddenly he is on duty. I ignore the question and he just goes on smiling and I ask him if he wants a beer. He smiles a negative, still in control.

"How old are you?"

"Just nineteen, Alex" He has that infuriating habit of repeating your name every time he addresses you.

"Would you like to have a look at one of our leaflets, Alex?"

He is a Seventh Day Adventist. The leaflet superimposes scripture on pastoral scenes of green valleys and smiling cows. A Dali-esque sun wobbles in the Heavens.

"Alex, I would like to pray for you." The words drop solemnly out of his prissy mouth and bounce back at me off the marble floor. He is already on his knees in front of me, his eyes shut. I should just read my book over his head. Or slap him with it. But I can't - it would just be too rude. Enslaved by a middle class training I drop my book to my lap and lower my head a touch as he begins to pray.

"Drop in for a burger sometime," he says as he gets up to leave.

"Thanks. Where are you from in America?"

"I'm not, I'm from Canada."

"Oh, sorry – don't all Canadians hate being mistaken for Americans?"

"No problem." Still smiling, still in control.

"Are your parents happy about you being here?" I ask, hoping to mist his eyes over with memories of mom baking cookies in a gingham apron.

"They brought me here. Dad's mission leader." A family of lunatics.

SUNDAY 31ˢᵀ DECEMBER
NEW YEARS EVE

> *The supreme organs of the Party of Labour of Albania and the state are located in Tirana. There are too the Palace of Congresses, the Academy of Sciences, the Computer Centre, the Enver Hoxha University of Tirana, the Higher Institutes of Agriculture, Art and Physical Culture, the Opera and Ballet Theatre, the People's Drama Theatre, the New Albania Film Studios, the National Museum, the Lenin-Stalin Museum, the Cemetery of Martyrs of the Homeland, the Museum of Natural Sciences, the Art Gallery and the Museum dedicated to the life and work of Comrade Enver Hoxha is under construction.* (AGO, pp. 67-68)

Busy Skanderberg Square wakes me up. After a breakfast of shortcake and coffee I set out into the Square. The winter sunlight is blinding and I feel suddenly nervous of the noise and the people. Half way across the Square I look wistfully back at the tall hotel. I feel like I am leaving the womb. But the real world of Tirana brings me to with the harsh efficiency of a midwife's smack. I narrowly avoid being run over by a truck loaded with aggregates. It curses me with a rude blare of its horn and I shake my stick at its rear, like some furious old man. Back on the pavement I am targeted by the string of handicapped beggars lying grotesque on strips of cardboard outside the Palace of Culture. A western cripple - rich pickings. But I have the advantage of masked speed and soon they are fumbling furiously in my wake.

Turning out of the Square I follow Tirana's Champs Élysées, Deshmoret ë Kombit Boulevard, down towards Tirana Park. Directly behind me is the Hotel and its stubborn memory over my shoulder is somehow re-assuring. The boulevard is wide and lined with tall pines. A banner decorated with clumsy berries and holly hangs overhead. 'Merry Christmas' it wishes the passers-by in English. Beneath it squat a few traders, their goods laid out on the pavement, including Christmas cards with messages written in English. Behind a copse of pines stands the Dajti. On the other side of the boulevard spreads a small park, full of coffee shops (known locally as kiosks). Most have been designed with escape in mind – alpine chalets or fairytale cottages, built at the end of twee paths, among ferns and small pools. Far away from Tirana.

I cross a dirty canal, the 'river' Lana. On the far side is a massive, pink marble pyramid, originally built as a 'life and times' museum to Enver Hoxha in 1988, the eightieth anniversary of his birth. Designed by the dictator's architect daughter, Pranvera, it stands among flower beds and marble steps and more (empty) fountains. Today it is used as a nightclub.

Past the pyramid, grey ministry buildings face each other across the boulevard. At the end of the boulevard, behind another defunct fountain, is the university, stained with graffiti and empty looking. Beyond spreads the city's park. In the middle of the park is a lake, where a couple of men are fishing from a rowing boat. Behind them a damp meadow, hills and fringes of grey woodland. Watching the fishermen, all trace of the city suddenly recedes - there is not a telegraph pole or the sound of traffic. Just a piece of water and two men fishing in a wilderness.

Back in Skanderberg Square I wander around an enormous hole dug next door to the Tirana. According to my Blue Guide it is known as Hajim's Hole, named after the Kosovan who dug it soon after the fall of communism, as the foundations for a new Sheraton Hotel. But before Hajim could fill his hole he quietly left the country with a lot of investor's money. Now he is in prison in Switzerland, his millions no doubt confiscated by the KLA and his hole remains unfilled, full of green water.

A drunk walks up to me and shouts something very loudly. He has long hair and a beard. He is filthy and when he shouts drops of saliva land like rain on my face. He has a gun in his belt. What is it about me that attracts unstable Albanians carrying weapons? After another outburst he sways off across the Square. Suddenly sick of this scruffy country and its damaged people I follow him, heading for the Hotel. I have had enough and go up to my room to gaze stupidly at Italian TV and read. Later, I have a lonely supper in the hotel dining room - an omelette, cooked in what tastes like Fier crude and a bottle of Albanian merlot which stains my teeth purple.

Around two I'm woken up by the screech of tyres and sounds of a fight. A police van is drawn up below, blocking the path of a small car. Policemen are chasing two men across the square, whom they catch and beat. One of the men struggles and is thrown violently into one of the pools. The fountains have been switched off for the night. One policeman gets into the small car, the rest drive away the night's catch. Next door someone is violently sick out of the window. Dance music is throbbing in Hoxha's pyramid and a searchlight plays against the sky. It is New Year.

JANUARY

There is an Englishman eating breakfast in the dining room. He is wearing a blazer and spotted tie. I ask if I can join him.

"Please do," he says, his words muffled by a mouthful of boiled egg. "Glad to have some company - I thought I was the only Englishman in Tirana." His name is Richard Grey.

"Came out on Boxing Day. Meant to be with my assistant but the poor chap broke his back skiing. What a place to spend New Year, eh! I went to the opera last night - heard a lovely Traviata. It cost me three pounds. Plus a one pound tip to one of those little scamps outside who looked set to throw a stone at me. Still I'm off home tomorrow. Back to Somerset."

Richard is an international business consultant. He has won an EU contract to organise a conference on investment opportunities in Albania. It will be post-communist Albania's first proper chance to sell itself to the outside world. The conference takes place in May.

I am intrigued by the idea of Albania as the next emerging market.

"I don't suppose it will be easy?"

Richard shakes his head.

"You said it. This place is a shambles. Government's got to attract private cash to get the economy moving - foreign money and expertise is the only thing that can get the place back on its feet, create jobs, pep up the provinces and show ordinary Albanians that capitalism is more fun than communism. The country's got potential: cheap labour, political will, proximity to western European markets, natural resources, good beaches. But so far western firms are hanging back - they think the place's still in chaos, bureaucratic minefield, corruption... That's where the Conference comes in. Boost the image - show the outside world what's here. Not that it will be easy. Goodness knows what I've taken on. But enough about me, what on earth are you doing here?"

I tell him about Sarajevo, and Maurice and the Professor.

"I've heard about Pace. He's big in Bulgaria, close friends with the mafia there. I know he's got plenty of interests in Russia too; minerals are his thing, and oil. I bet he's as bent as a screw... so you're going to work for the Professor! The great hero of the revolution! That should be an experience. But it doesn't sound like a full-time appointment; he's out of the country a lot for a start..."

Richard is sipping his coffee, his eyes fixed on me. "...tell you what! How about working for me as well? It would be bloody useful to have someone on the ground, who can keep things moving along in my absence, co-ordinate the thing at this end. Especially someone with your connections! What do you think? I can't pay you a fortune but I could get you something... And I could definitely swing you an office at the Ministry of Finance."

Ten minutes later my first ever job interview is over and Richard and I are toasting our collaboration with a fresh pot of coffee.

Richard has other jobs on the go in Russia and Macao. He will, he has told me, be coming and going. Meanwhile, I'll be in the Ministry of Finance, 'holding the fort'.

TUESDAY 2ND JANUARY
HOLDING THE FORT

Richard has gone home. He will be back in a couple of weeks, bringing me a new set of clothes. I'm going to need something smart.

"It's good to have you on board you know. Hell of a weight off my mind. I was beginning to worry that I was having to spend months in this bloody place."

Contemplating months in this bloody place I watch him hail a taxi to the airport and fight the urge to run after him and resign on the spot.

I try to ring the Professor this evening but there is no answer.

WEDNESDAY 3RD JANUARY
ITCHY FEET

I have found out that the Professor is in Greece until the weekend. In his absence I have nothing to do. It's time to stretch my legs. Richard has recommended Pogradec, a town by a lake on the Macedonian border.

"Tremendous place, ringed by mountains. Full of fish. Had a lovely drive there last August. Real holiday spot."

It sounds perfect.

Half an hour south of Tirana the Pogradec bus, an old Ford Transit van, climbs a series of hairpins until we are on the spine of a mountain range. Below us fields and small villages run adrift in folded, lion-coloured country. Groups of young men sit by the roadside selling roast potatoes. Down the other side of the range sprawls Elbasan, once the heavy industrial capital of Albania, spread out across the flat Shkumbini valley. A rusting intestine of pipes and empty warehouses, railway lines and chimneys (the tallest in the Balkans) mark the *Steel of the Party* refinery. Built with Chinese aid during the 1960's and 70's it was zappily dubbed 'the second national liberation of Albania' by Enver Hoxha. It was filthy by all accounts, polluting the air to dangerous levels and destroying the soil. Even Hoxha's party bosses were shocked by Chinese indifference to the welfare of the Elbasan's inhabitants.

In the shade of citadel walls there is time for a coffee while the bus fills up again and then we are off. The road heads east, shadowing the Shkumbini river. We are on the old Via Egnatia, once one of the most important roads in the Roman Empire, linking Durres and the

Adriatic coast with Constantinople, via Lake Ohrid and Macedonia. Gradually the valley becomes wooded and narrows and the road is squeezed between the river and a railway line. Damp leaves stick to the surface of the road and we come across a white car that has fallen, headlong, onto the rail track. We stop, have a good look and, a little later, wave down a police car. The policeman looks appalled and gets urgently onto the radio. He must know the train timetable.

Steadily the road climbs, the Shkumbini gets thinner and faster, the trees get thicker and the valley sides get higher and steeper. Over a narrow pass Lake Ohrid stretches below us, still and silver. Ohrid is the deepest lake in the Balkans (310 metres at its deepest point). Its cold waters swim with the koran, according to Richard a delicious and prehistoric cousin of the trout. Beyond soar the snowy peaks of Macedonia. It is beautifully clear and bright. Down by the lakeside there are more groups of men, this time optimistically holding out fish to the few cars on the road. Our driver buys some for lunch. The lake is bordered by empty cafes and empty holiday homes. The cafes have fancy pontoons built into the water. Pogradec is Albania's smart place to holiday and, like the Cote d'Azur, is full of all the best kind of people in August. Both Hoxha and King Zog had holiday homes there.

After I have found Albturist's Hotel Pogradec, a pink and green concrete block of communist mediocrity standing right on the waterfront, I order a prehistoric koran for lunch in a lakeside restaurant. It is, as Richard promised, delicious - pink (like the hotel) and full of flavour. It is also very big and I eat the lot, settling back in my chair with raki and a great sigh when it is all over.

When I can move comfortably again I stroll through the town. Ringed by mountains, by a well stocked lake and with an invigorating highland climate, Pogradec sounds like the sort of resort that kept Monsieur Poirot so busy during the twenties. But close up it is disappointing - not a casino or a shapely widow's ankle in sight. Instead derelict buildings, muddy parks scattered with broken glass, pavement blackened by small fires, gypsy boys begging barefoot in December, emaciated donkeys, flooded sewers, ripped-down trees, hillsides scarred by worked-out mine shafts, baying flocks of seagulls, queues for bread and buses, a score of drab boats still on the water, piles of rubbish, folds of human shit, potholes, political graffiti, groups of silent, useless men.

I walk back to the hotel. It is colder inside the hotel than out, which might explain why it is deserted. My first choice of room - one looking out over the lake - was deemed too cold to risk by the old manager, a retired English teacher called Ibrahim. My new room is no warmer. The sheets are off-white and damp. All the light bulbs seem to be broken. Ibrahim tells me that he pays his staff US$1 a day.

It is 5.00 pm and I lie on my damp bed in my cold hotel room listening to the World Service. I feel sick after my koran and too much coffee. I am very cold despite the fact that I have all my clothes on. This place makes Tirana feel spring-like. Peruvian terrorists have taken over the Japanese Embassy in Lima, ambushing an diplomatic reception. Their catch is a rich one: scores of ambassadors in white tie. The terrorists are now demanding the release of their comrades from Peru's jails. At this lonely moment I would happily swap places with a nervous first secretary, cowering under a table on Japanese soil.

Later, I walk around the dark streets, full of pale figures moving in muffled groups like ghosts. A few kiosks are open, their cheap shelves lit up by paraffin lamps casting elephantine images onto the street. By the lake I stop to smoke a cigarette. The movement of small boats near the shore creaks like rope. A ghastly laugh rises out of a group sitting around a fire. One of the group shouts at me.

"Hey! Fucking American!"

I head back to the hotel, spooked. I have had too much sinister and cold for one day. I suddenly feel horribly exposed, an uncomfortable distance from those that I love and who love me.

Behind the hotel's reception desk a man and woman, with no English, play cards in a warm fug. A tartan rug is spread over their knees. They point towards the bar. Ibrahim is waiting in the gloom, sitting alone at a round table. Nearby a couple of other tables are busy with old men arguing and smoking. Ibrahim is staring into a glass of raki and looking glum. I have lost my appetite in the cold and so the two of us share a bowl of olives and drink our way through a bottle of raki. It seems the only clever thing to do in the circumstances. I certainly won't be able to sleep sober.

The glass is broken in two of the tall windows that look out onto the street and the cold pours in, beating back a frayed net curtain. I alone among the other drinkers have taken off my jacket, leaving T-shirt, shirt, two jerseys, silk long johns, jeans and two pairs of socks. The jacket stays off for about five minutes. Opposite me, Ibrahim is wearing a woolly hat and scarf.

Ibrahim started out in the Albanian diplomatic service - rather a contradiction in terms for a country which, by the late 1970's, had literally not a friend in the world. He remained in the service only two years. These were spent in Cuba, where he soon got into trouble. Tears fill his rheumy old eyes as he remembers stolen days spent at the beaches with Cuban girls.

"Good days, good days." His enthusiasm for the beach often led him to go about alone, something that was against Embassy rules. These insisted that all Albanian diplomats travel in pairs so that one might keep an eye on the other. Ibrahim was duly sent home and given a teaching job in a dissident village in northern Puka. These villages were built as punishment zones for suspect families and were spitefully located on poor, isolated land, a long way from amenities like electricity and roads. Barren Puka was a long way from the conchitas but there he stayed, with his family, for five years, working as the village schoolmaster.

"Looking back, I don't know how I survived." After the collapse of communism he taught in Tirana and then Pogradec, where he stayed. Now, inexplicably, he is manager of this hotel which, he whispers, as if he is being vulgar, is up for sale. In fact it's been for sale for a couple of years but no one's interested in buying it. In the meantime the government has no money to fund refurbishment. Or central heating.

After the raki has gone, Ibrahim and I part company. I circle out into the lobby and tap my stick up the stairs in some kindergarten rhythm. In the dark corridor, smelling of woodsmoke, a tabby cat is staring intently at the foot of the door to 113 - the escape route, I guess, of a rare, cold mouse. The cat flees as it hears me looming through the darkness.

Back in my room, I turn on the noisy fan heater that Ibrahim has kindly found for me. It rattles slowly into action. A power cut rattles it slowly out of action and I fumble my way through my jacket pockets to find a torch bought in Athens for just this tedious moment. In the pockets I also discover the peel of a tangerine given to me by my neighbour in the bus from Tirana. I nibble it among raki fumes. Pulling back the bedclothes I climb gingerly inside. It is like lying in an ice box. Half an hour later the power comes back on and with it the rattling heater. It is still going when I wake up. Miraculously, it is light and my breath is once again steaming in the cold.

THURSDAY 4TH JANUARY
POGRADEC - KORCA

Back in the bar Ibrahim is waiting for me. I feel wretched. Ibrahim has

81

ordered 'brekfist' and toast arrives along with delicious creamy butter and plum jam. We sit sipping coffee, a pair of old men. He thumbs my Blue Guide with interest, examining the pages on Pogradec. Spotting 'errors' he clicks his teeth and murmurs to himself, as if he was inspecting a disappointing piece of homework. He is horrified by the Guide's verdict on his hotel ('badly managed, drab, ugly and cold').

"But Alex…"(he is momentarily lost for words), "you have been here! You know these things are untrue. You must visit the author when you return to London. You must speak with them. This is an injustice."

An hour later I am slumped across the back of another battered Transit van, headed for Korca, the capital of south-east Albania. Armed with bottles of mineral water and a bag of plum jam sandwiches I survey a new landscape of fruit trees, haystacks shaped like giant bearskins and small, prosperous-looking farms as the bus climbs away from the lake into rolling hills. Pogradec is soon a smudge on the water's edge and the lake itself is almost small enough to hold in one hand. It sits beautifully polished by the sun, a glacier prison - useless and unwanted.

A twenty minute climb takes us up onto the billiard flat Plain of Korca. A wide plateau ringed by mountains, the Plain is said to throw fantastic skies at the traveller, reminiscent (according to my wonderful Blue Guide) of the American Midwest. I have been looking forward to this all morning. I have never been to the American Midwest and am anxious to experience its skies. But today the plain is covered by an impenetrable fog and I can see no further than the edge of the road.

Korca is the main city in the zone of the south-eastern depression. It lies at the foot of the Morava Mountain at an altitude of 866m above sea level… Korca has been transformed into one of the most important industrial centres of the country, especially for the knitwear, food-stuffs, engineering and electrical power industry. The

industry in Korca turns out seven per cent of the total
industrial production of the country. Korca is famous
for its artistic handicraft products, carpets and rugs. The
holiday hostel for working people has been built on the
Partizan Hills.   (AGO pp. 71-72)

The bus drops me on the outskirts of the town, by the entrance
to a sooty power station. Korca's streets are busy. People smile. In the
town centre there are some surprisingly smart shops - a confectioners
that would not shame Paris, a Greek travel agency and small private
bank faced in marble with a polished brass plaque. The Greek influence
is strong here - we are only about thirty kilometres from the border.
Korca seems to have a great many barbers' shops, full of sharpfaced
men wielding cut-throat razors. I offer myself up to one of them and
spend a dizzy few minutes reclined in his chair. There can be no better
hangover cure than the scraping rhythms of the blade and the tingle of
lavender cologne.

Afterwards I walk into a handsome quarter of large Ottoman
townhouses, built on high ground on the edge of town. Cobbled streets
connect courtyards hung with vines and cats sunbathing. I come across
a flight of giant steps, leading up the steep hillside to the martyrs'
cemetery. By now the sky is clear and the sun is astonishingly hot for
December. At the top of the steps I collapse at the feet of an enormous
partisan hero, moulded fantastically in stone, his great fist raised towards
the hero city of Tirana. The air feels beautifully clean up here and the
view is breathtaking. At my feet spreads Korca, glinting rooftops,
chimney stacks, the green plain and, beyond, the snowy Morava
mountains. The champagne air makes me jubilant and light headed.
The gloom of Pogradec is forgotten.

I buy Korca beer from a small wooden hut on the road. It is ale-
coloured and I smack my lips at the thought of it. I eat kebabs and goats

83

cheese at a Greek restaurant, its walls covered in posters of waterfalls and dewy glades. Under the stairs is a bath full of shiny intestine, lemon-sized testicles, and pebble-bright brains bobbing about in cold water.

Back outside the power station a bus bound for Elbasan is waiting. By the time I reach Elbasan it is dark, though there are many people on the streets taking their constitutional. The bus stops in the town's old square, opposite the fat old walls of the citadel. A gypsy boy shows me the way to the Akelida Hotel, where a gauche old manager is clearing out a fish tank. At the bottom there are wrecked ships and doric columns among which the fish make merry.

SATURDAY 6TH JANUARY
POSITIVE THINKING

The Professor is back from Greece. I spoke to him on the phone this morning.

"Come tomorrow afternoon, Alexi. Maurice has told me all about you. I am looking forward to meeting you."

This afternoon, after dark, I throw my stick into Hajim's hole and march back into the Tirana talking to myself about a 'fresh start' and 'making a go of it'. With the Professor in town and Richard's return a few days closer this place feels a good deal friendlier. Soon I must find somewhere else to live. The Tirana's about to close for a post-communist facelift and, anyhow, it's too expensive.

SUNDAY 7TH JANUARY
THE PROFESSOR

I find Gzim outside the Dajti. "I want to go to the Professor's house. Do you know where it is?"

"The Professor! All people in Tirana know the Professor."

We cross the River Lana, grey green and dismal in its concrete

84

canal and turn left, following it upstream. Hoxha's pyramid waddles past on the right. Down a muddy side road we stop outside a high wall. Beyond I can make out the dirty yellow outline of a two-storey house, square and Italian. Gzim gets out and opens a pair of bent metal gates and we drive in along a puddled drive, past a garden of orange and lemon trees.

Inside the house the Professor and his family are watching English football on the television. Liverpool are pushing deep into someone's half on a cold January afternoon.

It is a modern, comfortable room, nothing like the peasant simplicity of Fier. There are sofas and a coffee table and a large pot plant in one corner. The Professor gets to his feet. He is younger than I expected, wearing jeans, flip flops and an old sweater, his hair is an untidy grey mass. Handsome in a rugged, cigarette smoker's kind of way, he looks clever and strong and his handshake is full of iron.

"Welcome to Albania, Alex" he drawls in a slow melody all of his own, rich with tobacco undertones. In front of the television sits his plump son, Haxi, and his tired-looking wife. A glass of raki is pressed into my hand and the Professor suggests a toast.

"To our two great countries," says the Professor with the hint of a grin. "And to friendship."

I tell the Professor about Richard and the Conference and he looks slightly put out, as if he had expected to have me all to himself. But he is good, funny company, chain smoking and sipping raki, listening carefully to what I say.

"You see Alex, the trouble with this country is that it's not a democracy, not a real democracy. Our President has the mentality of a dictator. And our people do not know any better."

"That's why I had to leave the government," he explains "because I am too much in love with what you British call fair play. I am not making myself very popular, but at least I am being heard."

Suddenly there is a power cut and the room is full of blue tobacco smoke trails suspended in the fragile light of a few candles. A now empty bottle of raki stands on the table. We sit in the darkness, listening to the radio as the rain rattles on old windows in the kitchen. The Professor's cousin, another academic turned DP government minister, is in danger. Like the Professor he has fallen out with the President. Now he is facing corruption charges (which the Professor insists have been fabricated). This evening, at a special session, parliament will vote on a government motion calling for the removal of his parliamentary immunity. Without it the President will be able to put him in prison. The result of the vote is expected any minute.

This is just how I had imagined political Tirana in dark January - sinister, clandestine, a little frightening. I remember my first meeting with Maurice and his ghoulish stories and listen for the rap of a secret policeman's knuckles on the front door. But there is good news on the radio. Parliament, in a rare demonstration of independence, has defied the government – the Professor's cousin is safe. Like a balloon popping, the tension goes out of the room. The Professor makes a joke, pours more raki and lights another cigarette. His wife goes off to cook supper.

TUESDAY 9TH JANUARY
THE IGLOO

The Professor wants me close to him. Around the corner from his house lives a lady in a tiny brick bungalow with a spare bedroom. She is fat and old and sleeps on a sofa in her kitchen, which smells of onion and boiled cabbage. She speaks not a word of English and I never remember her name. Her house is the coldest I have ever stayed in. My bedclothes are damp and my breath turns to thick steam in an instant. There is no electric light in my room. On one wall hangs a wounded crucifix.

Britain is not allowed an Embassy in Tirana. In 1945 a Royal Navy destroyer hit a mine in the Corfu straits and went down with around 40 sailors. The British blamed Albania. As reparation, a batch of Albanian gold, stored deep in the vaults of Threadneedle Street for the duration of the war, was confiscated. Now the Albanians want it back, but Britain wants an apology first. Until there is a settlement, full diplomatic relations are on hold and the British have to make do with a Chargé d'Affaires.

I have been looking forward to this visit. I am quietly confident that the Chargé, lonely and a long way from home, will welcome me with open arms and insist on sharing the contents of his FCO hampers and inviting me on hush-hush expeditions to Kosovo.

His office is in a modern white building, off a muddy road full of holes and vagrant children. Outside someone is washing a green Land Rover Discovery. A union flag flies from the roof and above the door hangs an enamel coat of arms. Inside I am shown into a small office, where a man in a v-neck jersey introduces himself as the Chargé.

"So, when did you arrive?" he says suspiciously.

"A few days ago, on the bus from Fier. I was mugged as soon as I got off it."

"Oh dear, I am sorry. No bones broken I hope…" He pauses, as if he wants to give me time to check. "And why, if you don't mind me asking, are you here?"

I tell him about Oslobedjenje, the Professor and Maurice and my job in the Ministry of Finance.

"Sarajevo! Well you have come a long way. What the hell was Maurice doing there…" he shifts uneasily in his chair. "Do you know if he's coming back?" He might have been talking about the black death.

"I haven't a clue," I reply. "I didn't know he had left."

Conversation is hard work. I move onto the Professor, but this only provides him with a fresh source of disappointment.

"But what are you actually going to do for him?" he protests.

"I don't know yet. We haven't really started."

"And what's this about the Ministry of Finance?"

"Well, I'll be helping to organise this investment conference. But I don't know any more than that. Sorry." I feel like asking him what he actually does.

"You're not here to... write, are you Alex? It's just we've had some very troublesome journalists recently and it really does become very time consuming."

"I don't have any plans to."

This seems to cheer him up a bit. "Good. So let me get this straight: you're working part-time for the Professor, and part time for Grey in the Ministry. And you're living with the old woman. Splendid. Excellent…That's all jolly useful to know... well then…" he rubs his hands together. It is clearly time that I left.

"I was wondering whether I might be able to leave my money and passport with you, I'm not too happy keeping it all at the house."

He seems to need someone's permission before he can reply and leaves the office to find out. "No" is the answer when he returns. "I'm afraid it's against regulations."

Aubrey Herbert began his career in the Foreign office, and left it disillusioned. *"I am not sure that it is a life I should always care to go on with,"* he wrote in a letter to his brother Bron from the embassy at Constantinople in 1910 *"... At most posts the ministers are simply glorified telegraph clerks and it is a service that has made an idol of that filthy thing the status quo."*

I speak to Richard on the telephone. He is delayed in Washington. He asks me to attend a meeting at the Ministry without him.

"Is there anything I should say. Or not say?"

"Try not to say anything. Just take notes and look interested," he tells me across the buzz of static.

On either side of the boulevard sit old men minding bathroom scales. For a few lek you can weigh yourself. That is all they do all day. I feel similarly redundant. The Professor is busy, dining at Embassies or with friends and leaves me to my own devices. He has a speech he wants to work on but it is always '... tomorrow, tomorrow'. There seems to be no prospect of an expatriate gin and tonic at the Residency. The meeting at the Ministry is a week away. The weather is foul. At night the streets are dark and, after the mugging, I am still jumpy. Aimless - no, bored, for the first time since I left London, I spend my empty days reading and navel gazing.

Boredom was something my great grandfather (paternal) Charles knew all about. He was only eighteen when he joined the Royal Navy. It was 1882. His ship was the brand new ironclad, HMS Invincible, a revolutionary ship in her day. I wonder how he felt, the day he joined the Invincible. Standing on the quay at Portsmouth, in his bell bottoms, a handsome, square-built young man with a big jaw and a kind look about his eyes. Staring up at the Invincible, with its tar-black hull and its orderly skyline. Excited? Scared? Bored? He certainly complained of boredom on ship, of hours spent mending ropes, or scrubbing down decks, and creaking hours on watch in the rigging.

I know a lot about my father's family. Compensation, I suppose. An attempt to retain some sense of him, to protect my link with his past. I find his family's story fascinating. Partly because it is my story too, and because its players share a surname that has an electric quality to me. 'Hickman'. Easily wobbled by prep school headmasters or boisterous friends into 'Hiccers'. Occasionally thumped into 'Dickman'. Once agonisingly re-packaged as 'Hickperson'.

Hickman literally means 'Richard's man', a servant of King Richard. Earliest records of the name occur in the West Midlands - especially Shropshire and Worcestershire. A good yeoman name. Pretty unusual. Friendly. Unpretentious. How pleasing, therefore, that the first memory of my clan is set not set among apple trees, or hay bales or the stock pens of some cup-sized market town. Instead it takes place on a foreign sea, under a hot sun, with infidels in sight and pressing colonial ambitions behind.

Shortly after Charles joined the Invincible, she completed her steam trials and left the south coast of England for Alexandria.

'The fleet consists of Alexandria (flag), Superb, Temeraire, Invincible, Falcon and Condor gunboats,' recorded Charles in his diary. Captain, later First Sea Lord, Fisher was in command.

Britain and France's dual control of Egypt, exercised through the rule of the Turkish Khedive, was under threat. A nationalist uprising, led by native officers in the Egyptian army, threatened European hegemony in Egypt and left the vital Suez canal, India's life-line, exposed. Five years earlier, William Gladstone, then prime minister, had predicted that Britain's engagement in Egypt would prove the 'egg' of its African empire. As the fleet pushed across the Channel towards the Bay of Biscay and the blue Med, the scramble for Africa was on, and by 1914 almost all of its wilderness would be the property of the five major European powers.

Ten days later, the fleet moored off the Egyptian coast. Its first objective was to rescue the puppet ruler.

'HM the Khedive arrived from Cairo. Dressed ship and fired salute of 21 guns at 3.30pm. Rebels still keep charge of town and are killing all Europeans they can lay their hands on,' Charles wrote on the 14th June. In retaliation for the massacre Fisher ordered his fleet to prepare to bombard the port. The attack took place early in July, razing much of Alexandria's beautiful old town to the ground. On the 15th Fisher sent in a landing party *'in all about 3000… Invincible's men... took charge of the (Khedive's) Palace'* recorded Charles, who had been among the landing party, sharpened cutlass in hand. They found the port in ruins, much of it was on fire. Rebel soldiers and looters roamed about but most of the nationalists had fallen back inland. After a few days spent working on fire duty - pulling down burning buildings – Charles and other members of the crew were ordered to build an armoured train in order to secure the railway line to Cairo.

'Went up line at 4.30pm,' records Charles on the 10th of August, *'fired a few shells into enemy to destroy their work with 40 pounds. They returned it with vigour (shell and rockets). The two last shells sent by enemy, one passed between the trucks of our train and the other striking the ground close by us and threw dust in our faces and exploding, hurting no-one. Returned 7.25pm.'*

The next day was a little quieter. *'Went up line at 3pm, taking Admiral Seymour to see and be received by Duke of Connaught at the position where we took the guns. The Duke looked well and he had a good look at us.'*

By Christmas the Khedive was safely back in his Palace. Pax Britannica restored, Charles and the Invincible continued up the Suez canal to Ceylon and Singapore. Charles didn't return to Britain until 1885, when he left the navy and took a job on a Thames barge running coal up the east coast of England. He used to spend his holidays in Clapham, where his father John worked for Pulsometer, an engineering company which produced machine parts at a local foundry. One holiday Charles started courting Jessie Watkinson, one of eight sisters who lived nearby. In 1889 they married, and moved to Staffordshire where Charles worked for a mining company. A few years later they followed John down to Reading, where Pulsometer had opened a new foundry. John had found Charles a job.

Settled in Reading Charles and Jessie began to build a family. They had four children; Nancy, Angela, Jack and May. Meanwhile, Charles became a popular figure at the 'Pulso', and by the time Jack was eight he had been promoted to foreman. He became an expert in making alloys.

"That boy," said John, "is a wizard with his metals."

Charles kept his 'spells' at home – in a black notebook full of formula and chemical symbols which he hid in his collar box. One day, he used to promise Jessie, he would go it alone and make them all rich.

But there was much more to his life than the Pulso. He kept an allotment on the edge of town, where he grew vegetables for Jessie. His plot was next to St George's church, where he worshipped every Sunday. Charles' faith played an important part in his life. It gave him a routine beyond his life at the Pulso. And it politicised him. He became an active Christian Socialist and then a Fabian, speaking regularly at the Reading 'butts', where archery contests used to be held. He was a romantic man, Charles. I like to think he thought of himself as a modern day Robin Hood.

When the Balkan spark set fire to Europe in 1914 Charles cut short the family's summer holiday in Ryde to enlist in his beloved Navy. But at fifty he was told he was too old for active service. Disappointed, Charles returned to the Pulso, now busy producing ordinance for Kitchener's army. The next summer he took Jessie and May back to the Isle of Wight. They stayed in their favourite boarding house, on the front at Ryde and the weather was perfect for the whole week. But Charles was miserable. He would stand on the front, licking an ice-cream and looking over the Solent towards France and the North Sea, where Dreadnought-class battleships, heirs to the ironclad Invincible, prowled the German coast. On the last day of the holiday he dived into a swimming pool and drowned. He was fifty-two.

Charles' body was carried back to mainland by steamer, in a black coffin covered in pink roses. He was escorted by Jessie and her brother-in-law, who had been granted compassionate leave from his regiment, the Royal Berkshires. At a sunlit station outside Reading Jessie's sister, Louise, was waiting on the platform.

"Well, have you got your black?" she whispered, as they watched Charles being lifted off the train. Louise, by all accounts, was like that.

The next day Charles was buried. Six men from the Pulso carried his coffin, draped in a union flag. The works came to a halt as the entourage crawled past, the men, their heads bowed, standing ten deep in the forecourt. At St George's church a sailor sounded the Last Post as Charles was buried just by the deserted allotment.

"Well, he died a sailor's death," sighed Jessie. "He would have liked that."

"Will Mrs Hickman be... comfortable?" the Pulso's manager asked Louise after the funeral.

"Of course I told him that Charles had left you well provided for," she told Jessie later, "I'm sure it's what Jack would have wanted me to say - I couldn't tell him the truth. It would be too shaming."

The truth was that Charles hadn't left Jessie much more than a penny. Although Nancy and Angela were now married, Jessie still had Jack (seventeen) and May (eight) to provide for. When a Fabian friend of Charles asked to buy two of his suits, brand new and barely worn, it was enough to keep Jessie out of debt for a few weeks. But it was the vicar's wife who rescued her, by suggesting that she take in a paying guest.

"The poor young men at the officers' infirmary are always asking me to find somewhere suitable for their wives to stay," she told Jessie. "Just give me a day or two."

She was as good as her word.

"I've found you an American lady, my dear. The daughter of a Philadelphia judge. Her husband is an infantry Captain. He's very fragile I'm afraid. Shellshock."

So my great grandmother's house lost a male voice, with its sea-salt passions and its alchemist's charms and gained an American, who wanted to be near her shattered husband. The arrangement worked well - Jessie and the American became friends and gave each other the company they needed. In the spring of 1916, the doctors at the infirmary proscribed the fragile Captain a convalescence in the country. Rudyard Kipling, who had recently lost his only son at Loos, invited him to use a neglected farmhouse he owned at Burwash, his Sussex estate.

"Would you come with us Mrs Hickman?" his wife asked Jessie. "I don't think I'll be able to cope on my own."

Jessie found Jack lodgings near the Kendrick, his grammer school, let the house and took May off to Sussex. It was strawberry time when they arrived by train at Tunbridge Wells. Kipling had sent a horse and cart to carry take them to Dugwell Farm; it was waiting for them outside the station. May remembers the months that followed as happy ones. It was good to be out of Reading, which always seemed so close during summer, and away from her home that seemed so quiet without Charles. And Burwash, named after the the river that ran through it, was a lovely estate. Day after day the sun shone. Each morning May would cross a plank over a tributary of the Burwash to fetch eggs from a man called Rudd who kept Kipling's hens. She attended the village school and in the afternoons would go exploring the woods around the farm, or help her mother in the kitchen. On the odd weekend Jack would come to stay and fish in the river.

Kipling was often to be seen riding about the estate. He was a kindly old figure, in a Norfolk jacket and voluminous whiskers.

"How is the patient today?" he would ask Jessie, leaning off his horse to peer through the window of the kitchen. "Well I hope? And yourself, Mrs Hickman?" Sometimes he had pies or a ham sent down to the farm.

One day May was playing by a stream when he rode by.

"Do you see the newts?" he asked her.

May did not, so he got down from his horse and grabbing her by the small of her dress, held her flat over the water so that she would see the black and orange newts below the surface.

The only dark planet in this universe was the nervous state of the Captain. He would often cry out at night, or wake sobbing. May used to hear his wife soothing him, or reading to him. One July morning May woke at dawn and, bored of lying in bed, tiptoed downstairs. The front door was open and outside she found the Captain. He had carried an armchair from the sitting room and placed it on the lawn. May could see his footprints in the dew. He was smoking a cigarette, staring out across the valley. The night sky was just turning violet and mist shrouded the runs of hedges and the woods. A tall oak loomed out of the next field.

"Hello," said the Captain to May "can't sleep?" May shook her head.

"Me neither. Dreadful business, sleep... will you keep me company?"

May nodded, and smiling, he fetched her a chair from the kitchen.

He set it next to his own and the two of them sat there, wrapped in blankets, listening to the clapping of the wood pigeon in the rafters of a copse.

Alone I walk the wet streets, the collar of my jacket turned up, the traffic shushing through the brown potholes. At the same restaurant I eat pizza and read books, talking to noone. Tiny, surprisingly green Tirana remains a closed city to me.

Back home I shudder open the heavy metal gate, disturbing Loti, the old woman's fearsome mongrel bitch. She hates me and I her. Hunching forward, she shows her teeth and starts barking and snapping. Meanwhile, I slowly take back my right foot, or pick up a stone. Confrontation usually begins with this kind of stand-off followed by Loti's attack. On one occasion she bites me on the ankle and I swing her off her feet.

"Loteee, oh Loteee," intervenes the fat woman, picking Loti up and holding her to her bosom. Slowly Loti will stop growling and, making faces at her, I make my way back into the cold of my bedroom.

Inside a power cut means no light. It is too cold to wash. Wearing long-johns, socks and a couple of shirts I climb in between my damp sheets and listen to the World Service or read by torch light. So uncomfortable is the simple reality of being awake in these surroundings that I sometimes take a sleeping pill to escape them. One night I wake up to a heavy drumming sound. Through chemical stupidity I realise that someone is thumping on the metal gates. I hear the front door open and shouts, the bolts are rattled back and an old diesel engine throbs into the yard. The next day a fat young man is asleep on the sofa in the kitchen. It is the old lady's son, back, if I understand his miming correctly, from the sea. As I enter the kitchen he leaps up and shakes my hand, while the other rubs down his tousled hair. He has a friendly, weak smile and the arms that hold the blanket around him are heavy with folds of blubber. I later find out from the Professor that he smuggles cigarettes between Montenegro and Italy. He does not stay another night, though his car stays parked in the yard.

SUNDAY 14TH JANUARY
MORE INERTIA

I wake at nine and lie still, listening to the radio and the sounds of this Balkan town. Outside the old woman is washing, or cooking or lying on her couch in the kitchen watching television. A dog barks, a child shouts. Into the potholes scattered about the road, cars splash. One hoots its horn and across the cold air scatters the voices of wrapped up old men chatting in the coffee shop. At ten I force myself out of the warm bed. The tiled floor is icy. Outside it is drizzling. Through the window I scowl at Loti, shivering in her kennel. I wash in the bath room, with painfully cold water pouring from a piece of black hosepipe.

In the evening I eat supper at the Dajti Hotel. I have discovered its dining room - rows of tables laid with heavy linen, candlelight and not a soul in sight. There is good olive oil in glass bottles on the tables, and parmesan cheese that smells of dishcloth. But it tastes alright on spaghetti bolognaise, alongside a bottle of Albanian Merlot.

Jack was seventeen when his father died, a scholarship boy at the Kendrick. He was a lanky, good looking fellow, bright enough but his real love was games.

Even at sixteen he was the fastest runner at the Kendrick and at the school sports day, held in June 1915, Jack's heats were deliberately staged just before the finals, in order to handicap him. Charles, watching from the grass bank above the athletics track, was furious.

"You could make him run backwards and have done with it!" he shouted at the Headmaster before stalking back up to where he had left Jessie sitting on the bank. An hour later Jack had romped home in the 100, 200 and 400 metres.

Jack left the Kendrick in 1917, and was immediately called up. It was the Headmaster who suggested to Jack that he join the Inns of Court Territorials, a cavalry regiment based at Champneys in Buckinghamshire.

"I know the Colonel a little - we were at varsity together. He'll keep an eye on you my boy. It's a fine regiment."

So Jack packed his bags and after a weekend with Jessie and May at Burwash, arrived at Champneys, one of forty new recruits.

"Right you miserable buggers," screamed the Sergeant from behind his moustaches, one early morning after physical jerks on the parade ground. "I'm going to make troopers out of you. And its going to fucking 'urt."

One of Jack's fellow recruits, an apprentice butcher called Barrow, was terrified of horses.

"You see, I was bitten by one of 'em blighters. Bitten on the arse I was, when I was thirteen. Just bending down I was, to get it a carrot an' all when 'wup', he sinks his dirty great teeth into me behind," he explained to Jack, "and then when I was sixteen a shire horse stood on me foot. It swelled up like a football - I thought I was gonna die! I tell you Jack, horses don't like Jim Barrow."

Barrow was not cut out for the cavalry. He was a feeble soul, with a face like a weasel, a permanently sniffling nose and a habit of cadging cigarettes. And he was terrified of horses.

Two weeks into training the platoon's mounts arrived.

"I've got a real beauty for you Barrow, nice and quiet," said the sergeant and had a heavy old bay walked over "...press-ganged out of a juicy little patch of Kentish clover just for you, me lad. Just enjoying his retirement, and you come along. Now let's see you step on board. Least you can do."

Barrow took a step back.

"'Eel bite me Sarge, I know 'ee will. Don't make me climb up on it."

The horse found a new patch of grass and shuffled a little, causing Barrow to jump and the Sergeant to lose his temper.

"Get up on this 'orse Barrow. That's an order."

"But Sarge...look...he's as vicious as anything."

"Up naaaa! Hickman - come and give Barrow an 'and."

Jack helped Barrow clamber up into the saddle. The horse looked up from its grazing and adjusted its footing. Barrow sat stock still, grey with terror, holding onto the front of the saddle with both hands.

"Now, wot about takin' a little bit of a walk, Barrow?" said the Sergeant.

Barrow shook his head and squeezed the saddle even tighter.

"I shan't be moving Sarge. It's bad enough when it's stopped. If we move I reckon I'll piss meeself."

"Aw you might as well just fuck orff inside, Barrow, and lock the bladdy daw. All the bladdy good you'll be to the rest of us!" He turned to his corporal "What's the fucking point, eh? 'Ow we ever going to beat the Hun with this lot?"

MONDAY 15TH JANUARY
ACTION

It is raining and cold. In a chocolate brown suit borrowed from the Professor, I nip past Loti and slam the heavy metal gate behind me. Beneath it pokes her snout, snapping and barking. Outside the world is muddy and drab and I have to pick my way between brimming potholes. I am on my way to my first meeting in the Ministry.

The pink flanks of Hoxha's pyramid glisten with rain. Next door stands the Ministry of Finance. I am challenged by a young conscript standing in a wet poncho. I smile and guess that I need to say something like "Ministry Finanzia" purposefully. It works and he lets me pass. Outside the entrance to the Ministry stands a crowd of men and women. They press against the door, where a policeman holds them back. What are they waiting for? Missing tax rebates, compensation for years of communist gruel? Me? I smile at the policeman and pace up the steps. Inside a dark hallway is a reception desk. Behind the desk sit a woman and a man, slumped on their elbows, talking.

"Minister Xhaja?" They point silently upstairs.

On the first floor the light is a little better but many of the windows are broken. From the loos comes the smell of stale urine. Next door sit two men and two women at computers. The room is fuggy from a heater in the corner, which has misted the windows. One of the men is on a bright red plastic phone. I am late he tells me, putting his hand over the mouthpiece. He waves down the corridor

"Xhaja is the last on the right, just knock and go in."

Outside the door I hesitate. I have never taken part in meeting with a real Minister, in a real Ministry, before. What is the protocol? Should my tone be energetic Anglo-Saxon? Deferential Ottoman? Egalitarian communist?

"Just be polite," I hear my mother telling me in some faraway kitchen. I knock. There is a muffled reply and I push open the door.

At a low table sit three men. They rise as I enter. A mean-faced man, wearing glasses, introduces himself as Gregor Xhaja. I apologise for being late, adding 'Minister' uselessly to the end of my sentence. Xhaja makes introductions in a reluctant sort of way: Anetsi (Xhaja's deputy), Arben Popoli (a jolly, impish, looking man in an anorak and dark glasses from something called the Albanian Centre for Foreign Investment Promotion or ACFIP) and someone from the Prime Minister's office. All here to discuss plans for the Conference.

We all sit down.

"Welcome to Albania, Alex. Where are you staying?" asks Xhaja. "In the Dajti perhaps?"

"No with an old lady. She has a spare room."

"Ahh, so you already know some people in Tirana."

"Well, sort of. The Professor, actually."

"The Professor!" splutters Xhaja.

"A great economist..." says Popoli.

"And a fool..." interrupts the man from the Prime Minister's office.

"We have a mutual friend in London," I say, trying not to look at the man from the Prime Minister's office.

"I see," says Xhaja slowly. The man from the Prime Minister's office is scribbling something in a slim notebook.

"And you too are an economist?" asks Xhaja.

"Mmm," I reply, hoping 'Mmm' sounds like modesty, not the hesitation of an 'A' level economist (grade 'A').

"BA or MA?" he asks.

"MA," I smile back at him. (In history from Edinburgh University).

"I too am MA," says Xhaja.

I bow my head, as if to say 'naturally'.

"And I too," says Anetsi. Xhaja and I bow our heads...

"Patriotic service in the army prevented me from taking MA," said the man from the Prime Minister's office setting his jaw in my direction.

"Well, I am PhD. I am Dr Popoli" says the man from the ACFIP, giggling.

"Shall we proceed with the meeting," suggests Xhaja stiffly. I hunt for my notebook. Finding it, I sit back and cross my legs. Government.

TUESDAY 16TH JANUARY
MINISTRY OF FINANCE

My first day at the Ministry. Anetsi holds court, waving his cigarette around the bright red phone as if it was a baton. He introduces his team: Halit is a friendly economist in his early thirties who is studying for an MBA with one of the American business schools. Every other month they send him a fresh course of tapes. Because of the tapes he speaks mechanical, business English with a clean Virginia accent.

Leda and Katrina share Halit's office. Leda is in her late twenties, bright, another economist. Leda has raven hair and coal-black eyes and is beguiling in a fierce, pointed kind of way. But her face is sad - she is aloof, and the rest are a little wary of her. Katrina is Leda's opposite. She has a fresh, pretty face that looks like it belongs outdoors. Her smile is warm, she giggles easily and Anetsi is continually wrapping his arms around her.

Anetsi is the boss. He is in his late forties, a large man with communist hair – wavy and heavy with grease – sad eyes, plump arms that move slowly around a large stomach. He has an office next door to Xhaja. He shares it with a man in sunglasses who rarely speaks. The man was Hoxha's favourite statistician, so brilliant that even the President can't do without him.

He and Anetsi are great friends - go into their office and the two of them will be grinning and grinding their cigarettes out on the wooden floor, or Anetsi will be whispering some piece of Ministry gossip, slapping his thighs and creasing up at the punch line.

"Welcome Alexi" says Anetsi shyly, after the introductions are finished. And everyone gets back to work.

Richard arrives, tall and distinguished in a Burberry mac. I meet him at the Dajti, where he is staying. There he stands at the reception desk, the mac dripping a small pool on the floor.

"How are you, fella?" he cries, shaking my hand. He has a noble face, with its aquiline nose and intelligent eyes, scanning you from underneath thick eyebrows. His hair is light brown, brushed flat across his head. He would make a good-looking General, though I shouldn't think he's got a nasty bone in his body. It is good to see him.

"Brought your new wardrobe. You'll be the best bloody dressed man in Tirana," he says, handing me a suitcase.

Minutes later we are at the Ministry, racing up and down the corridor, saying hellos. Richard wants to see Xhaja, who is away at a meeting of the Council of Ministers (the government's extended cabinet). Instead we walk over to the ACFIP. We walk at a tremendous pace, Richard's tremendous pace.

"Only way to get things done around here," he mutters, his Burberry flapping out behind him. "Got to go at it like a bloody steam train."

The ACFIP's offices are down a muddy alleyway, behind a lorry park. A stupid place to put an organisation charged with persuading wary foreigners that they should take Albania seriously.

"Richard!" roars Popoli as we put our head round his door, and leaps to his feet. They got to know one another during Richard's trip in December. Popoli howls with pleasure.

"Well, it's good to see you!" and punches Richard hard in the back.

Richard grimaces.

"And you, fella. Do you know Alex, my right hand man?"

"Yes, I have already met Alex. At the Ministry. We were talking about the famous investment conference. Alex has a disreputable friend. He will get you talked about, Richard, if you are not careful."

And he roars again with laughter and slaps Richard on the back of his Burberry mac.

Outside it is dark. We walk along the Lana towards the Dajti.

"Who's your 'disreputable friend' - the Professor?"

I describe the meeting at the Ministry and the man from the Prime Minister's office.

"Well for Christ's sake don't get caught up in anything political – this place can be vicious."

THURSDAY 18TH JANUARY
MINISTRY OF FINANCE

Richard and I have been given an office in the roof of the Ministry. On the door of the office is an inscription in Albanian.

"What does it mean?" I ask Anetsi.

"It says *Director for Public Administration.*"

"What does that mean?" asks Richard. Anetsi shrugs.

"Well, you must be the youngest yet," grins Richard.

Anetsi hands over a bronze key, rubbed smooth by generations of Directors.

The office is dusty and contains two wooden desks, two phones (one of which works), one chair and grey metal filing cabinets. The floors are bare and the taps in the sink don't work - apparently the water can't make it this far up. Shelves run down the side of one wall, heaped with old documents. The walls are grey, the floor is made up of dark wooden tiles, unpolished. The window does not shut. It looks out onto a piece of grimy wasteland leading to the back of the National Statistics Institute. In the drawers of the desk are a number of cards - a World Banker, a German from Siemens, someone from the Ministry of Trade. There is also a box of rusty paper clips. No state secrets, no pleasing bits of propaganda or discarded pieces of East German pornography. Just dusty anonymity - I try to imagine the man who occupied the office before me but all I can picture are his shoes - black and covered in mud, and the frayed bottoms of his trousers. Don't ask me why.

"What a find!" says Richard, clapping his hands. "You'll be cosy in here."

He unpacks his lap top and shows me a copy of the invitation to the Conference:

On behalf of the Government of Albania and the G-24, we are writing to invite you to an International Conference which is taking place on 16th - 18th May in Tirana to consider the investment prospects in Albania. The Conference is being held at a key point in Albania's transition. Following the initial phase of stabilisation and economic adjustment since the collapse of communism in 1992, the Government is now pushing ahead with a range of changes to increase the flow of investment into the country. The purpose of the conference is to review the framework for investment and consider ways of securing greater foreign investment in manufacturing and the service sectors and participation in major infrastructure projects. The Conference has been planned by the Government of

Albania and the G-24 Secretariat in Brussels. The conference will be opened by the President of Albania. Other speakers will include relevant Ministers, Vice-Ministers and heads of government agencies and departments, foreign experts, and chief executives of companies who have invested in Albania.

The letter is signed by a Spaniard, who is Co Chairman of 'the G-24 Secretariat at the European Commission'. The other signatory is our very own Gregor Xhaja.

FRIDAY 19ᵀᴴ JANUARY
PAX EUROPA

Outside the headquarters of the EU delegation flunkies soak a row of shiny Land Rovers in soapsuds. Inside, the blond wood, the carpets and leather furniture are impressive - these are known to be the best offices in Tirana. In the background whirrs air conditioning. There is that executive hush that belongs to the top floors of merchant banks and oil companies. On the tables lie this week's Time and Economist. It could be Vienna or Stockholm, Edinburgh or Milan. But we are in Tirana and I wonder whether the money cannot be better spent.

Upstairs, in a large office full of large pieces of furniture, sits the head of delegation, an Italian with the rank of Ambassador. A General in the new army of occupation, one of the most important men in the colony. He wears a lime green suit and sassy brown shoes. His dark hair has a purple tint and a thin white cigarette curls smoke between his fingers.

The Ambassador moves us across to a deep leather sofa. The Conference is being funded by the EU, the Ambassador needs to be briefed on progress. But he doesn't seem very interested.

"I am so busy, Richard," he keeps saying with cigarette smoke leaking through his front teeth. "The World Bank this, the Americans that. Everywhere big problems. I haven't been back to Bologna for a fortnight." He shakes his head.

As we leave he gives me a flashing smile and clasps my hand.

"If there is anything I can do to help..."

Behind him, on the coffee table, his abandoned cigarette pours itself quietly into the air. The Ambassador is impatient to get back to it.

Next door sits the Political Secretary, a chic Frenchman in his late twenties who used to be in the Navy. I can well imagine him in splendid white ducks and a peaked cap, standing on the bridge of a French cruiser as it slips into Marseilles or Tunis. Now he is in a navy three-piece suit, beautifully cut... and spats! His hair is lacquered back thirties-style and he smokes a cigarette which he draws from a silver case. He smokes it in a holder, between elegant fingers. What a find in grubby Tirana.

SUNDAY 21ST JANUARY
GUNFIRE

Mount Dajti is a fabled place for the Albanians - their Mount Rushmore or Eiffel Tower. Richard and I hire a taxi and wind our way up out of Tirana. On the outskirts stands a classical arch and colonnades and what looks like a zany aircraft hanger. It is the New Albania film studios, which once made epics about Enver and the struggle. Now they are empty.

Up into brown countryside. It is another bright, winter's day, full of sharp, fragile sunlight. The road climbs into the treeline. Birch and pine filter the sunlight into green pools. The Lana, enjoying a loud and carefree adolescence, blazes under the road. Above the treeline the road ends in a wide field of dirty grass gathered in by silvers birches. Rocks lie about. Off the road a number of cars are parked and a bus, which has no glass in its windows. The contents of the bus are playing football at one end of the plateau. Piles of coats and jerseys make up goal posts. Families picnic by their cars.

Close up the plateau is filthy. Broken glass lies everywhere, and scraps of loo paper and empty cans and other rubbish. Above the plateau stands the gutted ruin of a hotel, dressed in peeling yellow paint. A long flight of steps leading up to the hotel is overgrown with weed and soot stains lick above its ground floor windows. Behind the hotel the final heights of the slope sharpen towards the sky. A pair of television masts stand on the summit.

Standing at the bottom of the steps is a group of conscripts. As we approach they stop talking and stare at us. One asks me for a cigarette. I hold out my packet and his face breaks into a guarded smile as he takes a cigarette in his fingers. The nails are split and dirty and his wiry hair pushes out underneath his green cap. He looks my age and I wonder if I can make him understand me. But I do not understand myself, and he retreats to the mystery of his friends.

At the edge of the plateau there is a view of Tirana and the valley floor. Beyond float mountains and hills. I take a photograph of Richard with his camera, snapping him against the muffled horizon in a pleasingly absurd pair of sunglasses. We walk back to where we left the car. It has gone. Far away there is a report like machine-gunfire. Minutes later our car tears towards us across the field, scattering the footballers. It is full of conscripts and our driver, who brings the car to a sliding stop. The conscripts clamber out, looking very serious. They are drunk, an empty bottle of raki lies on the back seat.

"Tirana," says Richard firmly as we climb inside. The driver salutes and pulls off. I am only half in and just manage to stop my right leg being run over by the back wheel. Around the corner a red-faced policeman is standing in the middle of the road with a pistol in his hand. Behind him another is running to catch up. They leap inside and shout at the driver, who sets off at a ferocious pace down the hillside. Richard and I, separated by the red-faced policeman, are thrown about in the back as we skittle around the U-bends. The wooded hillside flashes past.

"What the bloody hell is going on!" Richard shouts to the driver, who seems to have sobered up.

"Presidente, Presidente!" he screams, pointing into the hillside and pointing his fingers like a pistol. The President has a residence somewhere on the mountainside and the gunshots that we heard have alerted the local police, who fear an assassination attempt. The policemen are terrifically excited. The one sitting next to our driver waves his cap out of the window and shouts "policia! policia!" to the silent trees as we race down the road. His red-faced companion licks his lips nervously, like an actor about to go on stage.

Halfway down the mountainside, police cars have formed a road block. Our policemen tumble out and shout dramatically at their colleagues. Our boot is searched and we are each frisked. Then we are waved on. Moments later the driver almost crashes into a truck carrying army reinforcements. The soldiers sit quietly in the back, wearing metal helmets, their guns between their legs.

We stop the driver next to a roadside restaurant overlooking a ravine and the thin glitter of the Lana. The excitement has given us both an appetite.

"Bloody fool," shouts Richard, shaking his fist as the car speeds away.

Inside the restaurant, sitting at a table, is Leda, the sad-faced girl from the Ministry. She is with university friends: a journalist, an engineer and a trainee vet. They are discussing Russian poetry. They all sound so tired and cynical, yet none of them can be more than thirty.

I eat fried fish and chips and listen to them. The vet has a puppy inside his orange puffa jacket. Everyone pets it like a baby, pulling at its ears and cupping it in their hands while they argue about Pushkin's *Tatyana*.

Leda tells me about her escape route - an MBA scholarship that she has applied for in America. What a thing to achieve: escape from glass strewn football pitches and drunks and bored, ugly conscripts. For a moment she looks enthused, almost excited, but only for a moment. Staring down into the ravine, the smoke from her cigarette curls about her hard lips and the adult glaze of her eyes.

"Do you think you'll stay there?"

"Of course. If it is possible." It was a stupid question.

"Perhaps you will marry an American," says the vet in a flat voice and Leda looks up and raises her eyebrows as if to say 'what's it got to do with you?'

MONDAY 22ND JANUARY
DRITAN

Richard and I meet people in a terrific rush. First on the list is Mr Rama, head of Albtelecom, the state-owned telecommunications utility (Albania has 52,000 telephone lines for its three plus million people) and then Skenderi, head of KESH, the state-owned power utility (hydroelectric, mainly in the north and east, power cuts regular part of life, noone ever pays their bills). Both utilities need massive investment, and that will have to come from abroad. Both men want to speak at the Conference. After a meeting at the Ministry of Industry, Trade and Transport with a civil servant (very deaf) we meet a team of World Bank consultants for lunch. They are Americans; serious, quiet men, just back from Durres where the World Bank is preparing the docks for privatisation. The World Bank is hoping to find some buyers at the Conference.

Dritan is sitting in the lobby of the Dajti. He is gentle-looking, about thirty-five with dark hair over a swarthy, smiling face. Dritan is the Chargé's driver. I have seen him before, washing the Chargé's Land Rover. Dritan has a spare room.

"I am happy to meet Alexi. Dritan likes English very much."

Outside, Dritan's brother, Dylber, is chatting with Gzim. Nearby the Wolvo gleams in a brown puddle. As he gossips, Gzim flicks the bonnet of Dylber's old Fiat with his duster.

Dritan lives in an apartment built onto his mother's house. Dylber lives next door. Their street is quiet. Opposite is a large building surrounded by wasteland. A basketball hoop is a giveaway. It is a school, windowless and dirty. Dritan's apartment stands in a small compound bound in by the now familiar clang of a metal door. In front of the apartment runs a terrace and in one corner of the compound stands a lemon tree. Dritan's older brother, Dashamir, a giant of a man with long hair and a slow, sad smile, has a small shop out front.

Inside, Dritan's house is comfortable and clean. Bright paintings hang on the wall and in a corner is a tv and video. The paintings are by Dylber's wife, who is an artist, now living in Germany. In the small hall hangs a photograph of the Queen and Prince Philip. Dritan pours raki and then makes Turkish coffee. He speaks halting English, shyly. Silent Dylber has withdrawn to the sofa. He has big shoulders like a rugby prop. There is something romantic about his reticence – as if he's read a good deal of books, can name wild flowers and would come into his own in a fight.

"Alexi like?" asks Dritan, waving his arms around the room.

It is perfect. The three of us chink our tumblers of raki.

Dritan and Dylber arrive this morning, the Fiat rattling outside in the alleyway. I carry out my rucksack and go back inside to get my wallet which, as usual, I have forgotten. On my way back Loti lashes out of her kennel. I catch her a fierce kick on the arse which sends her skidding across the yard. Turning slowly, she races at me, a scruffy white ball of fury. Just in time Dritan catches her on the nose with a stone. Leaving Loti gathered to the fat woman's bosom I march smiling into sunlight.

WEDNESDAY 24TH JANUARY
THE PEACE DIVIDEND

The British 'embassy' is bustling with activity - phones ringing, raised voices, faxes pouring out pieces of paper. Lord Rothschild is about to enter Albanian waters in his yacht. He is coming across from Corfu to inspect archeological digs at Butrint, an Illyrian coastal settlement, which he is funding. The Chargé seems to be acting as a kind of upmarket river pilot, dashing about waving telegrams, his v-neck jettisoned in the melee.

Dritan has a girlfriend. She is called Suzana. She's in her twenties, a secretary at one of the ministries. She rides a bike to work and lives with Dritan. Suzana has a sharp, high-pitched voice and a shrill laugh. She wears bright pink make-up. This evening she cooks an enormous supper of meatballs and cabbage. We eat together, squashed on a sofa, watching the telly.

THURSDAY 25TH JANUARY
THE GENERAL

Richard and I spend the morning in our office. He hands me a recent Financial Times survey on Albania.

"Any good to you?" he wonders, "background, that kind of thing. Could have some useful for stuff the conference briefing papers."

I flick through it. On the back page is an advert for a company called Vari. It claims to be Albania's largest private company – controlling (among other things) Tirana's main brewery, travel agencies, a string of shops, a construction firm and the ferry line to Italy.

Richard is looking over my shoulder.

"Ahh, I know Vari. Run by a chap called Maksim Halili. Used to be an NCO in the army, now calls himself 'the General'. He's one of the most powerful men in Albania. Definitely the richest. No one seems to know how he did it. Very close to the President. Mysterious bugger from all accounts – surrounded by bodyguards the whole time."

"We ought to track the General down. He'd be a star turn at the Conference." But the General is as elusive as a mouse.

SATURDAY 27ᵀᴴ JANUARY
DRITAN'S HOUSE

The air is sharp and grey and smells of rain. Down Dritan's street there is a market. I buy provisions: olive oil, coffee, cheese, bread, vegetables, rice, a bit of meat. Then chocolate, almonds and pistachios from an expensive shop for expatriates and mafiosi. I stop at Dashamir's shop to buy some beer. My room, which leads into Dritan's small kitchen, is warm. My suitcase is unpacked, my father's old suit is hanging by the window. I love the smiling girl in the photograph. Those are my books on the table. I feel at home.

The moustachioed sergeant needn't have worried: neither Barrow nor Jack ever saw service; by armistice the regiment had got no closer to the front line than a fortnight's exercise on Salisbury Plain. Early in 1919 Jack went to live with Nancy and her husband Eddie in Luton, where Eddie worked for an engineering firm. Jack got a job there as a clerk, and studied accountancy in the evening. A few years later he met Doris Wright at his tennis club. Doris' family owned Wright Brothers, a prosperous local hat factory. The family was rumoured to be the richest in Luton.

'Get ahead get a hat' read the sign in front of the factory gates.

The moment he met Jack, Doris' father always said, he wanted him for a son-in-law. He got his way in 1926, when Doris and Jack married and moved into a house given to them by the Wrights. By now Jack was working for the family business, travelling the country, winning big orders from department stores like C&A and Harrods. A few years later Jack built himself a house on Harpenden Common, eight miles away. It was a fine house but Doris hated living so far from her parents and her nine sisters, and she would often walk into town to see them. Within a month she claimed the worry and the walking had lost her a stone in weight.

But Jack and Doris gradually settled down. They joined the local golf club. In the summer they played tennis. By the mid nineteen-thirties Jack was bringing in so much business that he was made a partner in the firm, which changed its name to Wright Bros. & Hickman in the same year that Jack became captain of the golf club. When the Second World War broke out Jack volunteered, but the army turned him down on account of his deafness. His ears hadn't been right since his time with the Inns of Court. Jack blamed an injection of cocaine he was given during exercises on Salisbury Plain. The company vet, a known drunk, had used the most enormous needle. Jack always maintained that the powerful concoction, which had knocked him out for days, was meant for his sick horse.

So Jack, like Charles, also missed his war. Instead he became an air raid warden, and during the day he worked at Wright's, where he became managing director in the absence of his brother-in-laws. It was a bad time for hats - demand was down and Wright's prices were being undercut by new producers making the most of the cheap immigrant labour available in the East End. But they kept going supplying the Ministry of Defence with berets, and dyeing hats funeral black for the bereaved.

In 1940 Doris gave birth to identical twins, John and Roger. Three years later Jack bought a farm at Bourn outside Cambridge. The privation of war and an uncertain future made self-sufficiency attractive to Jack. He loved the idea of owning his own land. And the arrival of the boys concentrated his mind. He wanted them to be farmers - he thought it a useful, happy kind of existence.

Six years later, the war over, they were sent off to a nearby prep school. Jack, now a rich man, thought it the thing to do. But John and Roger were miserable. And so, increasingly, were Jack and Doris. They missed the boys, and Jack was becoming bored by the comfortable routines of middle class life, the golf club gossip and what he called the 'lounge lizards' that he met at his club and in town. Privilege and peace, he complained, encouraged indolence in young men. Jack didn't want his boys turning out like that.

In 1952 Jack took the boys out of school, sold up and the family set sail for a new life in New Zealand. After six months touring the country they settled in South Island, where Jack built himself a house, overlooking Tahona Bay. It was 'the house with the million dollar view' reported the local paper. Behind the house the land rose to a range of snowy mountains; there were bright rivers full of trout and golden beaches. It was a long way from Hertfordshire.

But it didn't work out. The boys were unhappy at their school in Nelson, which Doris thought too rough – full of pioneers sons and cane-wielding teachers. And the boys wanted to be doctors, not farmers.

To make matters worse, Doris was homesick. Eight miles from her family had been bad enough, now they were separated by thousands of miles of ocean. The nearest house was several miles away, where an Ulster couple grazed hundreds of sheep. Despite Jack's romantic imagination, Doris knew that they didn't belong. Two years later she persuaded him to sell up and the family moved home.

Jack never went back to Wright's. In fact he never worked again, choosing instead to live off what Charles would have derided, one afternoon at the Reading butts, as 'unearned income'. I suppose the disappointment of New Zealand knocked the stuffing out of him. And his hearing was deteriorating. Meanwhile the boys were sent off to Greshams, a boarding school on the north Norfolk coast. It was an unsettling time for them: they had been half way around the world and back again, and they had fallen behind in their schoolwork. But at Greshams the boys had a rare headmaster, a former Scottish rugby international, who took them under his wing and they flourished. They were both sporty and bright, which is the right order for success in a public school. John eventually became head boy, captain of the fifteen and Sergeant Major in the cadet corps. *'Dear Hickman,'* reads a note I found in his trunk the other day, *'please could I have the honour of being your fag next term? Respectfully yours, Roddy Scott'*.

In 1958 John went up to Cambridge to read medicine. Roger repeated a year. The twins had been together all their lives – Jack thought it best to put a bit of space between them. The next year Roger too became head boy and followed John to Cambridge the year after, to the same college, also reading medicine.

After Cambridge John and Roger both finished their training at the Middlesex hospital. It was at the Middlesex that John met Veronica Higginson, a social worker. They married in 1968 in the Tower of London. Roger was John's best man.

"*I understand,*" said John in his speech "*that there is some confusion as to the identity of the bridegroom.*" He and Roger were strikingly alike.

John was a talented and ambitious young doctor. After he qualified he spent some years in research, looking at blood cells and how they clotted, before applying himself to career medicine. He was quickly made senior registrar at the Brompton, and began to teach at the London. He and Veronica bought a house in Putney, with a garden running down to the river. In May 1971 they had someone to share it with. Me.

> '*Veronica produces a son weighing 8lb 4oz. It was a hectic day. Preparing to speak at St Mary's Hospital, visiting the labour ward, going to St Mary's, losing my notes, back to the labour ward, away to a restaurant in Addison Avenue, back to the labour ward. The little creature didn't seem overjoyed to leave its uterine pad, crying and clucking to itself. His face was blue for a bit and he spent his first night on dry land in the intensive care ward. It is night, a balmy summers night, I write this in a candlelit eyrie. The river is quiet, a pregnant cat has looked in en passant, its eyes flickering in the candlelight. I feared for a bit that it would tread on my sweet pea plants. Ducks squabble on the river, from the house JC Bach, all, very nearly all, is well for the world tonight.*'

A year later John became the youngest ever consultant at the London Hospital. Rooms in Wimpole Street began to support a thriving private practice, buoyed by the large number of sickly and oil-rich arabs. I was joined by Tom and then James, and we bought a cottage in Norfolk, only a few miles from Greshams. The cottage looked out across haunting marshes full of dykes. The marshes teemed with rare birds, which John loved to watch, and nearby were Brancaster links, set among samphire flats on the very edge of the sea.

SUNDAY 28TH JANUARY
MRS HETA

Dritan talks a good deal about his mother. And frequently alludes to her presence somewhere off. But I have yet to meet her – or even set eyes on her. I can point to a couple of windows, visible from the courtyard, that I know belong to her. Occasionally a light is turned on, or a curtain twitches. There is a door in the hall, which opens onto a dim corridor. Dritan will disappear down it for an hour or so, I presume to visit her. But it is all done with great mystery – he creeps away and once, when he emerged from the door just as I was passing he looked terribly guilty and, shrugging his shoulders, simply said 'mother'.

MONDAY 29TH JANUARY
THE DAJTI

Striding into the Dajti Hotel to meet Richard for breakfast, swinging my umbrella and feeling gay, I notice a group of British soldiers sitting in one corner looking at me. They are playing cards. Around them Bergens are piled high. I look at them astonished and wonder what on earth they are doing here. They stare back, hostile.

"Bonjour Alex," says Spartac, the Dajti's manager. Spartac is a charming old rogue who wears his greasy hair long like a seventies footballer. His face is fishy, with bobble eyes and chubby little lips. We are great friends and we always speak to one another in bad French.

"Bonjour Spartac, ça va? Ou est Ricard?"

"Dans le salle de manger, Alex."

"Tres bien Spartac. A bientot!"

Thanks to Richard (and Spartac) I have come to love the Dajti. Despite impressive inefficiencies, dirt and surliness, Spartac's hotel manages to just about look after your needs and somehow, at the same time, charm you. It has a 'je ne sais pas', a reassuring Balkan integrity, if there is such a thing.

Step past Gzim and the other sleepy taxi drivers, through the shade cast by tall pines and up the grey marble steps into the large, gloomy lobby and you find yourself in an older, less predictable world. It is mid afternoon. It is always mid afternoon in the Dajti. Behind the reception desk, there may or may not be someone to look after you. There, in the money changing booth, there may or may not be a woman able to change your money. In the corner, near the barber's shop (who may or may not...), the lavatory cleaners sit in their housecoats playing cards and charging to let you into the loo. Opposite them the phone booths are locked.

In a corner of the foyer sits an old man in a long coat and a corduroy cap. He will try to sell you an old Longines pocket watch that no one ever seems to buy despite the fact that it is rather fine. He also has a lot of coins from the Italian occupation and a few more which he claims are Roman. Elsewhere in the foyer sit groups of moody Albanian men, sipping coffee and not saying much. One or two will be watching the television that plays all day in the corner, usually MTV or American films with German subtitles. You will find more in the bar, where cigarette smoke hangs heavy in blue clouds and the conversations are a little more animated. Here plots are hatched.

In the 'salle de manger' Richard is sitting at a window table. We have breakfast together every morning when he's here. I walk over from Dritan's and meet him in the dining room at 7.30, when I drink two cups of coffee and eat two boiled eggs as we discuss the day ahead. Then Richard says "on on!" and we march off towards the Ministry.

Richard leaves for Somerset this afternoon. He is back in a month. In his absence the Professor will keep me busy. We have an article to write on Albania's transition from communism for an American magazine.

The Professor has made a good start on the article over the weekend.

"There, what do you think?" he says, handing me a number of typed pages. "It's about the dictatorship."

I begin to wade through the first paragraph which is too long and meanders about like spaghetti. My heart sinks at the prospect of the next two weeks.

I have to handle the Professor carefully. Being Albanian he dislikes criticism. Changes to the text have to posed diplomatically, or planted in his head for him to bring them forth with an impatient flourish.

"Great idea!" I reply and start typing. But sometimes he ignores my suggestions.

"No. I like it like that". And there is no more to be said. This morning it is difficult to get him going. He seems depressed and indifferent. He drinks whisky and plays Chopin on the hi-fi.

By lunchtime we have reached a compromise on the first few paragraphs. As usual the Professor has the President firmly in his sights:

> *The President's popularity in the country immediately after he was elected in 1992 was immense. He was hailed as saviour, the hero of the anti-communist movement. He accepted power in a mood of magnanimity and tolerance. It was time, he argued, to heal the wounds of communism.*
>
> *"I will govern for the whole country," he told the*

120

people. It set just the right tone. It was time to rebuild Albania, the past must be forgotten. Only the future was important. He made friends with international leaders, gave the peasants back their land, and the townspeople their houses, encouraged people to start up their own businesses and talked about a privatisation programme and foreign investment. And he praised Albania and Albanians to the skies - Albania, he promised, would be the next Taiwan. The people loved him for it.

But the President was not, by training, a democrat. Like all Albanians of his generation he grew up in a world of dictat and oppression. So, when he became leader of democratic Albania, he had no idea what democracy actually looked like, or felt like. And he ruled a country that respected strong leaders but had good reason to hate authoritarians. He had a fine line to tread.

Combine all this with the President's background - he comes from Tropoja, a poor northern region famous for its blood feuds and its banditry - and the size of his party's majority over an unpopular opposition, and one can understand how he came to believe that his own position was unassailable, and that his will best personified that of the Albanian people.

The first sign of trouble was when he began to dispose of his old allies, powerful men like the Professor, who made awkward bedfellows in government. And he had his old enemies, like Alia (Hoxha's heir) and Fatos Nano, his prime minister, thrown in prison.

Last November, a national referendum designed to strengthen the President's powers was unexpectedly

121

defeated. The electorate was sick of the government's promises of prosperity tomorrow, and the President's high-handed referendum campaign: his Mercedes motorcade and flanks of smart-suited aides looked incongruous, especially in the poor villages. So the President's spell was broken – he suddenly looked mortal, out of touch. He was furious, and threw a tantrum which wrecked his office and forced his doctors to knock him out with tranquillisers.

There is little evidence of the President's magnanimity nowadays. His attitude towards opposition parties, and especially the Socialist Party (the new name for Hoxha's AWP) is anything but inclusive. He vilifies them at every opportunity. They are "the red terror", "Marxists", "assassins", "guilty of genocide", "a threat to liberty and prosperity". The President dismisses the opposition press as "liars and troublemakers".

Bullyboys from the President's secret police force, ShIK - recruited in Tropoja and identifiable by their black leather jackets - pay visits to the President's enemies. The grimy windows of the Ministry of Interior and its tall custard coloured walls have begun to look sinister again. Albania is the only ex-communist country in Europe to ban private television and radio stations.

Around noon the Professor's wife walks in, dressed in a smart suit.

"We must be at the Embassy in half an hour." They are having lunch with the Italian Ambassador.

Before they leave she looks him up and down, tut tutting and straightening his tie.

I get home late, fry myself some eggs and sit down exhausted in front of the evening news. It is Albanian TV but I do not have the energy to turn over. And it is (visually) interesting. The President *is* the news - making a handsome speech in the morning, inspecting a factory after lunch and that evening welcoming a party of German parliamentarians to State House. He is everywhere.

WEDNESDAY 31ST JANUARY
ANETSI

I head for the Professor's house, via the Ministry to pick up some papers. It rains all the way and by the time I arrive the Ministry's corridors are slippery and filthy. Anetsi sits by a bar-heater, his jacket steaming in the heat. The room smells of singed wool.

"Nice day."

"What do expect. This is fucking Albania." He puffs on his cigarette and shakes his head. Poor Anetsi. Who is keen on dumplings and prunes and maudlin when drunk. Who has a stupor to his voice as if he can barely see the point of speaking. Leather pads on his elbows, endlessly patient with his children, two rotten old ties to his name. Working day and night in the Ministry.

This evening Suzana and I have to be especially quiet because mother is sick. Dritan hurries back and forth through the connecting door with steaming kettles of water and pots of tea.

FEBRUARY

The Professor is in a bad mood. After a frustrating morning in front of the computer, he takes me out to lunch. He drives the wrong way across Skanderberg Square and a policeman blows a whistle and flags us down. When he recognises the Professor he salutes and we speed on.

"Is Albania going to be OK Alex? Do you think?" he asks me over lunch. Before I can answer he continues.

"Sometimes I think no. This place is scarred. The people are too scarred - their heads are loose after decades of persecution and fear. They don't trust the state, they don't understand capitalism. They are wary of each other - they don't know how to relate to one another in a democratic context. Hoxha regulated social discourse, he created his own, how do you say - etiquette: what you could and could not say, how much pleasure you could seek, who you had to obey or vilify. It made life simple. Now the people are free to behave as they want - and they find it too difficult.

Sure, they are trying to change, to enjoy being free and become fucking capitalists. They want money and video players - they want to be like people in Britain or Italy. But they think capitalism is some magic, that it is a miracle. And what if capitalism doesn't work for Albania? What if the government make a mistake? Then there will be nothing for my people to believe in. I tell you Alex. If things don't get better soon they'll go mad again, like they did after communism."

"But there are people like you to stop that happening."

"Don't think I can stop anything, Alex. I am just an observer - I have a voice, I can say things but I can't make people listen. And who listens to me; no one but my enemies. Sometimes I wonder what the fuck I am doing here."

The Professor has been invited to address a seminar at Chatham House on modernising Albania. I am also invited. The Professor chortles as he hands me the envelope. Maurice is in the Chair.

Which means that I arrive wet at the Dajti, where I am meeting Mike Frost, a retired British army officer. I sit in the lobby, damp and reading (appropriately enough) *Memoirs of an Infantry Officer*.

The Chargé wanders in wearing a green cape and an impressive hat with a feather in it. He greets a group of men who look like British civil servants, and leads them dramatically into the night, where Dritan no doubt is waiting in the Land Rover. Then Gzim rushes up, gripping my arm with his fat fingers.

"Eh, Alexi ... taxi?"

At last Mike walks in, large and English-looking, the shoulders of his sports jacket dark with rain.

"Welcome to Albania," he says squeezing my hand, "rainy season I'm afraid."

Gzim's out of luck, Mike doesn't take taxis. Luckily it's stopped raining. He leads me across the road to a bar he knows.

"Run by Kosovans," he explains as we sit down. "Bit of research." Mike is in charge of the European Community Monitoring Mission (ECMM). The Mission is made up of active and recently retired military and police officers from EU-member countries. ECMM's job is to observe the integrity of Albania's northern borders with Serb-controlled Montenegro and Kosovo, and its eastern border with Macedonia. There is, after all, a war going on in Yugoslavia and all three borders are frequently trespassed by smugglers and refugees. Ethnic rivalries, as well as the frequency of armed patrols on either side, mean that there are regular incursions and shootings. ECMM teams, based in strategic border towns, work closely with the local border authorities, observing their activities, monitoring border stability and investigating 'incidents'. The monitors are unarmed, and depend upon their official status and their Albanian guards for safety.

On the way to a fish restaurant Mike knows nearby we are approached by a group of urchins on patrol. Dressed in torn clothes and broken shoes, they live in a pack near the Tirana hotel. They run towards us, hands outstretched. Mike reaches into his pocket and hands them each a few Lek.

"You want to watch that lot." He says, looking after them as they scamper off down the pavement. "Never take them on. They're dangerous."

"They're a ruthless bunch - they make bad enemies. There was a Greek diplomat out here last year, useless bugger. Anyway he hated being followed and hassled by them, day in, day out. He had a real thing about it. One night he was walking back from a restaurant, blotto, and a couple of boys asked him for money. When he refused one tried to snatch a pen out of his trouser pocket. The Greek turned on the boy and beat him - broke his leg. The Greek was quite proud of himself, 'now they will pay me some respect' he boasted to me the next day. A week later the Greek's Land Rover was found burnt out in Tirana Park. Inside they found two bodies - the Greek and a prostitute. Outside was an empty jerrycan."

"And it was the urchins?"

"What do you think?"

We sit at a corner table. A group of well dressed Kosovans walk in and Mike gets up to have a chat with them.

"Mafia, from Pristina. Another example of good friends and terrible enemies." He grins.

Mike is an old drinking partner of the Professor. "He's a complicated man. What do you know about his background?"

"Not much more than that he taught economics at Tirana University, set up the DP with the President. Then, briefly in government before he and the President fell out. Now persona non grata."

"All true, but go a bit further back and things get even more interesting. His father was a leading light in the AWP, one of Hoxha's right-hand men. The Professor grew up in the communist aristocracy. Gives him a big credibility problem; this place is obsessed with burying its past. Not that there aren't question marks hanging over the President. He was a young zealot in the AWP - received part of his medical training in France. Foreign trips and education weren't given out to everyone. Certainly not to troublemakers and likely dissidents. After France the President became Hoxha's personal physician and, some say, his confidante."

"Do you think the Professor could ever get back into power?"

"Unlikely. A week is a long time in politics and all that, but he hasn't a chance as long as the President's in charge. They hate each other. And when he goes? Well 'when?' is the question. At the moment the President's looking as safe as houses - Washington loves him, so do the European powers, his people still think he's got what it takes to turn Albania around, money pouring in, economy on the up, your Conference coming up ... Not to say there aren't plenty of problems; government's authoritarian and riddled with corruption, the mafia's growing, most people are still piss poor, Kosovo. But for the time being the President's on a roll, and things are going to have to go spectacularly wrong to knock him off balance."

"What are you doing next weekend?"

I shrug my shoulders.

"Why don't you come up with me to the Kosovan border. I'm taking some British aid workers to look at a health-care project they're funding. Come along. You'll be fascinated. It's another world up there," says Mike. "It's the nineteenth bloody century."

SATURDAY 3RD FEBRUARY
MUSLIMS

I am woken by the Muslim call to prayer. There is a mosque nearby, I pass it every morning on my way to work, a few old men padding about inside in their socks. It's easy to forget that this is a Muslim country - and a member of the Islamic Conference, a Muslim club that includes Iran, Saudi Arabia and the Gulf States. Iran has a handsome old Ottoman townhouse for its Embassy and the Saudis and Kuwaitis are pouring aid money into the country, especially the impoverished north.

My father built a large private practice treating fragile Arabs and their families. His patients included government ministers from Iraq, Dubai ... even Ethiopia. One or two became friends - in particular a Dubai sheikh, whom we called Mr Redwani. My father used to fly out to Dubai to treat him and other members of the government, and to lecture at Dubai's main teaching hospital. Redwani lived in a big piece of desert, surrounded by a white wall. He had his own oasis where he built a great house with a swimming pool. Everytime one of his sons or daughters married, he built them a house in some distant glade. I have photographs of my father smoking a hookah with Redwani, underneath the palms of his oasis.

One summer, while Mr Redwani was in London, we visited him and his family at the Dorchester. Redwani had asked specially to meet us. In his suite he presented Tom and I with a table football - unimaginable luxury. But we rather spoilt it by bursting into tears when he clapped for his wives to join us. They were in purdah and looked like ghouls in their beaked masks.

The next time I met him was in Essex. It was 1988. It was a wet June day, grey and unpleasantly cold. Mr Redwani was in Britain and he had asked us for lunch.

"Come to my house," he told mum. "It is in Essex." So we drove to Essex, mum, James and I. Tom was in France on a French exchange. Redwani's house was a pretty Palladian pile, with yet another swimming pool and large, fussy gardens. In the drive was a dark blue Rolls Royce. Inside the house was rather sad. There was a minimum of furniture, and little on the walls except gaudy wallpaper. Redwani was smaller than I remembered - a slight figure in a robe and a pin-striped suit jacket. He had just returned from a shopping expedition with his two wives.

"They have nothing to buy in the desert," he explained.

We sat on the floor on a silk carpet and a servant brought great quantities of steaming saffron rice and mutton, which we ate with our hands. Afterwards we sipped coffee flavoured with cardamom and some of Redwani's wives and daughters joined us.

"This is the wife and sons of Dr Hickman," he told them. And to our horror they all started crying and wringing their hands. Redwani watched impassively, the brass filter of his hookah hanging between his wet lips. Then he turned to my mother and, his eyes bright with tears, bowed his head.

"Your husband saved my life," he told us. "They are eternally grateful."

SUNDAY 4TH FEBRUARY
PAUL

Dritan has been skiing with the Chargé on Mount Dajti and his thighs are very sore. His cheeks and nose are red. I picture the Chargé shushing along, the tails of his cape flapping out behind him, his felt hat pressed tight over his ears.

"I want to go skiing," I whinge, stamping my feet like a spoilt child.

"Do you know of Paul, Alexi?" asks Dritan as we drink coffee and burp up reminders of Suzana's supper. Paul Coat is a young British diplomat, recently posted here. He is staying in the Dajti, and learning Albanian from a professor at the university.

"He is lonely, like you."

Dritan and I have given up smoking.

MONDAY 5TH FEBRUARY
LIONS AND SHADOWS

Passing the Dajti I leave a message for Paul, suggesting supper on Wednesday.

Then I hurry on. It is a grey day and an icy wind blows down the Lana. Somehow I sense I am being followed. A man in a black leather jacket paces himself behind me. Across the street, on a bench by the river, sits another man reading a newspaper. I eye him and he eyes me back. This is a ludicrous. As I turn into the Professor's street the man in the leather jacket is a little way behind me. I stop to loiter outside a shop in order to have a look at him. Not in the window, few Albanian shops have windows, but over my shoulder as I bend down to pick up some change, dropped and glittering across the pavement. He is standing across the road from me, a fat oaf with a moustache, smoking a cigarette. Just before I push open the gate into the Professor's drive I risk one last look back. There he is, leaning down into the window of a parked mercedes. Two men inside. Well that's that. They're ShIK. I am being followed.

The Professor is in his office. Among the piles of books and overflowing ashtrays, he is furiously opening his mail. He looks up and shouts at me.

"This is persecution Alexi," waving a buff envelope from Athens. Every letter in this morning's post has been clumsily opened by ShIK. He scatters the papers across his desk, furious.

"They tap my phone, they read my letters. Those bastards. Those fucking bastards. A fucking tyranny."

He seizes the phone. "A FUCKING tyranny!" He shouts into the mouthpiece.

I walk home. It is gloomy and cold. It is Tirana's rush hour and the crowds are reassuring.

"I'm safe enough here," I tell myself like some lonely traveller in a le Carré novel. Back at Dritan's I eat fried egg sandwiches in front of Italian TV. Raki and the application of cold logic: I am a conspicuous, foreign, young man working in the Ministry, curious, eccentric perhaps, but harmless. They wouldn't dare… In fact it is all a bit of a game. I decide that there is no need or point in telling Dritan. When he gets back I make coffee and, together, we munch through piles of pistachios, fidgeting disconsolately with the shells. What a time to give up smoking.

TUESDAY 6TH FEBRUARY
THE BOSS

Anetsi and I are walking down the corridor towards Xhaja's office. Last night I drank too much raki with Dylber and Dritan and this morning my head is full of cotton wool.

A sharp-faced man, serious looking in a grey suit, walks past and stops, nods at Anetsi and addresses me.

"So you're the young economist from Britain who's working on the Investment Conference?"

Hearing myself addressed as an economist itches like a rash.

"You must have great knowledge about privatisation. We have learned so much from your government in this area. Of course, Britain's advice has had great influence on our mass privatisation programme. You have studied our programme?"

"Umm, of course."

"And what is your opinion, please. How is it?"

"Well, I'm afraid I'm not up to date with the detail, but from what I've seen I think it's excellent... courageous, realistic..." I have run out of adjectives and blurt the first thing that comes into my head "...just what the doctor ordered." Anetsi looks at his feet. The man pauses, as if to let my comments sink home. Then he holds out his hand.

"Thank you. Well, I am pleased to meet you. I am sure that we will meet again. Perhaps at the conference." He walks off down the corridor.

"Who," I ask Anetsi "was that?"

"The Minister of Finance."

After lunch I visit Mike at his office to receive my battle orders - we leave for the mountains on Friday. It is a short walk from the Ministry. All the ECMM officers are dressed in white. Their white trainers squeak on the parquet floor. It is like a lunatic asylum.

"Emphasises our neutral status," explains Mike. "Makes it easier for the goons on the hills not to shoot us."

Mike is pouring over a map. A radio whistles over his shoulder. He is busy.

"Friday at the Dajti. Seven thirty a.m. See you there. Meet Gergj. Gergj, meet Alex. He's coming with us to Peshkopje." Back to the map.

Gergj is Mike's assistant, a handsome, smiling Albanian who speaks beautiful English. He is in his late twenties, cheerful and clever.

"It is my pleasure to meet you Alex. I look forward to travelling with you."

Albanians say things like that to strangers and the magnificent thing is they mean it. They really mean it.

WEDNESDAY 7TH FEBRUARY
PAUL

The Professor has gone to Athens for a few days. Which is rather a relief. I am glad to lose the kind attentions of ShIK.

Paul takes me to an underground Italian restaurant he knows. The room is hung with paintings - amateur still lifes in oils and kitsch pastel cottages by the sea. We order red wine which comes cold in a jug. Paul is young-looking, round-faced with thinning brown hair. He is very civil service: careful in his speech, classless, bad shoes, punctual. He smokes long John Players and is very keen on ping-pong.

"I was Reading University champion, three years running," he tells me proudly. "I play a bit at the university here. They've got a table, bit ropy but it does. I play daily - keeps me in trim."

After supper we go to the London Bar, decorated with a union flag and there are silhouettes of the Houses of Parliament on the wall. I tell him about my ShIK tail.

"It's not exactly going to make you popular, hanging about with the Professor. Not the President's favourite politician you know."

After a glass of brandy or two we part, both tipsy, in the middle of a deserted Skanderberg Square.

"We must have a game of ping-pong sometime" he says, gripping my hand, "…good to find some fresh blood."

After work I walk to Fidel's Café, where I drink coffee and watch the world go by. Sometimes I meet the Professor there. Fidel was the Professor's official bodyguard when he was a minister in the DP government. Now he runs his kiosk, a popular meeting place for members of the Professor's party and opposition journalists. In his spare time Fidel manages Albania's wrestling team.

The Café has a good view of Skanderberg Square, which is always a source of entertainment. The square is the centre of Tirana and it means many things to the city's inhabitants. It is where they go to riot and protest. It is where they change their lek into dollars or vice versa. It is where a few of them go to enjoy the opera, the national museum, Albania's oldest mosque, the national library or even to have a coffee or cocktail at the Tirana Hotel. It is, in other words, a draw. And the beggars are still patrolling its pavements.

There is the plump gypsy woman sat with her baby daughter. The latter lies permanently on a sheet of cardboard ripped from a box, dribbling and sucking at a filthy ten lek note that she has been given as a kind of bait. The woman will not get up but is aggressive, shouting and scowling at passers by, raising her hands and pleading for money.

One beggar on the Square is particularly grotesque. He has no legs, just lumps of loose flesh like a pair of brown handbags hanging from his waist. The rest of his frame is bent and taut and he moves about by his hands, pushing himself along the pavement on callused knuckles. He moves surprisingly quickly. Once, he saw me coming and zeroed in. I was not in the mood to stop and shimmied to pass him. He turned instantly and cut me off, grabbing hold of the buckles of my shoes. I balanced the revulsion I felt at his appearance with that which I felt for myself. My liberties had been sorely abused, I had given him money before. But I did feel a bit like a running dog of capitalism. It came out at about evens. It took fifty lek to prise myself free. He tucked the note greedily down the front of his shirt and crabbed back into the centre of the pavement.

Today he catches a portly man who looks like a Swiss banker. Like me he has tried to evade him, and failed. But the Swiss banker resists, shaking himself free. In the process he steps smartly on the beggar's fingers, whose pride is hurt as much as his gnarled fingers. He swears and spits and shakes his callused hand at the fat Swiss derrière.

Back down Deshmoret ë Kombit Boulevard, you can walk all the way in the green shade of the tall pines that line the road. The kiosks in the park are playing their music, the newspaper sellers stand by their wares - piles of papers weighed down with a stone to keep the wind off. There is much traffic and the queues at the lights by the bridge are being worked by a couple of urchins, who wave a grubby rag over each windscreen before pointing sadly at their mouths. Over the grey river the Ministry is in sight through the trees and around the bulbous hips of Hoxha's pyramid. Along the pavement are parked several mercedes, the doors flayed open. The cars are full of longhaired young men. Many are asleep, others sit on the pavement smoking. They all wear denim or leather jackets. In one of the cars the stereo is playing and music thumps across the pavement. They are Kosovans and every one of them is up to no good, sleeping off last night's escapades. They are there everyday, cleaning their grubby nails with flick knives, laughing, shouting, sleeping. Two minutes walk from the Presidency gates and the white-gloved guards.

We are four in the Land Rover - Mike, Ian, Keith and me. Sarah, Gergj and Cathy are in a little Skoda jeep behind us. Mike drives, hands held high on the steering wheel over his big stomach, Ian sits beside him.

We are on our way to the mountainous north east, lost, as Mike puts it, somewhere in the nineteenth century. One aspect of the twentieth century that the communities are without is good medical facilities. Ian and Sarah want to put that right. Ian is an engineer - tough, capable, unsympathetic, with edges as rough as broken brick. Stocky, with a small head and a hard, organised face, Ian is good empire-building material, the sort of man who could be relied upon to put down rebellions viciously and repair locomotives under a hail of gunfire.

But there must be a soft heart under all that grit. It is Ian who has raised the money to build a new health centre in one of the villages. Now he wants to inspect the site chosen for the centre - a disused hospital. He has brought along an architect to recommend any structural changes. The architect is Keith, a plump, cosy sort of person from the London suburbs. Sarah runs a nursing charity in the UK. She wants to see whether the project will provide suitable opportunities for her nurses. If she likes what she sees, she will recruit a couple to work in the centre. Cathy is Sarah's coordinator in Albania. Mike is providing the Land Rovers, somewhere to stay, a bit of muscle and, in Gergj, an interpreter. So there we are. Angels of mercy and myself, riding into the mountains.

We head north out of Tirana, past the settlements of Gheg migrants from the barren mountainsides of Kukes and Tropoja. Whole families live in Hoxha's old bunkers, or in pathetic shacks fashioned out of Tirana's detritus. Their sons and daughters, with fierce eyes from squinting into sun and wind, walk along the side of the road. They move with grace, their limbs are wrapped in lean muscle, their hair is bleached and matted like old straw. Some carry water, others small stacks of feed for their cow or donkey. But they are going nowhere. They are feared by their new neighbours in the town. There is no work for them and little money to buy food. Far from home they cannot grow it. And so they slowly die – from cholera or cold or the vicious mathematics of some blood feud.

At Milot the road crosses the wide Mati river on a bridge built by the Italians during Zog's rule. Just before it we turn right and follow the river inland. The Mati is broad and silver grey and the road takes us up the valley side, high enough to have a long view of the wide river flowing out of snowy mountains on the horizon.

In the middle of a rolling, boulder-strewn plain we reach Burrel, a hill-top town which serves as the administrative centre of the Mati region. Zog came from the Mati and this was his power-base; here he built himself a garrison, as well as a prison for his enemies. The prison was later turned into a forced labour camp by the communists, where dissidents were forced to mine copper pyrite on windy terraces cut into the hillside. Conditions were so harsh that prisoners often mutilated themselves in order to get off work. They were crammed into punishment cells only two metres across, where the temperature could fall to – 12°C. Thin blankets were only allowed at night and rations were meagre - just enough to allow docile energy for the day's 'work'. Unruly prisoners would be stripped and hung in wooden cages above the river. The prison was closed in 1991.

Past Burrel we begin to climb again, towards snowy mountains, sharp-tipped in the distance. We pass a squad of young conscripts in white vests, running on the spot in the shade of poplar trees. Mike knows the commanding officer and stops for a chat. The officer shouts at his men to do press-ups and winks at Mike. We keep climbing, up a swollen river valley, then suddenly, we are on the roof and the snowy peaks seem almost in reach.

"Kosovo," points Mike. Up on this open moorland, the day has a wilder aspect. The sky is slate grey, a cold wind picks up, the road runs away across the empty plateau towards Kosovo.

Crouched in a khaki hollow, on the edge of the plateau, is a modern, battleship-grey town. I can see tenements and towers etched out against the cold sides of the hill. I suppose there must be electricity, slogging up a few taut lines from the power station below Burrel. Are there traffic lights and corner shops too? Could I buy fresh bread or yesterday's paper? At a crossroads a narrow road peels off to our left, trudging over the cold moor towards the town. There is a line of people walking down it. In the distance the women have the faces of crows and the men are canine and fanged. They carry parcels and push prams full of coal. I cannot believe human beings live in this mountain desolation where nothing grows and the wild horses have several coats to stand the wind.

To our right the road runs arrow-straight to a mess of low concrete buildings and machinery a mile or so away on the hillside. It is a coal mine, another former labour camp. Just to see it through the window of a moving Land Rover, safe and transitory, makes me shiver. This road is deserted, except for the pepper of a faraway motorbike. It is a crossroads of almost perfect sadness.

An hour later we reach the end of the plateau, the road falls towards Peshkopje and the landscape takes on a more human aspect. We come across hamlets and ploughed fields. Just before Peshkopje there are orchards and gullies full of streams. In the ever-distance are the snow-covered mountains of Kosovo. The air is thin and tart like lemon juice. There are bunkers scattered everywhere - this is border country.

"Don't they all get in each other's way?" I ask Mike, pointing at them.

"You should be a General," he replies, a little sarcastically.

Suddenly we are in Peshkopje, which will be our base for the weekend. There are no suburbs or outskirts, we just round a corner and find ourselves in the main square. We cross a charging river, the Black Drin, which flows through the town. The bridge is Ottoman, as are many of the houses gathered around the market square. It is picturesque and very poor. The town's mining and manufacturing industries have collapsed since 1991, around 17,000 jobs have disappeared, and nearly half of the population is now dependent on government benefit, which averages around US$18 a month per person.

The river bed is filthy. The gravel is covered with rubbish - plastic bottles and torn plastic bags caught on the stones, fluttering like prayer flags. Up above the town stands a villa in a compound. Here lived the officers of the occupying Italian army during the war and now it is home to more European soldiers – those of Mike's ECMM. Peshkopje is the administrative centre of the remote Dibra region and, from this HQ, ECMM officers patrol the sensitive mountain border with Kosovo. Inside, Tom, a Danish policeman, and Edmond, a French fighter pilot, are eating lunch. Their Albanian guard, Kristaq, is in trouble with Mike. Last week he got drunk at a cousin's wedding and shot a stray dog and a window in the town hall. The local chief of police has complained. Now Kristaq is sitting at one end of the table picking his teeth and sulking. Mike takes no notice.

It is warm in the sun and after lunch I sit out on the verandah writing letters. Kristaq, keen to make friends, brings me coffee and goes off with my camera. Below me the bulk of the town has solidity and I make out the main boulevard lined with trees and, far down the slope, the copse of a housing estate and a green square where a football match is being played. I can see where the river angles round in a deep gully. Across it brown plain runs out towards the snow-covered mountains.

Supper in a candle-lit restaurant. Tom and Edmond are still wearing their white uniforms. Edmond has a pair of slim sunglasses sitting on his head. He looks like a slip fielder, stretching his legs between balls. A weasel of a man arrives, his greasy hair pasted across his head. It is the doctor whose derelict has been chosen as the site for the new health centre. Behind him walk two men, who wear ankle length coats and have dark, hidden faces. They have a highwayman grace about them and speak reluctantly. The doctor introduces them as the village mayor and his deputy. All three have travelled specially to meet us here, and to escort us to their village tomorrow morning.

It is a good supper, lots of meat and a delicious local raki made from plums grown in the nearby orchards. We drink a lot of it and by the end of supper are (with the exception of Mike) drunk. The doctor gets creepier, the highwaymen slouch in their chairs and laugh in deep baritones. Then Cathy makes an impromptu speech about women's rights and looks forward to the day the village doctor, and even the mayor, will be women. The Albanians look cross. As Cathy sits down we all breathe a sigh of relief. She turns to Sarah and mouths something like 'I think that went rather well'. Sarah nods earnestly and squints back at her. Mike suggests it is time for bed.

Outside Cathy falls over in a heap, ending up giggling in the pool of her own skirt. Above her, the mayor and his friends stand in silence. The doctor, pale in the night, his shoes squeaking, fetches her up. Red-faced, Cathy says goodnight and wanders off towards the hotel. There is a broad grin on the mayor's face. Cathy has put emancipation back years in that little corner of Dibra. As we follow her back towards our hotel I bet the good mayor and his friends can't wait to get home and give their wives and daughters one hell of a thrashing. Just in case.

The plum raki gives me strange dreams of great landscapes and horsemen and booming waterfalls. I am woken by Ian rapping on the door.

"Get a fucking move on." It is six o'clock.

Downstairs everyone is eating cheese omelettes. Apart from us, and two workmen prising out a rotten window frame in the corner, the dining room is empty. Ian is smoking his Dunhill and peering inside his attaché case. The highwaymen appear with cigarettes between their teeth. This morning they both wear hats and look like a brace of Jesse James's. Then the doctor walks into the dining room, rubbing his hands and smiling. There is something Heepish about the doctor. It is rumoured that he has a past. Girlfriends on the side. Young girlfriends. His wife is pregnant with their second child. He is expecting her to give birth at any moment, he tells me, his mouth visibly full of cheese omelette. Twenty minutes later Mike, Gergj and Kristaq arrive with the Land Rovers and we are on our way to the village.

We drive through a broken country of muddy rivers, sharp hills and scrub. In the back of the Land Rover my hangover intensifies. Gradually I realise that I feel sick. Sick – in front of Mike. Impossible. It would mean disgrace. Coventry. The Tower. I imagine a court martial, on a quiet bluff above the Black Drin, Gergj unable to look me in the eye, Ian beating a deadly tattoo on a little drum and Mike passing sentence, grim faced, with a black handkerchief planted askance on his head.

"Send him down!"

We pass a lonely hamlet, half brick, half mud houses and a school with a dented earth football pitch and a basketball hoop. Trying to take my mind off my heaving stomach, I ask Mike about Maurice.

"That man is a bloody lunatic."

"Why's the Chargé so frightened of him?"

"I think it's more that he's embarrassed. They're old friends. Maurice was in the FO, a high flyer posted to Czechoslovakia, until he got caught trading semtex and blackmailing God knows who. Story goes he had dirt on someone in the British Cabinet and managed to get the whole thing hushed up. Traded his way out with some kind of honourable discharge. He's got a brilliant brain."

"What's he up to now?"

"Using it. Making money all over the Balkans. He's a very big noise in Bulgaria - he's climbed into bed with one of the big mafia gangs. I'm not sure what he's doing in Albania, except mischief making and buying a few guns."

"Who for?"

"Rwanda. Where else? Big market in Rwanda."

"And what about the Professor? How come he's so close to the Professor?"

Mike thinks for a minute. "Three reasons. I know Pace has it in for the President, not sure why but he really has it in for him. There's reason one. He'd like to see the Professor at the helm – part of some long game he's playing – he'll want a source of cheap chrome for his Bulgarian car plant or something. There's reason two. And I think he likes the Professor. Rates him – reckons his heart's in the right place. Reason three. So Maurice can meddle and play with people, which he loves, and be on the side of the angels for once."

The road narrows between sheer rock and a clear drop to a river tumbling far below. Around a corner is a man and a donkey, which is loaded with hay. He moves it hard against the cliff face and we crawl past. At the bottom of the valley we ford the river and start up the other side. During the long winter the ford is often flooded, blocking the weekly bus service and cutting off the communities on the far side.

"Not far now," announces Mike. The nineteenth bloody century is just around the corner.

Mike parks the Land Rover up by a barn in the muddy village. There are a few houses visible – small, one-story, brick buildings. The rest of the village is hidden behind a spine of ground. Around us loom mountains. It is infinitely quiet. The mayor leads us into a tumbling building that turns out to be the village bar. Its walls are covered in pages cut from magazines. There is a radio attached to a piece of wire that runs up to the ceiling and the cold smell of woodsmoke. The mayor shouts a name. He looks agitated. Moments later a man comes running through the door and, mumbling apologies to the mayor, clambers over the counter. From behind it he produces glasses and a bottle of raki. It is nine thirty.

Half an hour later the doctor leads us towards a two storey building standing on a slim piece of open ground in front of the village. The building used to serve as the district hospital but the money ran out in 1990. Inside it is empty. The concrete floors are bare and covered in owl pellets and pools of water. Below the nose of the building the hillside falls away towards the valley floor and the view from the upstairs window is into lavender distance. Perfect for accelerating convalescence. And for fizzing golf balls.

Mike, Gergj and I leave Ian and his party to inspect the hospital. Mike leads us out of the village, to a tall mound standing on the very edge of the mountainside.

"Used to be a castle here. Medieval."

We sit on the old ramparts and Mike tells us about close scrapes in Bosnia while I throw stones at nothing in particular, remembering my time there. Drizzle runs the colour out of the grey sky and softens the granite sides of the mountains. Mike points out a number of passes and tracks on their flanks. They make for the border and trouble. I tell Mike about being followed to the Professor's and he looks at me carefully.

"I had the same treatment a couple of weeks ago. Chaps watching me from a parked car at the end of the Professor's street. Just marched straight up to them and introduced myself. Told them I was a good friend of the Minister of Defence and suggested I got in and they drove. Struck me as a jolly good idea – kind of a free taxi and total surveillance combined. Save everyone's time. They pissed off pretty quickly. But I thought they were watching me, not the Professor. The President must be turning up the heat. You'll tell me if they keep at it, won't you?"

Back in the middle of the village stand the mayor and his sidekick. Their long coats flap. Walking towards them feels like a scene from a Western. Who will draw first? The mayor invites us to lunch. Mike has already ruled this out. If we accept they will be obliged to kill a goat and provide us with the kind of hospitality that they cannot really afford.

"I know a good spot for lunch. Out of sight, out of mind," says Mike.

This is a desperately poor place. There isn't a man who is not over forty or under fourteen, the rest have left. The children are all a little pinched around the mouths and eyes. Four of them watch us climb into the Land Rovers, waving shyly back at Sarah. They all look about eight or nine, but Mike reckons they are about fourteen. He knows a nineteen year old soldier stationed further along the border whose voice hasn't broken.

We drive up above the village, along a rough track. A small field is enclosed by dry stone walls. On the wall leans a man, smoking. He nods as we drive by. Behind him in the field the bent figure of his wife is turning the heavy brown earth. Sarah and Cathy mutter in the back. We follow the track up a gully. It is U-shaped and at the top is a small round plateau. I can almost see the pin and a couple of bunkers.

"Make a good golf hole. Par three…about a seven iron," I mutter. There is silence in the cab.

"High enough," says Mike and we climb out and make a picnic. We lie out on a tarpaulin eating tomato and cheese sandwiches. It is surprisingly warm under the heavy sky.

"Time to go," says Mike, staring at the sky, and we begin to pack away the picnic. "There could be a storm coming."

I say something along the lines of 'excellent'. I like storms.

"A storm means flash floods, lightning, rain that you can't see through. The track would very quickly be impassable. We could be stranded, for the night."

"Mmm," I reply. "Good point."

On the way down, Mike points out the border station, laid out below us in a small valley. A few damp-looking buildings, a football pitch, a track leading out of site, parked vehicles. Here live the guardians of this lonely frontier – over the mountains is Kosovo and war. What a place.

I suppose there is electricity. But what can that do save heat the office of the fat commandant and cast a yellow light on the bullying, the buggery and the boredom that I presume rule the nine-to-five routine of the days down there. And for tea? Dry bread, sour milk, stale meat, old eggs. Then to sleep in a lousy, damp bed and up the next morning for physical jerks on a cold drill square. The station looks deserted – perhaps everyone has run away or an unnerved recruit has run amok and killed the lot of them.

Back in the village we gather in the mayor's office. His hat hangs on a nail in the wall. Beside him sits a telephone. It is made of faded baker-lite and looks like an ironic exhibit at a post-modern gallery somewhere in west London. Every so often the mayor looks at it. He is keen to make a call. Eventually we all fall on some excuse and he picks it up and turns a little handle on its base. The line is dead.

The children shout us out of the village. Keith and Cathy draw their Japanese cameras, as much a mark of modern northern visitors as crosses were on the chests of our crusading ancestors. The children pose, fighting one another to be nearest to the camera and staring it full in the face. They are standing on a pile of manure. It lends height to the pack.

"Look, Ian, they're standing on the shit," shouts Keith.

Ian, who seems to regard the rest of us (except Mike) as his own brood of dim and trying children, ignores him.

"I can't believe it. They're standing on shit. Uuurrgghh – two of them hasn't got any shoes on. Look! The shit's squeezing through their toes. I can't believe they're standing on shit."

They carry on standing on shit until we have finished taking photographs. Then they follow us back to the Land Rovers.

"I can't believe they were standing on shit. I just can't believe it. How come their mums didn't stop them." Keith is beside himself.

"That's enough Keith," says Mike, and nods us all into the Land Rovers.

SUNDAY 11TH FEBRUARY
PESHKOPJE - TIRANA

By midday our convoy arrives, dusty brown, at the Dajti. It has been a gruelling weekend. We were up most of last night drinking, leaving Peshkopje at six after a couple of hours sleep. I feel dizzy, disorientated and rather cross after over six hours on the road.

Paul is in the bar, practising his past tenses, a packet of John Players on the table in front of him.

"See that chap over there," nods Paul, his voice hushed. I glance slowly over my shoulder.

"Don't look, you fool," he hisses, too late. In the corner of the bar three rough-looking men are drinking whisky.

"Did you see him, the one with the shiny shirt?"

"And the chunky gold necklace?"

"That's the one. He's a smuggler. Mafia type from Vlora. I'm keeping an eye on him."

"Oh. Do you want me to go?"

"No, stay. Drink your coffee. You're creating good cover."

"What does he smuggle?" I whisper, leaning conspiratorially towards him.

Paul is annoyed.

"Alex, you must try and look more natural. Watch me..." He is leaning back in his chair, louchely blowing smoke at the ceiling.

"So what does he smuggle?" I ask, lounging back as I light one of his cigarettes.

"Drugs, girls, guns, refugees. All to Italy, which leaks like a damn sieve. The Albanians have got terrific speedboats – much too fast for the Italians."

"Why don't the Italians just shoot up a few boats," I ask impatiently "pour encourager les autres."

Paul crooks an eyebrow.

"That's a little excessive isn't it?" he says, leaning back to blow another jet of smoke lazily at the ceiling.

"Oh come on..." I reply irritated, and look up in time to watch Paul tip gently backwards in his chair, and crash to the floor.

Albanians are singular looking. At least the men are. To me their appearance is unique. I believe I could recognise an Albanian anywhere in the world, whether he was wearing a dinner jacket or a wet suit. How can I be so sure? Because I'm rash. And because Albanians really are very singular looking – a combination of height, head and hair.

First height. Albanian men tend to be pretty small. There aren't many six foot Albanians. One exception would be 'King' Leka (Zog's son and heir) who is set in the mould of de Gaulle – a hooked nose, haughty face and seven feet tall. That's pretty unusual – the consequence perhaps of his royal blood and the backbone that he was given at Sandhurst. And anyway, his mother was Hungarian so he doesn't count.

The back of an Albanian's head is unusually flat. Not 'ironing board' flat but flat compared to you or me. I don't know why this should be. I suppose that a people whose history has been so full of invasion and subjection might have received a fair few slaps on the back of the head from colonial masters and slave drivers - but enough to leave a hereditary scar? Or is it down to a shortage of pillows or an appetite for sleeping on hard floors. Whatever the reason, Albania's isolation over past centuries and the consequent confinement of the Albanian gene pool has kept the flat head in the family.

Hair. This is usually black and comes in two main varieties. The first variety is a complicated state of baldness. Being bald must be very bad news in Albania because most bald Albanian men (and there are lots of them) go to great lengths to disguise their baldness: growing one side-fringe ludicrously long and smoothing it back across the pate in a thick curtain. Even in still conditions, the curtain requires constant smoothing down or re-tugging. In a good wind it will ride about like a loose canvas. Let nature take its course, I say. The bald Albanian is an urban species and tends to be dark skinned, short and stocky with small feet and a large stomach. He works as taxi driver (Gzim is bald with a curtain), middling bureaucrat, customs official, junior army officer, money-changer and academic.

The other significant hair group is thick and wiry, often bleached with straw coloured highlights by the sun. This hair looks like it has been cut with a pair of sheep clippers and that is very likely to be the case. This is a Gheg look, most commonly found in the isolated communities of Kukes, Puka or Tropoja. Wiry, ill-cut hair goes with caves and cold mountainsides and clear rivers. The mayor and his deputy had it, though they kept it hidden below their hats.

Wiry, ill-cut hair also goes with the sunburnt features of Hollywood legends – high cheekbones, large chins, straight noses and crow's feet around the eyes. Men like the mayor spend much of their time squinting into the bright alpine sun looking for lost goats, wolves, mushrooms and rain clouds. Their skin is like leather, their nails are chipped. They wear mouldy tweed jackets and their shirt collars tend to be huge; they have iron on the soles of their boots and they are as hard a people as I have met. Woodsmoke fills their houses year round. Transport is on foot, the back of a truck or a dilapidated bus. Some will be playing out blood feuds and will pass them onto their children. Most will beat their wives to keep warm in winter and will carry their sheep, one under each arm, all the way to market.

Of course I'm generalising. Albanians don't all look the same, like, say, the Chinese might to the uninitiated. Which reminds me. Long before democracy, Dritan was Albania's cycling champion. His reward for winning a big race was selection for a cycling tour of China. I love the idea of Dritan's patient features surveying a cast of tiny thousands milling in Shanghai or Beijing, sounding their bicycle bells.

We have both given up giving up smoking.

I need to start putting together a list of invitees to the Conference. My first ports of call are the Embassies which will be able to provide me with the names of their companies interested in Albania.

The Polish First Secretary is a merry man with a beard. He is terrifically excited about the Conference and calls for vodka and a list of Polish companies.

He invites me to stay for lunch which lasts until three o'clock. We drink too much vodka in a happy state of Anglo-Polish friendship. The Pole tells me that the Embassy was used by the Italian army of occupation as a brothel.

"In this verrry room," shouts the grinning First Secretary "the Italian officers twirled their moustaches and swung from chandeliers."

Ping-pong with Paul in Tirana University's gymnasium. It is icy cold. Paul appears in whites that would not shame Wimbledon, a sweat band on each wrist. There is no net – instead an unsteady row of maths text books. I beat him four games to two. Paul complains of a bad knee.

I have been chasing the Egyptian Embassy for some days. No one ever answers the phone. Egypt is a big investor here and I need a list of Egyptian companies to invite to the Conference. I finally track down a man with good English at the Embassy. He agrees to see me and to try to arrange an interview with the Ambassador. I make an appointment for Monday.

To the EU delegation to dig out some statistics for a briefing paper I'm writing for the Conference. I track down a secretary who finds me the documents I need.

"Can I photocopy these please?" I whisper. It is like being in a library.

"Well, it is not normal," she replies.

"I'm on EU business. This is for the Investment Conference. I'm sure the Ambassador wouldn't mind."

"I'll go and find out for you."

I have to pay.

FRIDAY 16TH FEBRUARY
MINISTRY OF FINANCE

This morning, while crossing the bridge over the sad Lana, I come across a small shrine at the side of the road. I am on my way to work, it is wet and grey and the cars shuss along the cobbles. The shrine consists of a gilt-framed photograph of a young man, who looks about twenty, a glass jar of flowers and a number of fragile candles riding out the worst of a cold wind.

The shrine seems to touch the world around it. The hawker who sells chewing gum and sesame seeds has shuffled away, head bowed. So has the old man with the scales, leaving the shrine a dignified isolation. Around it the pedestrians move in a restrained way. Women in black, their hands full of shopping, mutter under their breath as they rock past.

In the Ministry, where the cold hangs about the corridors, I look for an explanation. Anetsi knew the dead boy, they all did. He had been at Tirana University, an economics student, bright and popular. But in recent months he had become hopeless and depressed, wore black, sat locked in his room listening to punk and getting stoned. He began to get

154

very drunk at parties, and shout at his friends and was disagreeable to a girl who loved him. Last night he was found lying cold under the bridge, where the homeless beggars take a piss.

"These are hard times, guy," says Halit, who had been at university with the boy's brother, in his waspy English.

Anetsi shrugs, he is embarrassed.

"It is the slow winter, Alexi. Our slow fucking winter."

My early memories come in snatches - and they just about reach back to 1977, to our walk along the cliff top. I remember going crabbing in Norfolk. And my father letting me, Tom and James stand on the back seat of his Renault Five with our heads sticking out of the sun-roof. A policeman stopped us by Wimbledon Common and gave my father a ticking off for being irresponsible. Another Renault memory is the sunny morning when the four of us sang *Brown girl in the ring* by Boney M all the way down the King's Road. I think that daddy had just picked Tom and me up from pottery class. I wet myself once at the class, as I raced down its steep wooden steps, too late for the loo. The prickly, warm sensation, and the resultant despair, is still horribly clear.

The same year, my father was diagnosed with leukaemia. He had felt bad for a bit, but put it down to over-work. During a holiday in Norfolk he realised it was something serious. He had been playing golf with a few friends at Brancaster. Roger was there, and Mark Fraser, who would one day become my step-father. They were eight of them – all doctors, friends from Cambridge or the Middlesex. It had been a happy weekend, played out in Autumn sunshine, the sea still and the sky a clear blue. My father had been swinging well, striking the ball clean and straight down Brancaster's narrow, sing-song fairways. So why, he wondered, wasn't he hitting the ball very far. Why did the perfect drive, sent fizzing into the clear blue, stop thirty yards short of

155

where it should?

Back in London he noticed strange bruises on his back and chest. The next day – Monday – he felt grotty. Later that morning, during a hospital round, a nursing sister told him he looked anaemic. Suddenly it all made sense – feeling tired, his lack of strength, his bruising. He took a sample of his own blood and submitted it under a false name to the hospital lab. It came back the next day – his red blood cell count was right down, picked off by his malfunctioning white blood cells. His bone marrow was producing predators instead of policemen, and they were destroying his own blood. Without an adequate red cell count his watery blood would be unable to clot – he was in serious danger of haemorrhage. Ambitious young doctor became patient overnight.

He was admitted to Westminster Hospital. Mum unpacked his suitcase in an upstairs ward – what had once amounted to his office now became his home. Tests soon proved he had a peculiarly vicious form of leukaemia. He was exposed to an intensive course of chemotherapy and radiotherapy, in an attempt to destroy the cancer in his blood. He grew weak, his hair fell out, he became sterile and vulnerable to the slightest infection.

Orthodox treatment proved useless, the cancer was too strong. But there was still hope. Bone marrow had recently been successfully transplanted in America. This revolutionary treatment had two phases: the wholesale destruction of the patient's diseased bone marrow, followed by the transplantation of healthy marrow from a donor. If the new marrow wasn't rejected, the patient could begin to produce new, harmless white blood cells. The operation was a risky one, and the chances of rejection very high. But my father had Roger – they were genetically identical. There was a good chance that his body would accept Roger's marrow.

He was transferred to the Royal Marsden at Sutton, where he

was shut in a sterilised room. The destruction of his bone marrow would leave him unable to produce white blood cells, destroying his immune system and making the mildest of infections potentially fatal. Visitors were not allowed into the room. Instead they had to talk to him through a glass window. His food had to be sterilised before it was served to him through a hatch. He complained that it took away the taste. Only the doctors, nurses and occasionally us were allowed in, wearing gowns and face masks.

My father kept a diary during his illness, which describes fevers and ulcers and nausea. His sense of isolation and inertia. But he managed to remain extraordinarily positive. He was able to take pleasure from simple things – the view of trees from his window, the sound of seagulls or the wind, the faces of the nurses. His friends visited him, and brought good things with them, like champagne and gossip, and chivvied him along.

Most of all he had mum. And I suppose, us. I well remember visits to the Marsden, which always seemed to take place on grey, wet days full of traffic jams. Tom, James and I didn't like wearing the masks, and we couldn't touch daddy even if we were allowed into his room because he bruised so easily and he was inevitably hooked up to some delicate contraption that was feeding drugs into his veins. And he seemed frightening – grey and bald, his cheeks puffy and his eyes a little bright. Instead we would talk to him through the glass, he looking absurdly elegant in silk pyjamas and a dressing gown, his legs crossed, one foot dangling a slipper, a heavy Rolex watch on his left wrist, while sitting in a wheel chair and absorbing some sinister clear fluid through a plastic tube that disappeared under his cuff.

Then suddenly he was allowed home. The transplant had been a success, daddy was well again. He set about his old duties at the London and in Wimpole Street, wiser, happier, determined to be a better doctor for his experiences. But the cancer had been biding its time in the slack water of some vein, and within months he was re-diagnosed. This time there was no cure. He didn't stay in hospital long; he wanted to be with us.

Mum once told May that his last few weeks were among the happiest they ever had together. All I remember is a bright red plastic bowl by his side of their bed, and groups of people gathered around it as they chatted to daddy in his pyjamas, and the way his sterilised clothes smelt. Then one evening Frances, our au pair, picked us up from our school in Chelsea and took us shopping.

"Daddy is a bit poorly," she explained. "Why don't you choose some toys. Have whatever you want."

Brought up on five pence pocket money a week and surveying the colourful shelves of a toy shop, the words were rather paralysing. I bought a yellow dumper truck – a solid thing made of metal, a Mickey Mouse that you wound up and set whirring along the floor and some lego. I loved lego.

Afterwards, we had supper with our next door neighbours. Muffy Stansfield was my best friend. The two of us regularly had fights with Boris and Edwin, blond twins from up the road, whom we once cornered and doused with an ice cold hose, and Merryll, a terrifying black girl who used to attack us with a cricket stump. By now I knew something was up, there was a quiet, a softness in everyone's manner towards us.

Inside our front door waited mum, red-eyed but smiling.

"I'm afraid daddy's died." That memory is like a photograph, her standing red-eyed in the hall, ridiculously brave, looking at her three boys. I felt winded by what she was saying, and acutely embarrassed.

We went up to our room and played with our toys. I sped past the closed door to my parents' bedroom. Inside lay my dead father. I wondered whether he had turned a funny colour. Sitting on the floor, pushing my dumper truck about, I felt pretty strange. Time passed so slowly. Mum came in with hot chocolate.

"Why have you brought hot chocolate?" I asked her, staring down at the carpet. "We don't usually have hot chocolate."

Mum asked us if we wanted to say goodbye to daddy. He was lying there, dead in his bed. I said no, so did James. Tom went. I wish I had. I wish I had to this day.

SATURDAY 17TH FEBRUARY
OPPOSITION

Maurice rings about the London seminar, giving the Professor an excuse to lambaste the President to his eavesdroppers.

"Yes, Alex is here, Maurice. He's doing a great job helping me write my speech for London." How nice of the Professor to acknowledge my place in his dissident community. And have the fact broadcast to the secret police.

"Bye you bastards," he shouts at the tappers as he puts the phone down.

It is awkward spending so much of my time among political malcontents like the Professor and Anetsi. Not that I mind their reasoning - I respect it, and their courage. But their political obsession is alien to me. And after six or so weeks in Albania I don't feel I know this place well enough to be zealous or confident in my beliefs. Or that I can identify with this country, and the Professor's cause, enough to put my neck on the line. It's a bit like learning to drive in an Aston Martin - one is constantly worried about crashing.

Before I leave the Professor's house that evening I ring my parents in Kent.

"How's it going?" asks mum.

"Fine."

"Is your work with the Professor interesting?"

I pause. The men from ShIK hold their breath, somewhere below stairs in the Interior Ministry.

"Quite." It is not an easy conversation.

SUNDAY 18TH FEBRUARY
LUNCH BY THE SEA

I am sitting next to Fidel in his black Mercedes heading for Durres. Behind us, driving in convoy, is the Professor. We are heading to the beach for lunch.

Fidel drives in the groove, as you'd expect an ex-bodyguard to drive. Almost too fast, very solid. He is built on a big scale, with heavy fists and enormous shoulders. His eyes are heavy and his mouth hard. Often he chews a toothpick. When I first met him I saw little more than an assassin and I thought he looked cold and stupid. In fact, he is shy, with a boyish smile, and before long he has shown me pictures of his daughter, Rosie. Because you know that Fidel could break your spine across his knee, it is a good feeling to get along with him.

Fidel speaks softly and carefully, checking each word before uttering it. He likes to talk of the countries he has visited. In London he accompanied the Professor on a visit to the EBRD. I imagine the Professor, proud and untidy, and dark Fidel in his tight black suit and toothpick, patting across a marble floor underneath the hanging gardens and atriums of a City bank. Did they flick their Balkan cigarettes into a spare fountain before risking the alien lift?

Today the Professor and his wife are cheerful and the sun is shining. This feels like a holiday. At Durres the Professor shows a pass to a teenage soldier with a shorn head and our convoy is waved into the compound that encloses Hoxha's old summer villa. There it is – catches

Sarajevo. The view from Roma and Sanda's apartment - November.

On route to Sarajevo airport, having been told to leave by the
Ambassador - December.

Fier. My first experience of post communist Albania - December.

Picnic near the Kosovan border - February.

Dritan, my best friend in Albania. Pictured on his roof, a top sunbathing spot - March.

Members of the Professor's entourage during our visit to his constituency - April.

Me and my father at my christening - Tower of London, 1971.

Roger and my father (identical twins) - Brancaster, 1977.

of yellow and pink marble glimpsed through the clumps of bamboo and laurel hedges. There are a few other villas, built for party deity and now owned by the handful of foreign investors committed enough to the country to afford perks for their expatriate staff. There are palm trees in the garden and, beyond, a granular beach and the milky blue Adriatic. We stop outside a restaurant, which is reserved for members of parliament and senior civil servants.

In front of the restaurant there is a terrace where Fidel plays an aggravating game of football with a tiny rubber ball and Haxi. Fidel laughs and leaps about and the Professor and I watch him from the warmth of the restaurant, through a plate glass window that looks over the terrace towards the sea.

We eat fried fish and drink Italian beer. An angry wind off the sea rattles the window. Nearby, other worthies eat lunch with their families. We rise to greet the Bulgarian Ambassador, recently out of hospital having survived an assassination attempt. His car was ambushed by gunmen on the way to Macedonia, sending it rolling down a hillside. The chauffeur was killed.

"Used to be a good friend of Maurice. Now his body is held together by bits of metal," whispers the Professor under his breath.

In the corner is the Minister of Interior, wielder of ShIK, tapping the Professor's phone and having me followed. He is sitting next to a small man, brown as a nut with oily hair.

"That's Ibrahim Rugova, leader of the Kosovars," explains the Professor, "making one of his secret little trips to the homeland. How interesting."

"Come and meet a friend of mine," says the Professor after coffee. His friend is a Frenchman named Vincent Quinz who lives in a grand villa on the seafront. One winter morning, a student at Edinburgh, I lay in the bath listening to a programme on Radio Four. A report filed by the BBC's Balkan correspondent talked about a Frenchman who had crossed into Albania on a whim in the last years of communist rule and discovered some peculiar resonance, and particular opportunities, that kept him there. The report described the man's growing business empire, and his villa by the sea, his servants and the suits of armour in the hall. The man was Vincent. Now, in front of me, was the same villa and there, in the open doorway, stood one of the servants.

Inside was France and at three o'clock on this Sunday afternoon France was *à table*. We could hear voices and laughter from the hall, where the suits of armour stood to attention on a polished wooden floor. And there, suddenly, was Vincent, a solid looking man with thinning hair and steel rimmed glasses. He wore a cerise polo shirt and had the kind of bland, open face that sometimes hides the hearts of torturers. There are rumours that one of Vincent's earliest deals was to arm the communist police force with riot gear. Now he owns an airline, an English language newspaper, a raki distillery...

On the dining table is good French cheese and fruit to eat and a bottle of Vincent's best brandy. Opposite sits someone from the French Embassy and next to him a Portuguese diplomat. The Professor, who speaks excellent French, grabs hold of the conversation and I sit back gratefully, to watch and listen. Next to me Vincent eats a peach without spilling a drop.

Coffee is served in a sitting room with views down the beach to the sea. A concerto plays in the background.

"Ah, Bach!" says the Professor, rubbing his hands with glee before accepting a balloon of brandy. There is a commotion in the hall and in walks a gorilla of a man in black leather trousers and jacket. He wears a leather armlet on one thick wrist, covered in silver studs. His head is shaven, he has an enormous beard and there is a fat gold earring in one ear. There he stands in the middle of the room, looking like a

162

colossal pirate.

"This man is a Frenchman, Alexi," whispers the Professor, enjoying his brandy, "and a smuggler. He has been in Durres prison for two weeks. Only today has he been released. I was hoping to meet him here."

The man fills one of Vincent's balloons up to the brim and sinks into the leather arm chair, his trousers creaking. He looks pretty fit on Albanian prison food - which can't be up to much. I suppose you see the inside of a few gaols in his line of work. He and Vincent begin to talk in animated French.

"He buys or steals antiques in distant countries and sells them in France for great profit. He has turned some of his adventures into best selling books - he is a national hero in France."

Last year he was almost killed by irate Amazon Indians whose gold he had stolen. This time a rare icon was found in his possession as he tried to catch a ferry to Italy.

MONDAY 19TH FEBRUARY
EGYPTIAN EMBASSY

The Egyptian Embassy lies in the Boulevard Embassadi. Policemen stand guard at either end. The boulevard is wide and quiet like an expensive American suburb. Behind the high fences and the neat gardens flutter the flags of France, Greece, China, Russia and others.

Inside the Embassy it is all smiles. A mincing young man, about my age, in a beige suit is called from upstairs. He takes me to a reception room, bare but for a couple of gaudy sofas and low tables covered in ornate white cloths. On the tables are copies of the Koran. The Ambassador will be down soon. Coffee is on its way. I flick through the Koran and, spotting my dusty shoes, clean them on one of the table cloths.

The man in the beige suit returns carrying papers. We chat about the Conference and he tells me that Egypt's involvement will be vital. In walks the Ambassador, a tubby, prosperous-looking man with pomade in his hair. There is an expensive gold watch around his wrist and kidney spots on the backs of his hands. Beige suit shoots up and shimmies about the room, puffing up cushions and ordering coffee for 'His Excellency'.

He starts talking about the Conference and about an Egyptian company which is a major investor in Albania.

"Very important company. One of the biggest in Egypt." H.E. clicks his fingers and beige suit produces a corporate brochure.

"It is written in English and French," grins H.E. "In Egypt, most people speak both languages fluently."

There are pictures of cans of fly spray and container ships.

"What does the company do in Albania, Your Excellency?" He feints surprise that I do not know. "Construction. Building famous road to Shkodra!"

He is inordinately proud of the company.

"Very good brochure, yes?" says the Ambassador, patting my knee. Meanwhile, beige suit gazes on. He seems inordinately proud of H.E.

"Your Excellency, I would like to interview the manager of this company and produce a report for the Conference."

The Ambassador looks horrified. "Interview me, not the manager. He is only merchant. I am diplomat. Ambassador!"

"With the greatest of respect Ambassador, the conference delegates will be more interested in the comments of a fellow businessman."

"Pah. Bye bye," and he rushes out.

Enough of the Embassies. It's time to find some home grown talent. Its time to track down the General.

By night his offices are marked by searchlights, which play the sky as if searching for the underbelly of a Lancaster. Daylight reveals a three-story town house, brick-built and grand by Tirana standards, flying the Vari and Albanian flags. Inside the gates sits the obligatory four-wheel drive, shiny and bulbous. In front of the gates stands a posse of bodyguards, dressed in leather jackets. Somewhere inside, sitting no doubt in a spongy leather chair in front of a grand map of the world, a white cat purring on his lap, is the General. I introduce myself to one of the guards.

"I am from the Ministry of Finance. I would like to arrange an interview with the General," I tell them slowly. I feel like a visitor from another planet. A man peels off and talks into a walkie talkie. The others eye me, bored. A minute later the man is back. He is a real cowboy, unshaven and tough. His breath reeks of garlic. The General will not see me.

"Fuck off" he tells me, in flawless Anglo-Saxon.

The well endowed 'Crime Column' in Vincent's Daily News explains this new fashion for bodyguards. It is full of stories of mayhem, slaughter and an incompetent police force: 'Whole Family Killed (mafia related murder in Tirana); 'Skeleton Found in Anti-aircraft Shelter' (a year old mutilated corpse discovered in Fier); 'Police Officer Killed From (sic) Recruit' (a nineteen year old recruit forgot to apply the safety catch on his machine gun during training); 'Five Policemen Tented (sic) to Kidnap Businessman' (the uniformed officers dragged a Tirana businessman into their car and demanded money before they released him); 'Six Injured in Weeding (sic)' (a fight between six people got out of hand and continued in the hospital where the wounded were taken for treatment); 'Policeman Accidentally Injures his Brother' (during celebratory gunfire at a wedding); Court Session Discovers that the Accused Escaped' (two old hands were discovered to have broken out of a 'high security' gaol on the eve of their trial).

I caught a pale flash at one of the windows last night, which I think was Dritan's mother peering out. I haven't heard about her for three weeks.

"How is your mother, Dritan? I hope she's better."

"She is better."

"She doesn't go out very much, does she?"

"No, she is inside."

"Does she have many friends in the area, who can visit her?"

"So many friends."

"Oh good."

Dritan is wonderfully mysterious about his mother.

WEDNESDAY 21ST FEBRUARY
PAX AMERICANA

Supper with Mike in a restaurant around the corner from the Dajti. We sit in a courtyard, behind fat Ottoman walls. The place does an excellent koran. In a corner is a crowd of jovial Americans. They are soldiers, big men with short hair. One is black, a rare sight here. The waiters cannot keep their eyes off him.

"They're from the airbase at Gjader. Part of the Predator crew," says Mike, watching them over his beer. "Running spy missions over Bosnia, keeping an eye on General Mladic and his friends."

Richard arrives for a two week visit. I meet him in the Dajti.

"Guess who I met in the passport queue at Rinas?" he asks me. "The Duke of Bedford!"

We are due at the Ministry of Foreign affairs at two o'clock. The Minister wants to discuss his speech at the Conference. We are late - it is already five past. Gzim is outside, reading a newspaper. We jump in and Gzim thrashes the old car over the Lana towards the Ministry. We are there in what seems like seconds.

"Bloody lunatic," mutters Richard under his breath as we climb out of the trembling Volvo.

The Ministry is a modern, ugly building standing on the Lana, behind a frieze of poplars. Inside the Minister is waiting. Mr Laco is a slippery-looking customer in a dapper blue suit. A balding man in his thirties, with a strong jaw and big hands. He speaks English with an American accent – he probably learnt it off the same tapes as Halit. Coffee is served along with a bitter liquor which is almost unpalatable and very strong. Laco is flanked by the head of the diplomatic service, a white haired man whom Laco introduces as 'the Doctor', and a skull-faced young aide called Godo.

"So, how are we doing with numbers?" asks Laco.

"OK, but we still need more," replies Richard.

"Could the Doctor instruct our Embassies around the world to provide their own invitation lists?" I suggest. "They must know of plenty of companies who have expressed an interest in Albania."

"Like it!" says punchy Mr Laco. "How long will you need, Doctor?"

"A few days," replies the Doctor, "as long as the telephones are working". He and I giggle. Laco looks sternly out of the window at the line of poplars, shaking his head, no doubt regretting that his American accent hasn't kept him in America.

"Well now Richard. About my speech..."

A meeting with Xhaja at the ministry. He is animated this morning, there is a rare smile on his face. He brandishes a photocopy taken from the New York Times. Popoli has sent it to him.

'The once isolated country of Albania is now free and democratic. For men of action this provides an exciting opportunity to get rich... in a country that lacks just about everything.'

So says Dr Gerhard Kurtz, resident of Hong Kong and author of *How to Get Rich in Albania.*

'You can live like a king under palm trees – even if at home you're drawing welfare, (in Albania) your pennies immediately turn into gold nuggets... Albania is one of the few countries left where you can enjoy a feudal lifestyle surrounded by undemanding domestic helpers. In the south the climate is as good as Florida's (without the hurricanes!)... After half a century of being the most repressed country in the world... practically everything is allowed... The Ministry of Education and Culture can offer you a restored noble title which can be entered officially in your passport - for the same cost as a mountain bike.'

Perhaps a mountain bike would be a little more practical, considering Albania's geography and the state of its roads. Men of action can obtain a copy of 'How to Get Rich in Albania', by faxing Privacy

Reports on Hong Kong 285C5502. Xhaja thinks it hilarious.

"Live like king - under palm trees!" he repeats, grinning dreadfully.

Many moons ago, probably during the anarchy that followed the collapse of communism, someone abandoned an old bus down the alley that leads to Dritan's gate.

A family of gypsies have made it their home. They are an unhappy family, much given to roaring at each other at night and smashing things. The husband and wife are well matched and have the stamina of mules.

We often meet in the alley, me usually coming back from work, they usually sitting about doing nothing very much. They will watch me suspiciously as I walk past, dad occasionally raising a stiff arm in greeting. My favourite is the most animated, a girl of about four. Her attitude towards me is unpredictable. Sometimes she will wave and run up to me, bubbling greetings down her chin, holding out her hand. Other times, she will just stop and stare, a look of complete incomprehension on her face. Or she will start screaming very loudly and not stop for several minutes.

Suzana is never happier than when passing on information. This time it is about Dritan's mother. It seems she is locked in a long-running legal dispute with the mayor's office over the ownership of the school buildings across the street. The land belonged to the Ademis before Hoxha came along and confiscated all private property. The President has promised to return all confiscated property and Mrs Ademi wants what's hers. Unfortunately, it's now a school.

Running around Tirana with Richard is one of the great joys of life.
After breakfast at the Dajti, we set off at a fine pace. Richard doesn't
like taxis unless there is an emergency: Tirana is too small and taxis
are too expensive and driven by bloody lunatics. So, every morning,
we jog past an ever-disappointed Gzim and the money lenders at the
gate and hurl ourselves into the helter-skelter of Deshmoret ë Kombit
Boulevard.

On the way we'll have some random conversation about inland
waterways or Tolstoy or the byzantine workings of DG24, all the time
dodging puddles and pedestrians at great speed. And then we'll arrive
at a ministry or the Albtelecom headquarters or the National
Privatisation Agency and there is the wonderful theatre of one of
Richard's meetings to look forward to.

The Albanian on the other side of the desk (a) knows Richard
already and (b) is intimidated. As he rises to shake Richard's hand
there will be a troubled look in his eye. Richard represents action,
forward movement, getting things done. Now. He is well known for it.
So when the Minister or Director General shakes his hand across the
desk he can feel the shock waves of Richard's animation disturbing the
carefully tended lethargy of his office. Quite suddenly he is operating
on London time or he could be in New York at a power breakfast. And
of course this sort of thing comes as a shock.

This atmosphere of time travel provides a constant tension to
the meeting. The Minister/ Director General knows that he is about to
receive some work, unless he is very senior and has aides to pass it
onto. And he is trying all the time to keep up with Richard's beautifully
crafted 'English for foreigners'. Richard only ever speaks to Albanians
in fast English and no matter what he is saying, or who is talking to, he

is always understood.

My abiding memory of Richard is the sight of him leaning towards a blushing ministry secretary or a government clerk, fixing them with his warm smile and saying, a little too loudly 'Hello, Richard Grey. Yes, R-i-c-h-a-r-d G-r-e-y. IS THE MINISTER ABOUT?' or 'I am hoping to get my hands on a copy of the '94 regional production figures, just a photocopy will do.'

He will then maintain eye contact, nodding and raising his eyebrows, which means 'OK?' and 'Go to it' at the same time.

I am standing behind him, giggling and marvelling at how fond I am of this man and knowing that this time they cannot understand. But sure enough the minister is in or out, the report appears and we head off, as if we have carried out a perfectly normal transaction.

Very occasionally, Richard fails to make himself understood and even his energetic attempts at sign language fail, the flashing arms and grimacing mouth causing alarm rather than enlightenment. At this moment, with a deep sigh, Richard will engage a bastard language all of his own.

'Allo. Je suis economista' he tells his astonished audience. 'Organisé el investment conferenzi', or sometimes 'Conferencé investementé' or 'INVESTMENT CONFERENCE.' 'Je me cherché EBRD reporta' (making him sound like a cockney) or 'la reporta EBRD?' or 'THE EBRD REPORT' followed by 'aaah grazzi', or occasionally an expansive 'merci beaucoup, ciao.'

So there is the Minister or the Director General, nervously watching Richard's lips and trying to nod in the right places. A speech will be discussed, or statistics for one of the conference briefing papers, or themes for one of the morning sessions.

Richard will rush the Albanian into agreement, exacting commitments to do x by y. Then the Albanian will relax and move the conversation onto more civilised subjects - the weather, diplomatic gossip, the war in the north. And Richard, his pound of flesh sitting wetly in his blazer pocket, will gracefully comply. When they part they are the best of friends and Tirana's corridors of power will not boast a more stalwart admirer of Richard Grey than the Minister or the Director General. 'That man,' he will say, shaking his head 'he really gets things done.'

TUESDAY 27TH FEBRUARY
SUMMONS

"Come and see us on Wednesday – eleven o'clock" says the beige suit at the Egyptian Embassy.

WEDNESDAY 28TH FEBRUARY
SPHINX

Security at the Egyptian Embassy eyes me suspiciously as I knock on the gates. I wait in the reception room for the beige suit to shimmy in. Ten minutes go by and he is nowhere to be seen, though there is great traffic on the stairs. Then a man I have never seen before enters the room. He looks embarrassed, exercised.

"Mr Hickman, you must leave Embassy immediately." There is a jump in his voice. Perhaps the Ambassador has had a turn, or an Egyptian killer bee has slipped in via the diplomatic bag and is loose in the building.

"But I have an appointment to see Mr –."

"I'm afraid he is unable to see you."

"But I spoke to him yesterday, we arranged a meeting. He told me to come now."

"He cannot see you."

"Why not?"

"The Ambassador says he cannot see you."

"Why not?" He shrugs. He is clearly embarrassed.

"Do you know why I've come here today. I'm arranging for Egyptian companies to participate in the Investment Conference. It is a very important conference. The President will be there and representatives of the European Union. Mr — is preparing a list of Egyptian companies that your Ambassador has asked me to invite. If I do not have the list I cannot invite them."

"I am sorry. I do not know anything of this. I have been told that His Excellency does not want you in Embassy. Ambassador says you are not good for Egypt."

Outside, security open the gates. Walking back to the Ministry I try to imagine what I have done to upset them all.

MARCH

The newly refurbished Tirana International Hotel is unveiled this afternoon. The outside has new mirrored windows, which reflect the blue sky back into Skanderberg Square below. Inside is Turin chic – minimalist, discreet, Italian. There is a cocktail party and ribbon cutting by the President. I have a few cold glasses of champagne. Everyone is there – ambassadors, the head of the EU delegation, politicians grateful to be outside their ministries, press, Albania's leading businessmen.

I chat to the chic French political secretary from the EU delegation. He is in a cream suit, double breasted. He offers me a cigarette from his silver case.

"Where do you get your haircut?" I ask him, bored. He is a brilliant sight – his hair slick and shiny like new shoes.

"Paris."

Richard walks up.

"There you are, fella! Been looking for you everywhere. Seen the General? He was here a minute ago. Bloody man's disappeared. Oh well, come and meet Vito. He's going to help run the Conference for us."

Vito is wonderful: round, Italian, beautifully dressed, gentle, generous and as bright as a button. He runs a conference management company in Bari which will handle the physical organisation of the Conference – invitations, venue, staff, marketing, catering etc. He's flown over to meet Richard and I and to have a look at the new-look Tirana, where we are holding the Conference. He's had a bad experience at the airport.

"Alex, it is a great pleasure. Richard has told me about you. I could not believe it when he told me you have been here since January.

You must be very strong. Or very mad. This place... this place is just crazy."

This afternoon the Professor flies to London for the seminar. I drop in on my way to the ministry to say goodbye. The man in the leather jacket follows me at a discreet distance. As I turn into the Professor's street I wave to him. He just stares right back.

The Professor is packing his briefcase in his office. He is excited about the trip. Albanians always look excited when they're about to leave their country.

"Hope the speech goes well…"

"Thank you Alexi. And thanks for your hard work. When I come back I'm going to give you a present."

"Oh. What's that?"

"A trip," he replies mysteriously, "an adventure."

On my way home from the market, Suzana's shopping basket full of spring onions, pistachios and a thick block of bacon, I run into the Egyptian who ushered me so gracefully out of the Embassy the other day. He wants to talk.

In a nearby coffee shop he apologises again. I ask him what had happened.

"The Ambassador a bad man. All the time he is very angry. All the time he is shouting. Very difficult."

"But what did I do to offend him?"

"Ambassador say you are spy, you want to spy on Egyptian

company for commercial secrets. He say: 'Mr Hickman is enemy of Egypt – he cannot come into Embassy again'."

"And what about Mr —?"

"Mr — very frightened of Ambassador. Mr — from rich family in Egypt. Same family as Ambassador. All diplomats from Egypt from rich families. Mr — is Ambassador's dog." He smiles curiously.

"Ambassador bad man. Ambassador friend of man who owns company. Ambassador works for company. He say you are spy for English government."

"Isn't it dangerous for you to be talking to an English spy?"

"I know you are not spy."

"How?" I ask, a little disappointed.

"You are too obvious. And you clean your shoes on our table cloth. Not, I think, James Bond."

MONDAY 5TH MARCH
ATHENS

I am back in this dreadful city for a few days. The Albanian Embassy is promoting the Conference hard to Greek businesses. Laco asked Richard to join a delegation he is leading to whip up interest in the business community. But Richard is in bed in Somerset, nursing a nasty bout of Asian flu so I have come in his place. Much to the envy of Anetsi.

As much as I 'dislike' Athens it is good to be in an ordinary city, with normal bustle, plenty of hot water and proper shops. At last I can phone Britain easily and at reasonable cost. All are well in London. I am missing nothing, except perhaps a week's skiing. But I've got holiday plans of my own.

It has been a boring week, full of presentations and meetings in ministries. It is an EU-sponsored jolly, barely justified but taken up enthusiastically by Laco's team who relish the chance to savour the inside of a three star Hilton and the city's porn cinemas.

Each smog-filled, overcast day we are treated like poor relations – kept waiting by minor officials, patronised when they arrive, ignored as soon as they leave. Like the Professor, Laco enjoys showing me off as his 'English assistant'. The Greek across the table just grunts and regards me with contempt.

There is nothing like a few days in Athens among brother Albanians to ignite a low Balkan fury. But I am sick of Laco and his mincing Godo. They make precious travel companions. Godo is jealous of me, fancying a rival to his master's ear. Which means elbows and shoulders everytime we get into a taxi together, Godo jockeying for a place next to Laco. Or clever little questions such as: 'Alex, presumably the Minister is so well known in your country?', asked last night, as we piled our plates high with wet prawns and rolled ham at the Hilton's Acropolis Buffet.

Meanwhile, the master pimps about in Aviator sunglasses and an overcoat draped over his shoulders (how Godo loves to remove it with a flourish!). Away from home Laco is a sycophant. He plays the snob to the Greeks.

"Of course we are an unsophisticated people," he apologises to his opposite number in the Greek Foreign Office who is cross about the state of Albania's roads and the contrariness of the young Fier girl his wife has engaged as a maid. "What can you expect from the peasants!"

Tomorrow Laco and his men fly back to Tirana. I want to travel back via boat to Corfu and Saranda, the capital of Albania's riveriera.

I want to see the ruins at Butrint, and explore the nearby city of Gjirokaster, where Hoxha was born. "Bloody marvellous," warns Richard. But we all know what he thought of Pogradec.

"Would you excuse me, Minister?" I ask Laco. We are on our way back from dinner with the Albanian Ambassador, during which I had stupidly told the story of the young diplomat leaning out of the window and telling me that Albania was closed.

"What's this!" Laco had roared at the news, his teeth stained purple by a bottle of Albanian Merlot, "deny me my English assistant!"

The poor man was called up from the staff kitchens. "Do you think your job is to turn people away from entering our country! This guy" pointing to me, "is a dam fine servant of Albania. He is an adviser to Ministers. A friend to the powerful. Especially myself." Standing, his head bowed, the man started sobbing. Next to him Godo played menacingly with a steak knife.

In the taxi I explain my plans to Laco.

"Richard Grey has asked me to see some people in Saranda and Gjirokaster," I lie. "And I am keen to see your beautiful Butrint."

"But Alex. How're you gonna travel. Hell, it means taking those buses. Have you seen inside one of those buses? And what about the boat to Saranda. It's little better than a bath-tub."

In the front seat Godo sulks.

THURSDAY 8TH MARCH
ADVENTURE

Patras is truck-driver dingy. Boarding the Corfu ferry I pass a herd of Albanians, alien and uncomfortable by the stern door. They are wearing damp-looking tweed jackets and have soil under their fingernails. The young customs official supervising them looks uncomfortable. His head is cropped to naval regulations, his face is haughty with distaste.

181

"Lice!" he is thinking, "cholera, herpes." He can smell the cold mountain air on their clothes. He is terrified of them.

> *The city is the economic administrative centre of the Saranda district. Prominent in the branches of its economy are the food-stuffs and light industry, the artistic handicrafts industry and the economic activity of the port. Saranda is an important holiday and tourist resort.*
>
> (AGO, p. 74)

I manage one hour's sleep among the cover of a few chairs in the corner of the foyer. At 4.30 I wake with a headache and the smell of crude oil in my nostrils. The ferry is throbbing and humming and the lights are bright and by my head is a pair of crossed feet which belong to a blond girl smoking a cigarette. Feeling foul I get up and shiver outside as the dark mouth of Corfu harbour opens to eat us up. There is little light on the quay. Around me the crew run about throwing each other bags of dirty laundry and bashing their feet up and down on the steel stairs.

On dry land it is cold, a cold that gets colder despite the dawn boilers firing up over the horizon. I leave the ferry alongside the group of shivering Albanians. They are carrying fertiliser bags over their shoulders and cardboard boxes tied up in string. I ask a customs officer where I catch the Saranda boat. He looks bemused and points me in the direction of an empty waiting room. Inside I sit down on a wooden bench. There are five hours to go before the ferry service to Saranda. Five hours. I light a cigarette and try to ignore the cold which gathers about me, heavy like water. I can almost see it ripple when I move my arms.

182

Albanians begin to trickle into the waiting room and I brace myself to meet them. They spread towards me, eyeing me softly. I offer cigarettes and biscuits and the atmosphere is broken. My little Albanian delights them. One man – small with broken teeth and strong hands – is called Abdyl. We get talking and he buys me a drink. Another buys me a coffee. They are such a humbling group of people. Abdyl looks about thirty-five but when we inspect each others passports we discover that he is just two months older than me.

"Young, young!" he cries, pinching my cheek. Organised games, square meals and central heating versus a peasant diet and days spent working poor fields. Abdyl has not had a BCG injection.

The sun rises, heating the room. At last a tobacco-stained old man in a bright orange coat and dripping black boots marches into the room and claps his hands. The Mimosa has arrived from Saranda.

The Mimosa is low slung and small, about the size of a Thames pleasure boat. About sixty of us huddle inside the cabin and begin to steam up the windows. At one end of the cabin is an improvised bar, where three men get cheerfully drunk. I walk out onto the deck. There is a fresh wind, just too warm to sting and I stand above the ash grey water and let the wind blow over me. We motor past small gorsey islands, then away towards Albania's broken shoreline. On the upper deck, sheltering from the wind behind the wheelhouse is a young man with western luggage. He turns out to be a Swede, a Baptist missionary, on his way to visit his fiancée, an Albanian girl he met last year. She lives in Korca.

"You must be very happy," I shout through the wind, wondering what happened to Daniel.

"Very happy," he replies, grinning with his hands on his knees and the wind shocking his hair across his face. Later, as Saranda defines itself into a thin line of terracotta buildings, broken tower blocks one end, what looks like a government hotel the other, palm trees in between, he waves his camera at me. He asks me to pose for him and I stand there, grinning stupidly. Instead of taking a photograph he adjusts something on the camera, nods and calls me over.

"Now you can take me" he says taking up my position at the bow.

In Saranda's harbour the water is calm and a translucent blue. The Mimosa circles and moors at a crumbling jetty. Around us rises Saranda. It is much smaller than I expected, and prettier. The town is drawn up close to the water, rising in neat tiers like the banked rows in a theatre. Afloat in the bay feels like being on stage. Most of the town seems to have come out of their houses to watch us dock. Young men perch on a road above the harbour gates like crows in a tree. On the Mimosa there is an enthusiastic crush as everyone surges towards the jetty before being hurled back by a cross-looking policeman. The Swede and I are called into the cabin for special treatment. Our passports are extravagantly stamped and flung at us like frisbees and we barge our way onto the jetty.

Above the quay sit the young men, watching. One by one they spot the Swede and I and begin to walk slowly down towards us. It is a sinister movement – the whole thing done to silence and a slow-paced roll of the shoulders. Then they are around me, feeling my sleeve, trying to take the rucksack from my back, taking the bag from my hand.

"Taxi, sir, to Tirana," says a smooth, dark-haired man in sunglasses. "Mercedes taxi – extra good," whispers another, leaning towards me like a persistent suitor. They are slow to absorb my refusals, especially as the Swede succumbs to the embrace of a gaunt youth and lets himself be led away towards a waiting transit van. Soon there is a crowd of five or six, kneading me slowly towards cars and minibuses. The gentle crush, the low melody of their imploring voices feels like a dry drowning. I long for my stick. I want to take off their heads with one sweep, like so many thistles.

According to my Blue Guide, Genc's Hotel, next to the bus station, is surprisingly comfortable. Genc, a cheerful character with a great mop of black hair, produces kebabs and retsina for lunch. Afterwards, his nephew and a friend take me to see nearby Butrint. Here, on the nub of Lake Butrint, just where a river feeds out towards the sea, lies the remains of a fortified settlement that dates back to the fourth century BC. The position of the hill outcrop, almost wholly surrounded by water and less than a kilometre from the sea later gave it strategic value to Illyrian, Greek, Roman, Venetian and Ottoman occupants.

We drive south out of Saranda, very slowly in an old Fiat. The road follows the contours of the coast. It is full of potholes. The two men, both in their early twenties seem shy and self-absorbed. The road turns away from the sea and the land becomes marshy and waterlogged. Duck push into the air on our left and skim low over the long marshy flat towards hills in the distance. Butrint's duck and snipe used to coax Victorian shots across from Corfu to wade about in these marshes.

A lake emerges on our left. Massive and still, a sheet of salt-water grey held between dun-coloured hills. A series of large wooden pens, floating on the lake's surface, run parallel with the road. They are the skeletons of a communist attempt at mussel farming. And then the lake is gone, hidden by hills as the road leaves it to seek out the sea. The going is up and down and wooded, small valleys and quiet woodland next to streams, an emerald world of shepherds and fairies. Landscape like this never lasts for very long and quickly we reach its edge, a great stretch of sky and far horizon confronts us and the road falls down a steep, gorse covered hillside into a new world of maritime space.

Below us stretches marshland, spreading west towards the sea and south towards low hills and Greece. At the bottom of the hill the road stops at an improvised jetty on the clear Vivari river. Beside the jetty is a small café. There is another, similarly decrepit jetty on the opposite bank, about forty metres away. Between them runs a ferry built of oil drums and railway sleepers. Between the jetties, the river runs softly to the sea. To our left, with a good view over the river, stands the old hill-town of Butrint.

Classical mythology has it that the first settlement here, Buthrotum, was founded by Helenus, son of Priam of Troy. Helenus, sailing along the coast of what was then Epirus and looking for somewhere to dock, orders the sacrifice of an ox to ensure his ship's safe landing. But before it could be killed, the terrified ox plunged overboard and swam into a hidden inlet. Seizing upon this omen, Helenus ordered his ship to follow the ox inland, up the Vivari into the sheltered lake. Here he found the ox, dead, lying on a beach at the foot of a hill where it had hauled itself out of the water. Helenus named the spot 'the wounded ox' or Buthrotos. And here he settled and married his love, Andromanche. In the *Aeniad*, Virgil describes how Aeneas, sailing up the Epirus coast comes to Helenus' Buthrothum, 'that hill city'. Now the hill city is deserted but evidence of past tenants remain – bits of late Roman baths and an acropolis, Illyrian walls, a Roman theatre and an early Christian baptistery with a fine floor of mosaics.

Among dripping silver birch we come across an amphitheatre. It is flooded and frogs plop about. Around us stand spare columns like stone tree trunks. My guides don't seem very interested in our surroundings and treat the place as an assault course, climbing about the Illyrian walls and disturbing the Roman brickwork. But I, a veteran of Tirana and Albania's tendency towards muck and disrepair, am captivated by the perfect beauty of this place and leave the pathway to walk along the water's edge. Around the knuckle of land turns the lake, still and primitive in the silence. Behind it hills rise suddenly, furry with bracken. A heron beats away across the water. Along the banks of the Vivari fishermen sit with static lines looking at the water. There are a couple more fishermen on the still water, rowing somewhere. The sounds of their oars crunch against the soft air in this magical place. It is the sound of peace.

Up on the roof of the acropolis there are palms and formal beds and paths. Here the Italians built a small fortress during the thirties. It looks a little theatrical, which is just how one would want it. There are iron gates, padlocked shut. Ebony cannon point south over the Vivari. We stop, muggy, to stare across the river and drained marshland towards Greece, which is little more than twenty kilometres away. In the light of late afternoon the green flats, scratched by irrigation channels, stretch away to foothills and the etched silhouettes of villages. Cow bells glitter from tiny necks walking towards the sea. The buzz of a motorbike picks out a hunched man moving minutely towards the ferry. Three horses canter, wild and silent, in a moated field. The air is clean and soft. Standing above this wide, rural stage I watch new figures act their tiny parts. Old women in black, a man on a slow donkey, another cutting wood on a block, shuddering echoes across the air towards us.

Perched on one of the cannon, I can see where the Vivari turns between two bluffs to flow into the sea. On one stands the ruins of another fort, a dream of tower and shouldered parapet. Suffused in the sea-salt breeze and the soft light, soothed by the secret noises of the marshland I experience something sublime. This place is exquisite, gentle, timeless. No pillboxes, tottering housing blocks, burnt-out buses or throbbing music just an arcadian scene. A benign way of life unchanged for centuries. It is a view of Albania's rural soul. But for how much longer? A Maltese company (expected, with baited breath, at the Conference) is keen to cover much of it with a golf course.

Just before Saranda we drive off the road and through a pauper village. The two boys want to show me something. They have serious faces.

"Special beach," repeats Genc's nephew, pointing towards the sea. Through the village, shoeless children and chickens scuttle out of our way. A woman cooks on a fire built in the engine well of an abandoned car. At the top of a slight hill, in a fenced-off compound, stands a round concrete building full of broken windows. Music is playing inside. It is a bar, just. Goodness knows who drinks there or how they pay. The café looks out to sea, which laps against orange rocks below us. There is a column of concrete steps leading down to the waters edge, escorted by rows of jaunty lamps, tall, silly and broken. Either side of the steps is pasture where goats munch. The scene has a jaunty, sea-side air –Brighton or Bournemouth resort humour, naughty cards and candy floss – in this rural scrapyard. I suppose in better days party members bathed from this pretty little beach and spied upon Corfu on the horizon. Did old generals, easing their piles in the cool water, plan the seizure of Corfu town. Where did they direct their artillery fire I wonder and how many submarines did they place at the harbour mouth?

Communicating in a sort of way we play ducks and drakes on the flat water. Genc's nephew wants to open a hotel nearby and sleep with girls from Italy and Germany. He believes they will come to him with a click of the fingers.

"Why is this beach special?"

From here, he explains, a friend of theirs set off for Greece one late evening during the dictatorship, a pair of flippers on his feet. He was a strong swimmer and had his clothes in a bag around his neck. They have never seen or heard of him since. It was at this spot that they last saw him alive. The story chills and the weather turns in sympathy. The bay changes colour, blue becomes grey, and the sea throws a punch of wind whispering through the thorn trees.

"He is talking," says Genc's nephew, looking at his feet.

When he was twenty seven, my father, an ambitious young doctor with a good brain and a curious frame of mind, spent some time researching the clotting mechanisms of blood cells. One day he decided to inject himself with a radioactive fluid which would enable him to label certain cells, and even certain parts of certain cells, in his own blood, and study their behaviour during clotting.

He had to drive to the government's atomic research centre at Amersham to collect the fluid. It wasn't the sort of stuff you could buy on the high street. Or even find in a hospital. And once he'd got it he squirted it into a vein in his arm. He produced a first-rate piece of research and had two papers published, ground breaking stuff, on how a substance called fibrinogen contributes to the clotting process.

Ten years later he died of leukaemia, a cancer of the blood that has often been associated with exposure to high radiation levels (communities situated near nuclear power stations, for example, often have unusually high incidences of child leukaemia). Did he bring on his own death? Did my father fall to some Icarian drowning, swamped by the malevolent, fizzing policemen in his own blood? I, who am twenty-seven as I write these words, don't know – nor do I want to.

SATURDAY 10TH MARCH
GJIROKASTER

The museum city of Gjirokaster is the biggest city in the southern part of Albania. It is a city of stone. The beloved and unforgettable leader of the Albanian people, Comrade Enver Hoxha, was born this city on October 16, 1908... Gjirokaster is a city of museums. They include the Museum of the Renaissance, the Museum of the National Liberation War and the National Museum of Weapons which has been set up in the castle. There is a higher pedagogical institute which includes the chair of Greek language in this city. Gjirokaster is important also as an economic centre (especially industrial) and as a communication junction for the whole south of the country. (AGO, pp.89-90)

Gjirokaster stands high up on one side of the Drinos valley, tiered ranks of timbered Ottoman houses built into the hillside. The proliferation of Ottoman architecture has persuaded UNESCO to make Gjirokaster a 'world heritage' city. In a square in front of the deserted Gjirokaster Hotel, Genc parks the Fiat beneath dripping horse chestnuts. Cobbled streets wind up the hill into the heart of the town. After Tirana, this is by far the most normal looking town I have seen in Albania. Leaving me in the square, Genc heads off to try and find his cousin, an army officer based in barracks outside town. We arrange to meet back here in an hour.

The Citadel stands above the town, built on a fist of black granite. Around it large Ottoman houses cling on to the hillside. Below them cascade tongues of rubbish where the families have emptied years of empty raki bottles and sardine tins. I walk around the high walls until I find an entrance, a small iron gateway which I rattle until an old man with a broom lets me in. He leads me through a dank hall, past a rusty display of Albanian cannon (the National Museum of Weapons) to the curator's office.

"Two hundred lek" smiles the woman sitting rosy-cheeked by an electric heater. I wonder when she last saw a tourist.

Out on the ramparts, past a row of what look like cells, stands a silver jet fighter stranded among nettles. Hoxha claimed it was an American plane, forced down while on a spying mission in the 1950s. In fact it was donated by the Chinese – apparently they had it spare from the Korean war. They're a generous bunch, the Chinese. Friends worth having.

Below lies the town, crumpled and wet. Up on the ramparts I look down over the Drinos valley. To the south it stretches down river, towards the Greek border. To the north its vast barrel emptiness leads into the belly of Albania. Opposite, snow-covered mountains push into the sky. It is easy to picture a squadron of tanks rutting up the valley and for a moment I watch a flight of bombers queuing at the top of the valley before, one-by-one, skewering down to meet them.

During communist rule the citadel was used as a prison. Up on a bleak, concrete exercise yard there are bullet holes sprayed across a wall. Below, cells lead off an L-shaped corridor. On the wall is a portrait of Hoxha and a number of quotations, painted in red paint, plucked no doubt from Hoxha's published works of political philosophy, designed to help the dissident think again. The cells are cramped and bare. Their doors open onto a slim terrace overlooking the Citadel's ramparts and the snowy mountains. Standing among the barbed wire in the exercise yard I try to imagine the tedium and discomfort of life as a prisoner. What would I have had to eat? Would my guards have hated me? And how painful would I have found the open view to the hills above Gjirokaster and the sounds of freedom in the town below me? And what about the towns people? Did they hear the crack of morning rifle fire and shiver? It must have been a cold spot.

Genc is sitting in the hotel dining room drinking a sickly brew of hot milk, sugar and cinnamon.

"Cousin?" I ask, raising my eyebrows like Richard.

"No good," says Genc emphatically and pretends to pull a trigger and roars gunfire. It seems Genc's cousin is on manoeuvres – or at war with someone. A young man with Down's syndrome asks me for money and Genc throws a spoon at him. Outside it is raining. The square is dark and cold. Horse chestnuts stand dead black across the square but blacker still is the mounted silhouette of the citadel riding tall and quiet above us.

The road back to Saranda crosses a range of khaki hills. As we dip down towards the coast I can see a deep blue reservoir below, hidden in woodland. Genc knows how to find it. Standing on a concrete platform set several metres into the reservoir we find a father and son fishing. Genc and I swing over the holes in the suspension bridge. Their lines lie soft on the still water, which is a brilliant blue like watered ink. They have a couple of fish in a plastic bag and chat happily to Genc. Around the dam trees grow to the water's edge. Clusters of grass-green lilies sit on the surface. It is an idyllic spot. In the distance I hear the tumble of a river.

Back over the bridge we drive towards the sound of water. The road winds its way between blackberry bushes. Around a corner we enter a wooded gully flooded by the foaming water. The track is passable, but only just. Further on is a fish farm, its rows of concrete tanks white against a wall of blackberry bushes. As we get out of the car a pair of vicious dogs come bounding towards us, showing their fangs. Genc lets out a tremendous yell and begins to scuttle back into the car. But a shout calls them off just in time, and we wave gratefully to a big man in waders and a thick yellow turtleneck. Genc has gone pale and mutters what sounds like 'mama mia' under his breath. The gates into the farm are locked, explains the man in waders, and he has lost the key to the padlock. So Genc, the dogs and I squeeze under them.

The fish farm buzzes with the sound of rushing water, which races in glacier blue channels into concrete troughs swarming with pebble-shiny trout. I am enchanted and wonder whether the farm is viable and imagine picking it up for a song and running it with friends. We could build a smoke-house and packing plant and fly smoked trout to Athens and Rome from Saranda's little aerodrome. Long hot summer days, spent swimming and fishing, and in the evenings drinking local reisling chilled in the river. Genc asks the man in waders whether the farm is for sale.

"No," he replies. It is owned by an Israeli company. The man offers a bottle of raki, and we take it in turn to swig from the bottle. He begins to tease Genc for being so afraid of the dogs, and Genc angrily tells him that he should keep them under control 'or someone will shoot them' aiming his trigger finger at the dogs, which are now tied to an iron ring embedded in the side of one of the tanks.

"Don't you shoot my dogs!" shouts the man in waders.

"Fuck your mongrel dogs," screams back Genc and suddenly the man in waders is striding purposefully towards the growling beasts, and Genc and I are running full pelt, arms pumping, towards the gate. Back in the car we sit wheezing and getting our breath back. The windows soon mist up but we can only open the windows a fraction as the dogs are slobbering outside, their front paws leaving pad marks on the windows.

Genc drops me outside the hotel and we say goodbye, both pleased with our expedition. I walk down to Saranda's sea-front where I eat a plate of fried shrimps and drink beer in a restaurant overlooking the harbour. In the distance is Corfu, and it is from the island that a storm whips up, bending the palms on the front and lightning the horizon. Corfu is soon invisible behind a curtain of grey rain. As I order coffee the Mimosa struggles gallantly into view. It must have been caught by the storm halfway home. It is pitching alarmingly into a milky sea. I imagine the passengers being thrown about in that steaming cabin, scented with mildew and damp earth, and am glad that I am safely on land, with my belly full of fried shrimps. But she reaches the calm of the harbour walls and by the time I ask for the bill its passengers are tottering onto the quay.

SUNDAY 11^H MARCH
SARANDA — TIRANA

By late afternoon we reach reach Kavaje and Lushnja, industrial satellite towns south of Tirana and the bus fills up. Men and women press into the aisle, bringing the smell of cold twilight into the fug of the bus. The new passengers are barracked by the same conductor who bullied me between Fier and Tirana. An old woman with a bag of onions and muddy potatoes in her hand accepts my offered seat but does not thank me. A soldier scowls. In Lushnja, we weave around the dormant shadows of empty factories and tilting apartment blocks. A mains has burst, flooding the road.

Before Durres the road runs parallel with the railway and there, beside us, is the sooty snout of the locomotive, travelling at the speed of a galloping horse. Behind it the carriages are dirty and windowless. Children sit in the doorways waving. It is good to be home.

MONDAY 12TH MARCH
GAZ

Walking back from the Ministry, a man, about my age, comes up. He has a face like a skeleton into which bright blue eyes are sunk. His fair hair is cropped short, he is wearing jeans and a tracksuit top. There is something startling about him. For a second I think that he is going to attack me. Or is this my new ShIK tail? He looks unstable, dangerous even.

"Come. We drink coffee together," he orders. And I agree. Just like that. In the Rambo Bar we sip our coffees and stare at one another.

"I have been watching you," he tells me. My heart sinks.

"My name is Gaz. What is yours?"

He plays with his cigarette box, turning it on one corner, round and round like a spinning top. He chain smokes and his teeth are brown. Gaz is eternally restless. And he has a habit of staring you full in the face, without blinking, without perceptible expression. He would make an effective interrogator, an excellent SS officer with his blue eyes and his fair hair.

He is a poor migrant from the north. His family lives in the Gheg enclave on the outskirts of town. He describes his house as 'very poor'.

"I would be too embarrassed to take you there." I picture a hovel with gaunt Gaz staring restlessly into space in one corner. Nearby, his grandmother lies dying. His father is ill, he tells me, his brothers are scattered across Greece, Italy, Albania. He is not ShIK. He has no job.

"I think we can be real friends. I think that we can really help each other," he says, playing with his cigarettes. "I really need a break. I work in Greece for some months last year but I have no visa. I have no money for visa now. Then I work for a Swiss lady, a journalist, to travel in north – Puka, Tropoja, Kukes. Very dangerous for western ladies in the north. I travel with her as guide. I am very correct. We were alone in the hills, I could do anything to her. But I am very correct."

He puts a matchstick in his mouth and moves it about his mouth with his tongue, staring at me all the time. His timing is urgent and spot on, like a young Richard Burton.

He puts his feet up on the table and leans back. I am not able to help Gaz and am not sure that I want to. But at the same time I feel drawn to him.

"If its money you want, I haven't got much myself" I tell him.

195

He raises his hands.

"It's not money I want. It's friendship. I want you to help me improve my English." Bullshit I say to myself but somehow I cannot say it to him. We arrange a time to meet next week. All the time I am thinking how pointless it will be. Gaz is emphatic about the location and time.

"If I am alive I will be there," he says, laying his hand over his heart. "If I am not, I am dead." It should have sounded awfully melodramatic but, strangely, the possibility of Gaz's disappearance felt plausible. I expect that his life is pretty cheap.

"Alex, this is my mother."

I am sitting on the terrace, enjoying a cup of coffee and early spring weather. The lemon tree will be heavy with lemon yellow fruit before too long. Mrs Ademi is younger then I expected, a little bent and very thin, with a froth of brown-black hair. She has a knowing smile and her wrists are covered in bangles. In her right hand she holds a cigarette. She speaks no English and is shy and after a bangle-clacking hand-shake and another smile, she retires down the corridor.

TUESDAY 13TH MARCH
VITO

Vito flies in from Bari for a meeting with the new Swiss manager of the Tirana International Hotel.

Vito loves his job and food and plenty of other good things. But Albania he regards as hostile territory. It is dirty, uncomfortable, uncompromisingly poor. The natives are not very friendly. Italians have a thing about Albania. They feel guilty for having colonised it, embarrassed because they didn't do a very good job of it, revolted by its uncouth manners, disturbed by its poverty and nervous of further mass emigrations across the Adriatic. In Italy, like Greece, Albanians provide newspapers and populist politicians with an easy target. They are looked upon as a caste apart. People who clean your car windscreen at the traffic lights, who lie in the gutter and scour rubbish dumps.

Vito is in awe of Richard for his ability to manipulate the natives. For getting so much done. He does not find it so easy. Being Italian, Vito shares his ups and downs with me and Richard. Which means that he is often very cross, shaking his head and chuckling in a nervous, knife-edge sort of way. Come midday he is usually more than ready for a good lunch.

This morning is no different and he leads us into the Tirana's dining room, muttering savagely under his breath. An hour later we leave him discussing PA systems with the Swiss manager.

WEDNESDAY 14TH MARCH
ROUSING THE PROVINCES

It is important that cities like Peshkopje, Gjirokaster, Korca, Durres, Shkodra and Elbasan get a look in at the Conference – to give them a chance to show off their minerals, cheap labour and clean beaches and promote themselves as possible investment locations for foreign companies.

"I think best place to start is mayor's office," suggests Anetsi, giving me a sorry smile.

I telephone the mayor's office to arrange a meeting.

A thin, reedy voice crackles onto the line.

"Hello please." I tell the voice about the Conference.

"Yes yes. I know Investmenti Conferenci," replies the voice.

"Shall I come and talk to you now," I suggest.

"Please come not. Please faxi your request," says the thin voice.

"Why? It would be simpler if I came to speak to you."

"I must first analyse faxi and explain faxi to mayor."

"Why do you need to talk to the mayor?"

"Faxi first. Then speak me."

"When is the mayor back?"

"FAXI PLEASE. Telephone week next."

I put the phone down and punch a deep divot in the Director for Public Administration's filing cabinet.

I send a fax, marking it URGENT. There's no way I'm waiting until next week. But that afternoon there is no answer at the mayor's office.

THURSDAY 15TH MARCH
LOOKING FOR THE MAYOR

"We are dealing with your faxi," says the thin voice down the phone.

"Can I see the mayor?"

"He is back day after today."

Vito went to the EU delegation this morning, to meet the purple-haired ambassador. They discussed the Conference agenda. The ambassador has suggested that we hold the Conference dinner at an 'excellent' restaurant he owns in Durres.

FRIDAY 16TH MARCH
THE MAYOR'S OFFICE

The mayor's office is in a muddled one storey building off Skanderberg Square. A power cut has thrown it into shadow. I have an appointment to see the mayor, I think.

A fat woman in bright lipstick smiles nervously at me from behind a desk.

"Please sit," she says. It is eight thirty in the morning. Just before nine a man walks in. He wears an expensive looking suit and carries a smart briefcase.

"Mr Mayor?" I ask, extending my hand. I have always wanted to call someone 'Mr Mayor'.

He smiles and shakes my hand. We talk about the Conference. He is all for it.

"There is someone you must meet, who can help you," he says, and calls up his secretary. Moments later in walks an awkward-looking man, small and bald with a ridiculous curtain of hair tugged across his scalp. He wears a cream shirt with enormous collars and sagging grey trousers. His sleeves are rolled up above his elbows. There is a peculiar air about him, the combination of dull evasiveness and stubbornness and an absolute lack of imagination. It is the air of the communist bureaucrat. He introduces himself in a thin voice.

"*Was* that the mayor?" I ask as we walk down a corridor and into his dank office. He turns to me and smiles and moves his head impenetrably. I want to thump him, but my knuckles are still sore from the filing cabinet. A bar heater glows in the corner. His breakfast sits on greaseproof paper on his desk – an orange and a piece of cold mutton that smells. Tea in a stained china cup. Wet boots steaming by the fire. His greasy hair shifting across his scalp as he sits down. Ghastly.

"Yes. What?" he asks, smiling at me across his desk.

"I sent you a faxi. I mean fax. You said that you were dealing with my request."

He looks hurt. "Please understand I am so busy."

"I am sure. But I am sure that you also understand that the Prime Minister wants me to prepare the Conference in good time. The Prime Minister wants the mayor's office to play an important part in the Conference. He wants the mayor's office to provide a list of the foreign companies that it would like me to invite to the Conference. He also wants you to arrange for Albania's other cities to participate in the Conference. The Prime Minister has asked me personally to see that all this is done."

"Making you list. Right away now!"

Walking home after lunch I pass Mrs Ademi. She is pushing down the middle of the road, dressed in a long black coat. Her hair is held in a white scarf. She is carrying a large brown envelope full of papers and there is a vicious, faraway look in her eye. She is on her way to the mayor's office.

SUNDAY 18TH MARCH
GYPSIES

The gypsies have a fine set-to this evening. Sitting on the terrace with Suzana and Dritan we follow the argument back and forth like spectators at a tennis match. The children start crying. The voices rise and then there is a scream of pure terror and a great metallic clang. Everyone, including the children, goes quiet. We run outside. The man is sprawled on the ground. In her hand the woman holds a frying pan.

MONDAY 19TH MARCH
GHOST

Gaz has not died. There he is, smiling like a corpse, in the shelter of a kiosk opposite the Dajti.

"I thank God you came. I've been here for two hours, just waiting and thinking about you."

"You didn't need to do that."

"You go for lunch and so I came here to wait for you."

"You've been following me?"

"Yes. This morning you leave Ministry to visit the Italian Embassy and after for lunch with the English soldier in Tirana Hotel."

He looks quite pleased with himself, like a schoolboy able to recite a difficult piece of Latin.

"Why are you following me?"

"Your life, it is better than mine."

"My life's not for sale, Gaz. Don't follow me again. If you follow me again this is the last time we meet. I've had enough of people following me."

"I am sorry."

He stares at me. He looks nervous.

"You said that you were correct, Gaz. It's not correct to follow people."

"You're a man. I don't need to be correct to men."

"Why not?"

"I'm sorry. Very sorry."

He asks for money for a visa to Greece. I don't have any to give him. What is the point of all this?

Gaz is an enigma. He looks like a stone-thrower, a gang member, a desperate thief. He has gnarled hands covered in sores and a light frame that somehow suggests great strength. He has few clothes. The very sight of him in Athens or Rome, striding down a pavement, would prompt a policeman to rest his hand on his revolver and demand to see his papers. Yet he speaks good English. He is engagingly frank and, I suspect, highly intelligent. His few clothes are clean. He never smells. There is something deep and questioning about him. Gaz has a measured delivery that suggests each word is well considered. When he has finished he pauses to let the thing sink in. That is the moment when he looks at you with those eyes of his. It is an incongruous mixture of power and vulnerability, dumb violence and sensitivity. There is a pale, haunting threat about him, an indecent poise that spooks me. I am glad that there aren't many Gaz's in the world.

This evening the gypsy husband has resumed his perch by the bus. I wave at him and say 'hello' and this time he waves unhappily back. There is a dirty bandage wrapped around his head.

TUESDAY 20TH MARCH
I HATE THE MAYOR'S OFFICE

The list arrives from the thin voice in the mayor's office. It is almost meaningless. There are the names of twelve companies, their industrial sector and their country of origin but no address or contact name. Several are multi-nationals with operations all over the world. One example is: Royal Shell Oil. United Kindom (sic)/ Netherlands.

"Thank you for your list," I tell the thin-voiced man in his office. It is cold today and he is wearing a blue woolly hat. He sits behind his desk sipping milky soup from a bowl.

He smiles archly. "No problem."

"Have you talked to the mayor's offices in other cities - Durres, Shkodra, Vlora...?" He stares into his soup.

"No time. Sorry. Perhaps you faxi mayors direct."

"Perhaps I beati you to a pulp," I mutter to myself. 'Do you want the Conference to be a success?' I feel like asking him. 'Shouldn't we try to hoodwink a few businessmen into investing in your country?'

Instead, I say, "If you have not organised for these cities to participate in the Conference by tomorrow afternoon you and your family will be thrown down a coal mine."

No, of course I don't. I simply tell him that I will be asking the Prime Minister to dismiss him. No, I didn't even say that. In fact I pick up the bowl of milky soup, tip it steaming over his woolly hat, and walk out of his dank office for the last time.

Paul has his head down preparing for his exams, but has told me that he can 'squeeze me in'. We meet in the same underground restaurant. He is in a blazer and beige trousers and looks like a touring hockey international. The Chargé is in London.

"Until he's back the buck stops here," Paul tells me, poking his chest.

I describe my recent trip to Athens, and the glories of Saranda and Butrint.

"Ahh, Saranda! I was there last month. Between you and me someone had a pop at me. Found a firebomb in the cellar. Close shave."

"Any idea who might want to firebomb you?"

"All sorts. I've been getting rather close to a few shady characters recently. Bit of a thorn in their sides – which leads me to assume that they might have wanted me out of the way."

"It sounds like Dick Barton."

Paul chuckles. "Fact is stranger than fiction, my lad. Always has been."

At the London Bar we drink more brandy. "What about another game of ping-pong?" I ask at the end of the evening, full of bon homme.

Paul shakes his head. "This bloody knee..."

Mrs Ademi's campaign has suffered a reverse: there is bad news from the mayor's office. This evening Dritan spends several hours down the corridor and while he is away I hear a great deal of thumping and shouting. Dritan returns ashen-faced.

"Mother sick. Very sick."

Vito arrives this morning, hopping across the Adriatic in one of Vincent's planes. I meet him for lunch in the Tirana Hotel. He has spent the morning inspecting the hotel's preparations for the Conference and seems satisfied. There is a cathedral silence as he considers the menu.

"Market research," he explains, rubbing his tummy. Over carpaccio, salads and cold beer we discuss English literature. Vito is an expert on E.M. Forster.

"Come and see Zog's palace," he smiles. "I want to check it out." Zog's Palace of Brigades, which stands among trees on the edge of the city, is used by the government for state functions. The Prime Minister has offered us the palace as the venue for the Conference dinner. It sounds ideal, as long as it's up to scratch. The only other possibility is the EU Ambassador's restaurant in Durres.

We climb into a waiting Mercedes ('these streets, Alex, they are so *dirty*!'). It is chilly inside. The seats are leather. Minutes later we are at the palace. A squad of soldiers run past in gym kit. At the bottom of stone steps an impressively smelly curator is waiting for us. Inside he shows us the palace's reception rooms. It is dark and he opens some shutters. Sunlight illuminates the dust showers that follow our clapping footsteps. The air is mouldy and old. The walls are hung with enormous mirrors.

The banqueting hall is huge. Tall windows looking over Tirana park, chandeliers, an ornate ceiling and heavy tapestries on the walls. Hot, heavy, ponderous, formal, gaudy, grand. Perfect. Vito is delighted and smacks me on the back as we walk back out into the sunlight.

"Yes, this is good Alex. This is really good."

Outside there is a fountain and a long, rectangular pond. Around it curls a gravel drive lined with Cypress trees. I can imagine Zog strolling in a canary silk dressing gown, a morning cigarette in an ebony holder clenched between his teeth. I can also see the tyre tread of a Nazi Benz in the gravel; the Colonel has gone hunting for boar, or to inspect a new batch of partisan prisoners. Things have happened here.

As we glide out of the gates a group of sentries snap to attention. The road back to Tirana runs past the palace grounds and there, under what looks like a tall metal mushroom, stands another sentry. He is reading a book.

TUESDAY 27TH MARCH
MINISTRY OF FINANCE

On Tuesday they burn the rubbish outside the Ministry. Fires are lit and the rubbish piled on top. On Tuesdays the civil servants arrive at the Ministry smelling of smoke. If there is a breeze their clothes are covered in smuts.

It is just one sort of dilapidation in Tirana. And just the sort of thing that makes everyone so gloomy. Dritan gives an exasperated smile and shrugs. The Italian-trained waiters in the Tirana Hotel exude it, as they squelch about in their rubber-soled shoes: "I know that I'm hopeless but I can't be bothered to do anything about it, what's the point, this is Albania." I shout it out in my attic office when the phone goes on the blink. "I hate Albania!"

Just before lunch I need Xhaja to sign something.

"Come in, come in," he waves impatiently as I knock and peer into his office. He is wearing an orange kipper tie and packing away some papers into a cardboard box on his desk.

"Going somewhere?" I ask him.

"Yes. America."

I take this as a deadpan joke and hear myself laughing mechanically as I leave the room.

Xhaja has resigned. He has won an MBA scholarship at an American university and flies off in a week or so. Six weeks before the Conference. I suppose it's called a brain-drain. Anetsi is taking over from Xhaja, which should cheer him up.

I spend the morning in Elbasan, briefing the city's mayor on the Conference.

After lunch at the Akelida it is time to get back to Tirana. It is cold again and a granite sky hangs low overhead. I ask the Akelida's manager to find me a taxi.

He grins. "I know good man. Very fast."

Minutes later a car rounds the bend and skids to a dramatic halt feet from the Shkumbini river, which runs past the Akelida in a dirty, concrete watercourse.

"I am Safet," announces the driver gravely. Safet looks remarkably like Peter Sellars. He drives an old silver Opel and wears dark glasses. I wonder how much he can see in this light.

"Come back soon!" says the manager. Safet hurls my briefcase in the boot and slams it hard several times in order to lock it. The noise echoes across the grey waters of the Shkumbini.

Up into the foothills we reach cruising speed. Safet sits hunched over the wheel, peering through his sunglasses as we roar hornet-fast towards Tirana. Ninety is perhaps a good speed for the M6 but on a slippery road full of hairpins and potholes it is not. At first I enjoy the speed but Safet is an unusually bad driver and it soon becomes oppressive and then properly frightening. I try to distract him, asking him about his family but after tossing me a sun-bleached photograph of a shiny gravestone he returns to the awful business of driving. I stare gloomily out at the flashing hillside. If I had been wearing a hat, I would have held onto it.

We hit a wild cat and Safet turns to me and cackles. I suggest we slow down. Safet wags his finger, *"Inshallah, inshallah!"* and points to a copy of the koran lying by the gearstick. We are in God's hands - to be reaped or spared at his merciful will.

Charging down the mountainside we just miss a motorcade of black Mercedes, police vans and outriders heading up the hill towards Elbasan.

"Presidente!" sneers Safet, spitting out of the window.

The motorcade reminds me of Comrade Mugabe's regal progress around Zimbabwe - troop carriers, more black Mercedes, more outriders, ambulances, sometimes even a helicopter. I well remember his entourage racing past the eighth green at Ruhr, sirens going, while I was trying to save par by chipping dead.

Safet drops me the Tirana. I need a drink, and settle down in the Terazza bar with a glass of raki and some paperwork.

"Hello."

In front of me stands a girl, about twenty, long black hair, too much make-up, pretty in a synthetic, doll-like way. I ignore her but she doesn't go away. I look at her again and this time notice her oddly smart clothes, the wet mud on her boots, the moustache lying above the sheer pink lips. She is thin and deathly pale. Her eyes are big and smudged. Another lunatic. At least she's not driving. The girl shuffles nervously towards me. She has the handshake of an asp.

"Hello - I can sit down please?"

She sits down.

"What is your name please? My name is Eda. I am student.

Welcome to Albania. Sorry. What is your name please? My name is Eda. Pleased to meet you. Welcome to Albania. Sorry. What is your name please? My name is Eda. I am student. Sorry - what is your name please. Alex, Alex! Where are you from, Alex? Welcome to Albania."

It is like talking to one of those dolls, programmed to repeat a few saccharine phrases, all the time smiling thinly. Although it isn't that simple. There is something sinister about her. Her limp voice, her fixed eyes. She doesn't know what she's saying. Perhaps she's stoned. What does she want? Why does she keep repeating these bland introductions? Why can't she remember my fucking name?

We sit there, looking at each other. Me trying to stop my eyes slipping down to read the report I am holding, she smiling insanely and sipping at her cappuccino. I feel tired and cold, I have work to do, it is raining and I hate her. Then her eyes light up, like a tongue-tied actress who has suddenly come across her lines.

"Are you married Alex?

"Yes, I have four children."

I rustle my report impatiently. Her eyes stare at me and she licks her lips, her tongue as neat and pink as a cats.

"You and me, we go to disco?"

"No, Eda, I must work."

"Please, we go to disco. Together." A pale hand reaches out to stroke my arm. Too much. This doll with her acid lips and tripping sentences unnerves me.

"Eda, I must go to a meeting." Her wide eyes cloud over. Fireworks. She becomes pathetic - I cannot go, I can go in ten minutes, she will come with me to the meeting, we must meet later in my hotel - in a restaurant - in a disco.

"I am having tea with the President. I must not be late. If you delay me he will have you shot."

Daylight penetrates the far corners of her doll skull and she becomes even more agitated.

"I give you my address," she says, pulling all sorts of rubbish out of her handbag.

"I give you present."

Out of her bag she pulls a selection of postcards. She selects one and writes her address on it in green ink. The postcard has a picture of a grotesque pink baby in shorts and a singlet and wearing a huge pair of sunglasses. 'To my baby' reads the caption. I shiver. I get another postcard, a picture of a blond model. "For gift," explains Eda.

"How nice. Thank you."

"Give me your address please."

I hurriedly write down the address of a friend, then cross it out and put down any old rubbish.

Paying for the coffee I leave her there, her glazed eyes pouring into the distance.

Later that evening I doze on my bed. Dritan and Suzana are out visiting friends. The phone rings.

"Alex. It is Eda. How are you?"

How the hell did she get Dritan's phone number. Stupid with sleep I say "Eda, go away".

"Alex, I come to your home tonight?"

"No, Eda, no, no."

"But Alex, Alex ... speak to my friend please."

"Is that Alex?" says a fake American accent.

"Yes."

"Look, Eda really wants to see you."

"Well, I don't want to see her, I told her. I have no interest in Eda – please tell her that."

"Oh come on! She just wants to talk to you. Why are you being so unreasonable? She's a young girl, just looking for a good time. What's so bad about that?"

"Fuck off."

I take the phone off the hook. I am furious – it's like being stalked. Spooked again, I imagine Eda's whey-faced smile gleaming through the window. Her bright red nails scratching on the door. I have a shower, my tired imagination tearing into the possibility of a set-up. A teary Eda pressing charges in Tirana's police station, men with prehistoric faces and dirty blue uniforms breaking my nose with their boots. Or modish Eda in muddy boots knocking on my door in London. Too much raki has made me paranoid.

FRIDAY 30TH MARCH
MAURICE AND THE PYRAMID SCHEMES

The Professor's back from London. He greets me at the front door.

"I flew back with Maurice. He has his own plane. Spencer is the pilot. It is sitting now at Rinas surrounded by policemen. So is Spencer." He looks tremendously pleased with life.

Maurice is sitting at the Professor's desk, smoking a cigar and talking to someone on the phone. He is wearing a pinstripe suit and talking in Albanian. Maurice waves his cigar at me as I enter. Moments later he puts down the phone.

"Damn good speech, Alex. Fair zipped along. Well done! Professor was the star of the show."

"What are you doing here?"

"On my way to Sofia. Dropped in to see a chap called the General. Owns Vari, Albania's largest company".

"I know Vari. We've asked the General to the Conference – we want him to speak. But so far we haven't heard back from him."

"You don't want him at your Conference, Alexi, he is a son of a bitch, he is stealing people's money" replies the Professor.

"Oh, come now," soothes Maurice, "the General isn't all bad – not yet anyway. And if he is a son of a bitch, he's a damned clever one."

"How clever?" I ask.

"He's the pyramid king of Albania – that's what Vari really is, you see. A bloody great pyramid scheme."

"What's a pyramid scheme?"

"They call themselves 'Investment Companies' but in fact they're money factories. There are several in Albania, but Vari's the biggest by a long way. You see, the General offers people massive interest rates on cash deposits – say 20% over three months, 40% over twelve. Because the banks are bust, and couldn't offer 2% over a year, and because Johnny Albanian is desperately poor, he begins to invest. Especially hard up public servants, pensioners, employees on pissy wages...in other words most Albanians. And three months later they've made 20% and are eating meat again, perhaps even bought a little car, and so their jealous neighbour invests and her cousin and his granny and her son working over in Berlin or Rome and, hey presto, suddenly the General's got millions of dollars under management."

"But how is Vari able to offer 40% a year?"

"The General'll tell you it's the fruit of wise investment, that he uses the money to build up his business empire – tourism, transport, shops, breweries, construction... an empire so profitable that he can pay his investors 40% a year – a bit like paying shareholders dividends."

"But..."

"But it's bollocks. OK, the General's got a few shops and factories and he builds a few houses but really Vari's a money factory: cash goes in one end and comes out the other, nothing really happens to it in the middle. The 40% is sustainable as long as there is more money

211

flowing into Vari than there is flowing out. A constant flow of cash from gullible investors pays the 40% on deposits made a year ago. But, in a year's time these investors are expecting their 40%. Which means he's got to have found more money by then..."

"But surely..."

"There's a limit to the amount of cash around. Spot on, old man. Gradually spare cash is used up, there are more and more schemes and they start a rates war, offering higher and higher interest rates in order to get their mits on the spare cash. Then one day all the money is gone, soaked up by the schemes. They've run dry, facing an impossible bill. The investors are ruined and the Generals of this world are on the first plane to Switzerland or Brazil with suitcases full of dollar bills. It's still quite a long way from that here – though Romania's getting close to the edge. It's already happened in Russia. The General's been trying to edge into Bulgaria. I'm here to persuade him not to – bit of a closed market, Bulgaria, not open to the likes of the General."

"What's the government doing about the schemes?"

"All for them. Spirit of private enterprise, taking pressure off the spending ministries, a safety net for the elderly... the General's got good access to the President. And of course, he's a generous friend – helps pay the bills. So the government stays away, doesn't ask any difficult questions. Everyone's happy. But one day the President will wish he'd never set eyes on the General. Just you wait. Prof, any chance of a drop of your terrible whisky? – I've given myself a thirst."

We sit down to lunch. Maurice teases me for turning down a bit of sheep's brain.

"Best part," he says, picking out the eyeball and popping it into his mouth as if it were a strawberry.

"Next week I am going to give you your present, Alex. To thank you for my speech."

I look up at the Professor. He is grinning like schoolboy.

"What's that?"

"A visit to Vlora. A tour of my constituency! It's time I paid them all a visit."

Beside me Maurice chokes on his eyeball.

Maurice drops me home. He has a driver and a bodyguard, who scours Mrs Ademi's schoolyard, hand on hip, as Maurice and I say our goodbyes.

"Good to see you looking so well, Alexi. Sorry I can't stay and show you round a bit. Some lovely chrome mines I know up in Puka. Went on strike once. Crammed with thousands of miners, refusing to come up until they were paid. Starving to death. Hell of a spectacle. Good place to die I told a few of them, really stunning country. Life and times eh! Good luck in Vlora. The Professor took me on one of his jaunts once, absolute fucking slaughter – couldn't focus for days. He's a bloody hooligan down there. Like the rest of them. Well, I'd better go or I'll be late for my little chat with the General. Toodle pip!"

SUNDAY 31ST MARCH
FUN FAIR

This evening Dritan and I stroll through butter yellow sunshine into town. Skanderberg Square is full of families, walking up and down together. Others sit in groups on the steps of the Opera House and in front of the National Museum. Walking across the middle of the Square I can feel hundreds of pairs of eyes watching me carelessly as hundreds of mouths gossip below. There are dodgems running in a corner of the square, where Hoxha's old statue used to stand. How splendid the gold leaf would have shone in this light. The dodgems skid about marvellously slowly but their young drivers scream with delight. This seems a happy, safe place tonight.

APRIL

We're back at Mike's favourite fish restaurant.

"Tell me about the pyramid schemes," I ask him, picking the bones out of a huge koran.

"Now there's a can of worms! How much do you know?"

"I know that Vari's a glorified money factory, and that if I had shares in Vari I'd have sold them by now."

"Well Vari's just the tip of the iceberg. There's lots more, none as big as Vari but all just as dangerous – timebombs ticking away. They're run by a queer bunch: the General; a former bricklayer owns something called the Guri Investment Company which has hoovered up most of the mafia money in Vlora; a gypsy woman – ex-nightclub singer – owns another. In Lushnja the Dardha Investment Company's made so much money that the owner's offered an Argentinian US$300,000 to coach the local football team. The pyramid bosses are the richest group of people in Albania – they just about control the economy. Some people say as many as fifty percent of families have invested money in the schemes – could total $500m or so. Hundreds of thousands depend on their income from the schemes. And when they run out of money God knows what's going to happen. That's where your Conference comes in I suppose, restore a little balance, pull in a bit of legit business which actually produces things, rather than just recycles dollar bills."

There was an explosion early this morning opposite the Dajti. A kiosk, recently and illegally constructed was blown up with an enormous charge of dynamite, leaving nothing but a smoking crater. An urchin was injured by a spray of tea-spoons. Now there is a great crowd around the hole and one distraught man, presumably the owner, is pacing about shouting his head off.

WEDNESDAY 3RD APRIL
THAW

Down the green Lana bubble hundreds of cabbages, chasing each other in the current. Sitting on the river bank having a coffee, feeling the sun warm my back, I watch them tumble over a rapid, where a jumble of logs, old oil drums and plastic detergent bottles block the current. They go on and on. Are they cast-offs, or has a lorry fallen off a bridge upstream? Already a group of gypsy boys are fishing them out of the water with a wooden plank. Behind them the muddy bank is scattered with daisies. Spring is coming and every day there is less snow on the mountains that stand guard over the city.

THURSDAY 4TH APRIL
FANTASY ECONOMICS

A quiet day in the Ministry. Anetsi is celebrating his birthday and we toast him with a bottle of raki at lunchtime. A little drunk, I wander upstairs to my office and fall asleep with my feet up on the desk.

At four I am woken by Halit.

"Hey guy!" he shouts in Americana and I come to with a jolt that would have given an older man a heart attack. Halit has brought me some papers to read. Afterwards I take him for a coffee in a nearby kiosk.

"What do you know about these pyramid schemes, Halit? Is Vari one of them."

Halit starts. "How do you know about the schemes?"

"Doesn't everyone?" I ask.

"Hardly, man! They're as close to damn a state secret!"

"Aren't they rather dangerous? I mean they're bound to fail."

Halit nods his head impatiently. "Bullshit they're going to fail. They're Albania's future!" he says with a conspiratorial grin.

"But they can't work – not for ever. It's mathematically impossible."

"OK... but Albania's schemes... what if they're special schemes?"

I stare at him hard, watching his face. He is smiling a clever, suggestive smile and he is quite serious. He is an American-trained economist working at the Finance Ministry. And he believes in the integrity of schemes that even my 'O' level maths recognise as a con. As if Albania has struck upon a magical way to recycle and churn out new money, a magical money factory. The General and the other pyramid owners: miracle workers, working abstract mathematics that no one really understands but that nonetheless make $2+2 = 4,000,000$. It reminds me of Willy Wonka and his chocolate factory and the childish fantasies it inspired in me. Halit has never heard of Roald Dahl but he knows all about the chocolate factory.

Tomorrow the Professor is taking me to his constituency.

"We'll make an early start" he has told me imperiously. "You'll be at my house by 6.30."

It will be good to get out of the Ministry.

FRIDAY 5TH APRIL
CONSTITUENCY VISITING

In this city the outstanding diplomatic patriot, Ismail Qemali (People's Hero) raised the flag and declared the independence of Albania (from the Turkish empire)

on November 28th 1912. The people's uprising which
burst out in Vlora on June 5, 1920 and lasted to
September 3, 1920 drove the Italian occupying forces
into the sea.

Before Liberation Vlora was a small administrative
centre mostly of an administrative character. Today it
has been transformed into an industrial city in which
the food-stuffs industry, the cement industry and the
chemical industry are important. For its outstanding
contribution all through the history of the Albanian
people Vlora has been proclaimed a 'Hero City'.

(AGO, pp. 70-71)

I knock on the Professor's door. There is long silence, then the padding of bare feet in the hallway and a shaggy head of hair leans around the door. The Professor takes ages to get ready. I am wearing my heavy, blue suit, appropriate, I hope, for constituency visiting. Peeing against a walnut tree in his garden I look at the clear blue sky and realise that it is going to be a beautiful day.

The crippled old houses and dusty streets of Tirana behind us, the Professor puts on his favourite classical music. He sucks on a cigarette and drives fast and not very well. We head west to Durres and then south, between the pine dunes and the railway line, where trains never go faster than a galloping horse. Across the drained marshes to Fier, with its familiar stink of crude oil, and past olive groves and fruit trees to Vlora. Just before we get there we pass a brand new petrol station, flying Vari's cambridge blue flags.

Albania's second 'Hero City' is also its smuggling capital, a terminus for Turkish heroin on its way north and refugees wanting to get into Italy. It is also the centre of Albania's cannabis production (the

220

climate is ideal). Criminality and a history of political independence have made Vlora rich and prickly, and turned it into Albania's urban Wild West. Most of its male citizens are cowboys – cocksure, violent, plenty of chutzpah. When the Professor won 80% of the Vlora vote at Albania's first ever multi-party elections he told a crowd of supporters that the communists '...who sucked our blood for years are finished'. 'Soon', he promised 'they will be in pieces'. He was declaring war on his father. He was flashing his spurs.

In a suburb of heavily armoured compounds we pick up Arben, the Professor's constituency agent. Arben is wearing a satin blue shirt. Around his neck hangs a chunky, gold necklace. He is unshaven, red-eyed, he has a scar across his neck – he looks fantastically dangerous. Arben is the man Paul was spying on in the Dajti, before he spoiled his cover by falling off his chair. I think Paul would describe this as a 'turn up for the books'.

"Arben used to be the Prime Minister's bodyguard," explains the Professor, as he drives us towards a café for coffee. "Now he's a businessman here in Vlora, aren't you Arben?"

Arben grunts and grins at me. In fact, Arben is one of the biggest businessmen around. He owns several, enormous, black speedboats. By day the boats bob about on Vlora's waterfront, their pilots in bed with girls or drinking whisky in the cafés. After nightfall the pilots climb into their boats, guns stuffed in their belts, and guide the hunched figures of refugees from Kurdistan, Iraq, China and Pakistan into the bow and stern. When all is set the on-board engines lift the boats' noses out of the water and the sleek black boats thieve across the water towards Italy and isolated coves or strips of coastline where the Carabiniere cannot hear. It sounds romantic but Arben's trade is a brutal one. There are stories of disorientated refugees being dropped a few miles up the Albanian coast, where they are abandoned believing the sand beach to be the beginning of Italy, or even being forced overboard at sea and left to drown.

Most of the Professor's constituency lies in poor agricultural land behind Vlora. After coffee and brandy Arben goes off to rouse one of his lieutenants and the Professor and I drive inland. We stop in a couple of villages to drink beer. The villagers are glad to see the Professor and we collect a small motorcade, an old van and two Fiats, which escort us down dusty roads, blaring their horns and waving at people working in the fields. At an isolated spot by a bridge crossing the wide channel of the Vjosa we stop for an impromptu meal with a constituent. Beer and raki, mutton and pickled peppers that sit like damp tongues on the plate.

Down by the river the water rolls chalky blue towards the sea. Across the channel men are shovelling gravel into the boot of a car. I take photographs of a nodding donkey oil well, long seized up. It is hot and my bladder is beginning to collapse under the diuretic onslaught of the beer. I glance nervously down the long road winding away into hills beyond the bridge and our brawny motorcade. They look like they have cast iron bladders.

Next stop, says the Professor as we climb into the car, is the largest town in the constituency. As we bump along the track he explains that the town used to work local bitumen reserves. Now the reserves are exhausted and the town depends upon subsistence agriculture and trading gravel dug from the Vjosa. Over the incessant hooting of the motorcade whines Vivaldi's *Four Seasons*. I ask the Professor how often he visits the constituency. He looks sheepish.

"Uurgh ... about once every three months."

My bladder begins to feel ominously heavy. I shift in my seat and pray for a short journey. Through the open window fine terracotta dust curls in a light spray. We smoke furiously.

The road runs on between rolling country filled with flat fields and bunkers. Far away rise the gentle hills and there is an impression of Russian steppe in the long, slow plain towards a distant horizon. We pass the shell of a large brick building, isolated and small in this vast plain.

"Old dormitory for collective workers," shouts the Professor over the music.

We climb into more interesting country – steep gullies covered in gorse and high peaks. By now my bladder is about to burst.

"How long until the town?"

"Five minutes."

I cross my legs. There must be few less comfortable feelings in the world for an adult, especially for a male adult in the company of boozed-up Albanians showing off to each other, than the prospect of wetting yourself like a nipper.

"I may have to go to the loo soon," I suggest weakly. The Professor ignores me.

In the distance I can see the town and soon we hit the random broken buildings and rubbish pits that signal urban poverty everywhere in this country. Round a bend we stare into the pocket of the town square, oddly formal and neat in its Wild West setting. Behind it, empty terraced fields climb an untidy hillside. Goats drift slowly among piles of rubbish. In the middle of the square stands a group of people. In a dreadful moment I realise I am staring at a reception committee. Our reception committee. Some bastard has warned the townsfolk of our arrival.

"Stop!"

To my eternal gratitude the Professor stops, the reception committee gazing in bewilderment barely forty yards away. Behind, the entourage comes to a halt, still hooting. Giving the reception committee as casual a wave as I can muster, I disappear behind a pigsty, a peculiar-looking visitor in a blue suit. Minutes later I join the Professor and the crowd in the centre of the square, walking towards them with as much dignity as I can muster. They are chuckling as the Professor explains my behaviour. The Professor makes the most of me – "this is my personal assistant from England," he says importantly and I shake hands with the local bigwigs. They are a poor-looking bunch – quite dark and small and wearing the Oxfam assortment of tweed jackets and shiny old trousers that is so popular in Tirana. And no wonder, their town forgotten at the end of a long drive across empty fields, a rare pile of verticals in this horizontal world.

The largest building is a sort of town hall. There are cows stabled on the ground floor. Upstairs is a bar. Here we sit among posters of John Travolta and Samantha Fox. Gaudy Christmas decorations hang from the roof. Below a group of staring young men pretend to play pool on a worn table. The girl who brings us beer doesn't look quite right. I watch her carrying bottles of beer back and forth as the Professor works the crowd. Soon he has everyone laughing. He is good at this.

The mayor has sent out orders for a meal to be prepared, bringing women in from the fields. When it is time to eat we cross the square, a party of drunk men blinking in the bright sunlight. Inside a blue painted room a long table has been laid. A candelabra of raki bottles stands in the middle. We sit down to salad and old olives and dry bread which we dip into bowls of sour yoghurt.

The toasting begins. Glass after glass of raki in honour of Albania, the Queen, Great Britain, Skanderberg, Churchill, the war against the Germans, my mother, father, brother, sister, Vari, the defeat of Serbia and the liberation of Kosovo, the Professor, the Professor's wife, the Guri Investment Company, the town, the mayor's family, victory against

Greece, the Professor's children, long life and fortune…

A whole sheep arrives on the table, surrounded by rice. For the Professor and his English aide there is half a skull, each holding a cooling piece of brain. I look into one opaque, stupid eye and wonder whether this is somehow Maurice's work. More toasts, singing, slaps on back, Everyone begins to eat, cramming handfuls of rice and greasy mutton into their mouths, shouting and laughing. Every toast brings glasses crashing to the table. Four men begin a loud song.

Soon we are so drunk that we toast old favourites again and again, interrupting our meal to stand up and raise our glasses. Anyone can raise a toast, and everyone has to respond – stand up, repeat after me, drain glass, cheer. The system is awfully abused. One old man, his beard full of rice and mutton grease, has us up and down every couple of minutes.

"Winstaaan Chercheel!!" he bays (he fought as a partisan alongside British commandos), "Queen Lizbath, Excellency Professor Minister President Number One… Albania!" Every time he raises the table to its feet he glows with pleasure. He has not had this kind of fun in years.

Back outside in the sunlit square we loll about, bouncing off one another, full of bonhomie. The old man meanders about, shouting his old toasts to the hills. The professor slaps me hard on the back.

"We know how to drink in this country, eh Alexi. Come on, we've got work to do. Want to drive?"

The townspeople gather in the square as the Professor and his entourage climb into the cars. There is a cheer as we drive away, the motorcade hooting furiously. Then the townspeople go home to sleep it off. We, on the other hand, have to drive as fast as possible down a dirt road, hooting our horns all the way. Twenty minutes later we stop at a half-built café. Nearby are other half-built houses. Around us the green plain stretches into infinity. The Professor has a bottle of whisky in the boot. It is one of a batch that he keeps at home in plain cardboard boxes called something silly like McTartan or Glenstag. Somewhere I have heard a rumour that he sells it in Kosovo. The members of the motorcade gather around a couple of tables and a few men join us from inside the bar.

With the whisky the sense of the day at last spills into the empty, sun-drenched landscape. I remember only an unsteady progress back to Vlora, from drink to drink. Soon I have heartburn and the cigarettes I smoke in a desperate attempt to retain some hold on my intelligence taste harsh and thick in my stinging throat. At a poor-looking house standing somewhere on its own above the Vjosa, we stop again. The Professor wants to pay his respects to a couple whose two sons recently drowned. There they are, standing in front of the house, grey and severe. Both weep as the Professor tells them how sorry he is. It happened in February, when the river was high and grey. My dancing brain pictures the terrible silent murder, the damp smudge of colourful bodies snagged on the bones of an old tree, or left on a strip of gravel.

Inside, their shy, pretty daughter makes us coffee. The room is bare save for the couch, a rug and some chairs. The man watches the Professor grimly and I guess he realises how drunk we all are. Suddenly, the two men are arguing. The wife and girl look on, their faces wide with concern. The Professor stands up quickly and walks outside. Following him we turn to say goodbye, which lasts several minutes as the two men patch things up. I want to plant a kiss on the lips of the girl which look as smooth as cream. Thankfully I don't – I'd probably have to marry her and spend my life as a herdsman among these lonely hills.

Back in the car, the Professor is indignant. He tells me what happened. The man had started abusing the Professor and his political class. Modern politicians were 'lazy' and 'corrupt'. They had no idea what former generations had suffered. They were neglecting old people. The man had been a partisan hero, then imprisoned as a dissident by the communists. When he reminded the Professor about his father's role in the dictatorship, the Professor lost his temper and walked out.

At Vlora, for no good reason other than that we have been drinking all day, we have more to drink. Out in the bay, the black speedboats wait for darkness. Sitting under a large umbrella somewhere on Vlora quay, a huge whisky in my hand, I watch the Professor inspect the engine of a new Mercedes parked on the front. It still carries German plates.

"We have all the best cars in Europe, Alexi. For free!" He thinks it a great joke. Which it is.

At last we set off for home. There is a beautiful evening light as we drive through pines and over the last of the dunes. The Professor drives with a kind of mechanical certainty. To synthetic violins we meander between lanes (we have a choice of two, one of which is ours).

The Professor is ranting about the dictatorship.

"Do you understand what is happening, Alexi. DO YOU UNDERSTAND?" he asks, turning to me to emphasise his point.

"Just keep your eyes on the fucking road," I yell.

Moments later the Professor overtakes a bus on a blind bend with a burst on the horn.

Merciful Fier is dark. In a private room of the Apollonia Hotel, sitting in the middle of a party of rogues and cut throats, is Arben. How or why I do not know. Perhaps he has nipped up the coast in one of his boats. Is it out there somewhere, waiting for his return, its load of Kurds cooking up chai in the bow?

"Nice shirt," I tell Arben and he promises to give it to me before I leave. On the table stand brand new bottles of whisky, brandy and raki. Around the table sit Arben's protegés, in suits and heavy gold watches. Somewhere close by lives John's family. Poor crippled Baba and his beautiful wife.

One of the men is a Vlora judge. He is twenty-five, a year older than me. The Professor pulls the top off a whisky bottle and throws it over his shoulder. There is a roar of approval and we're off again. By now I've reached that state of drunken trauma when one begins to worry about going blind. I sip at raki, which lights me up a bit, and chat to the judge who is full of questions about the English judiciary. I tell him that most judges in England are over sixty. He laughs and translates this for the benefit of one of Arben's mates who has a gun stuck in his belt. I ask the judge how he came to be appointed.

"I am a law graduate," he replies.

"Hanged anyone?"

"Not yet," he grins.

SATURDAY 6TH APRIL
CONVALESCENCE

I am still drunk when I wake. Dritan is sympathetic and makes me tea which Albanians regard as a gentle medicine. He is deeply impressed by my report of the trip.

"The Professor – he is a good man. So strong!"

I feel washed out. My legs ache and creek like old timber under sail, my kidneys hum and titter like nervous children and somewhere, somewhere inside me, I can feel my malcontent liver. I go for a stroll around Skanderberg Square. It is raining. There is a new beggar on the Square. He has been left in front of the Mosque. Some neurological disorder makes him ram his head up and down, his eyes fixed, his mouth dribbling. It is a violent movement and the muscles stand out on his neck. His hair is slicked wet by the rain. No one has time or money to care for him here. It is a desperate sight and, in my brittle state, I fancy waiting until dark and knocking him over the head with a brick.

In the afternoon I walk to the Ministry. It is deserted. Upstairs in my office I listen to a play on the World Service, incapable of working. Outside comes the roar of a crowd watching the European Cup game against Moldavia in the National Stadium. Albania lose 3-1. I never got my hands on Arben's shirt.

MONDAY 8TH APRIL
BRING BACK HOXHA

Richard is back for a week. Things are hotting up. We have supper with Mike in a pizza restaurant by the Dajti. Mike tells us that the border situation is fragile. There have been more killings near Kosovo.

Walking home late, yards from Dritan's house, I am attacked by the pack of dogs that live in the school. It is pitch dark and suddenly they are around me, about twelve of them, snapping and barking. Then one of them bites me in the calf. I kick him hard in the ribs and he runs off, whining. But the rest smell blood and I run for it, all the time calling melodramatically for Dritan. The gate, thank goodness, is open and I slam the door behind me. Dritan bursts out of the front door and together we pelt the pack with stones. There is a small cut in my leg. Under Hoxha armed patrols shot strays by night. Now the city is overrun.

TUESDAY 9TH APRIL
EVANGELISTS

On the way to the Ministry, I visit a clinic run by American evangelists. I am wearing my dogtooth suit, a pale blue shirt and a navy tie as I walk in off a road full of people pushing prams full of firewood and abandoned cars. What a sight.

The evangelist behind the reception smiles, showing all her front teeth. Inside a consulting room I pull up my trouser leg and a white haired doctor gently examines my calf. The wound now looks pathetically small and I feel rather sheepish and not at all rabid. He pronounces me fit and out of danger. A nurse beams on. I half expect them to offer up a prayer of thanksgiving. In the waiting room I ask the receptionist whether I can make a small contribution in return for the all-clear. She smiles and gives me a bill for $30.

Dritan's mother has bounced back. She has hired a lawyer, who is confident of success. This evening they plot their next steps on the terrace. I make coffee and encouraging noises. I want them to wipe the floor with the mayor's office.

THURSDAY 11TH APRIL
GAZ

Gaz is waiting for me outside the Ministry building. My heart sinks as I see him smoking by the rubbish pit. We go for a coffee.

"What can you do for me Alex? My life is really terrible. I don't know what to do."

I try to imagine what he does do every day. Walking about, bumming coffees off strangers. Does he ever get the odd day's work putting up a house or unloading a truck? What does he eat every day? Not much judging by how thin he is. Does he have any friends? Does he beguile other foreigners? He wants me to set him up with a foreign company.

"I am very correct. Good for driver, guard, guide."

I tell him that I cannot help him.

But he is persistent. "I think that my life is in your hands, Alex. You are the only person that can help me."

"You are the only person that can help you, Gaz." I am a poor civil servant working in a pissy ministry where the wind whistles through the broken windows and ministers of state wipe their backsides on yesterday's copy of Vincent's Daily News.

He looks sulky and I lose my temper. There are enough petty irritations to life in this tatty city. I am not going to add to them by accepting responsibility for this scarecrow. As I leave I give him a book that I cannot bear to read. It is a terrible historical romance in a hard cover.

"I want you to meet my friend. He is Swiss. He works in the Swiss Embassy."

His magic has not worn off. "OK. Next Tuesday, say about six o'clock."

"If I do not die I will be there. If I am not there I am dead." I leave him, hand on heart. The other clutches the book.

SATURDAY 13TH APRIL
THE EPICUREAN

Dritan has a passion for food. He loves to talk about it – what is good, what is bad, where the best food comes from. He has fastidious and disciplined tastes. He will only drink his cousin's raki, which he sends up from his farm near Kruja, in glass bottles stuck with ill-fitting corks. We drink it out of small tumblers, Dritan pouring precise measures of the clear, syrupy alcohol. In the tumbler the raki sparkles like trout water. And there is a delicate fragrance – of aniseed and hay and manure. Dritan will take up the glass with a frown and touch it to his lips, his little finger askance. Truly a connoisseur's moment, and it is a great relief when his face eases into a happy grin and he places the glass neatly back onto the table, satisfied.

Dritan drinks Turkish coffee, boiled with water and sugar in a small pot. The sugar, he insists, must be added at just the right time. He no longer lets me make coffee when he is around because I never quite get the sugar right.

"Dritan make good coffee," he reminds me, taking the pot gently out of my hand. In the kitchen he has the hands of a chef, neat and strong, and he holds a fork or a pan as it is meant to be held. Not too tight, not too loose, comfortably away from the body. It sounds like a good golf grip. Dritan is a pro in the kitchen.

Every morning Dritan sips one cup of coffee, and smokes a cigarette. Dritan's inability to separate coffee and cigarettes finally did for his attempts at giving up. Morning coffee is a silent ritual, usually played out by the lemon tree on the terrace. When he's finished, Dritan will grin and reach for his car keys. It is time to pick up the Chargé.

Dritan has a savoury tooth. He prefers dark Tirana beer to Italian lager. He will not touch chocolate or biscuits. Fried eggs disturb him. Tomato sauce is not his thing at all. Tomato salad with olive oil and thick chunks of onion is, as are meatballs, figs, poached fish, salty white cheese, peaches and spinach. He makes one of the best salads I have ever tasted: fresh oranges in olive oil, sprinkled with flakes of salt. When he eats something good he will look up, his eyes shining and almost giggle with pleasure. Sometimes he waves his hands in the air with delight.

Processed food is still scarce in Albania so that people haven't forgotten what real food looks like or how to make interesting dishes out of a few simple things. Food is a still a valued source of colour and fragrance. Certain foods are considered medicines, each with a particular benefit: that is good for the eyes, this makes your hair grow, that herb stops toothache. And food is not always available – so when you do get your hands on a nice bit of fish or some plums, it is an occasion for celebration and a reminder that the year is getting on and the seasons are changing.

I am late for Gaz and the Swiss. I had doubted the Swiss' existence but there they are sitting in the cafe. Gaz has a beer in front of him. The Swiss is wearing a complicated brown jersey and strict glasses. I have met him before. He spoke to me in cool English one day in his Embassy's reception room, when I asked to see the Ambassador.

"He is a busy man. Please put your request in writing." Instead I phoned the Ambassador direct and hours later, met him in his office. The Ambassador was avuncular and had a stuffed pheasant in a glass case behind his desk. When I asked him if he had shot it himself he looked horrified.

"It is too beautiful to shoot," he replied.

Now the Swiss and I smile thinly at one another. Gaz is astonished that we have met before. He goes on and on about it. The Swiss is drinking fanta. I order raki. The Swiss speaks five languages and is married to an Albanian. He is great friends with Gaz. What on earth do they talk about? Or is Gaz playing a long game for a Swiss visa. After twenty minutes of hardworked tedium I remember an overdue telephone call to London. The Swiss has not yet finished his fanta. I have drunk two glasses of raki which have fired my temper. I must never see either of them again. It would be too much.

It rained yesterday, all last night and it is still raining this morning. Warm spring rain. Lots of it. Tirana is a miserable place when it is raining. The sewers are broken or too small and the water has nowhere to go, so it runs in rivers down the sides of the road, gushes from holes in the pavement and streams down from the overflowing gutters. The pot holes in the roads fill up and standing water hides the ruts in the uneven pavement. Yesterday I saw a woman plunge one leg deep into an invisible pot hole, breaking her ankle. I held an umbrella over her head while a queue of cars stopped to help and fight over who should take her to hospital.

The Ministry want to see my list of delegates coming to the Conference. Or rather they want to see how many of 'their' names (supplied by Albania's handful of Embassies) are on it. Very few. Their list was little better than the drivel supplied by the mayor's office, and much too late so I've thrown it away. We're oversubscribed as it is.

Ghastly Godo has telephoned and asked me to send the delegate list ahead. Which I have. Now they have asked for an 'interview' so I borrow a car from the Finance Ministry pool. They are all red Peugeot 505s, cast-offs of the French fire service. I have seen an old British fire engine on Tirana's streets, as well as Royal Mail delivery vans and a Devon ambulance.

The Lana has broken its banks and the road leading to the Ministry is flooded. The poplars are getting their feet wet. The car creeps through the water with me urging the driver on, staring nervously at my watch and pretending I have a meeting with the Foreign Secretary. Twenty yards from the gates he stops. He is worried about pot holes. I am quietly astonished that I have got him this far. I open the door. The Lana, swollen with grey rain, rushes below. The water catches around the car's wheels where it bubbles and foams. I look up at the Ministry and across at the driver. He shakes his head adamantly. There is no alternative. I am already late – I am always late for appointments at the Ministry of Foreign Affairs.

The water is colder than I expected. I tread carefully. I cannot see my shoes which are completely submerged in the dirty Lana. I almost trip over the curb but recover to stumble through the Ministry gates dry from the ankles upwards. Godo is standing by the reception desk.

"I have been waiting for you, Alex," he says, rubbing his hands and grimacing.

"Funny you should say that," I mutter and point at my feet, which squelch impressively.

"I am sorry for inconvenience," he says "we have bad flooding." We both look at my shoes and he grimaces as I wiggle my toes.

"Come, the Doctor awaits."

He leads me into the main hall of the Ministry. There is a wet patch in front of the tall front doors, where water is seeping through. Up a marble staircase, down a corridor and we enter a large drawing room with a high ceiling and chandeliers. There are crude oils of Skanderberg and mountain castles with heavy gilded frames. In the middle of the room is a small congregation of furniture – ornate chairs painted white and touched up in gold leaf and a low table with clawed feet. On it stands a steaming pot of coffee and a plate of glucose biscuits. In one of the chairs sits the Doctor, his spectacles hanging from the corner of his mouth. I squelch towards him across the cream carpet. Godo guides me by the elbow, as if I need assistance or might be unsure of the way. The Doctor shoots up with great enthusiasm. He is alone. Laco is on an official trip to his beloved America. What are they up to, I wonder.

"I'm sorry I'm late," I say as I shake the Doctor's hand.

He points to my shoes and laughs. I have left footmarks on the carpet. "Please to sit down, Mr Hickman."

The Doctor is a funny, academic character – short and white-haired and scattily dressed like a mad professor in a Walt Disney cartoon. He is quite unable to finish a sentence. All this makes me impatient with him.

"Well," I ask, "did you like the list?"

They both look at each other. Godo as drawn up a chair next to the Doctor and together they face me, side by side. Sitting like that they look very close, like they are father and son.

"Mr Hickman," says Godo, his voicing rising slightly, "our companies are not on your list." He waves the list in his hand. It is damp and fraying at the edges.

"Yes, I'm sorry about that. We have sent them invitations but only recently. We haven't had any positive replies yet."

They both look at me carefully. They seem satisfied. The Doctor nods his head. Godo unwinds a little.

"So they have been all invited. You can confirm?"

"Yes. We are waiting for their replies."

"Good. Coffee?" says Godo.

There is something else on their minds. I can tell as Godo pours the coffee and the Doctor pushes the plate of biscuits towards me. Both men are nervous about something.

"Milk?" says Godo, arching his eyebrows impressively.

"Mr Hickman," begins the Doctor carefully, "I think that by now you understand Albania quite well. You know, how shall I say, our realities. For example, Mr Godo and myself. We have spent many years working hard for our country. We are loyal public servants. We feel a strong sense of duty."

I mutter something about that being obvious and how lucky Albania is. But as usual I have cut off the Doctor in mid-flow and he flutters his hands in protest.

"Thank you, thank you. You are most kind."

"But even loyal public servants like myself and Mr Godo (and he turns to sweep an inclusive hand towards his young colleague) have to eat... and our families have to eat." He smiles benignly at me.

"Sadly, our salaries here at the Ministry are small. The

government is poor. It does not have the money to pay us what we are, perhaps, worth. As a result, we are forced to think of our futures."

Godo leans forward in his seat, the veins standing out across his macabre forehead, watching the Doctor.

"You shall be meeting the representatives of many foreign companies during the Conference. You shall have considerable access to them." He is stabbing his glasses at the floor with each syllable.

"These companies, if they should choose to invest, will need capable people to help them on the ground. They might well raise this very issue with you, Mr Hickman. And we should like you to know that there are members of the Civil Service, first class members, Mr Hickman, who are available." He looks at me knowingly and his eyebrows arch like Godo's. Perhaps they are father and son, in disguise.

"In short, Mr Hickman, Mr Godo and I might be interested in alternative employment."

At last it is over. The Doctor sinks back, exhausted by the effort of selling himself to a twenty-four year old in squelching shoes. In fact, we all sink back exhausted with the strain and, when Godo suggests 'more coffee', we drain our cups as if in toast to private sector enterprise, rattling our saucers to clear the air.

MONDAY 22ND APRIL
MINISTRY OF FINANCE

Over two thousand Conference invitations have been sent out to companies in forty seven countries. The take-up has been much greater than we anticipated and we are preparing for nearly three hundred delegates. The Conference room only seats two hundred and fifty. Vito is organising another room next door, which will accommodate the spill-over. Events in the conference room will be broadcast on closed-circuit television. We are all buoyed by the unexpectedly large numbers.

There is no sign of life at the Professor's house. His car is gone.

"Gone away," explains his neighbour. "Outside."

He has taken his family and vanished. Followed Xhaja to America, according to Anetsi, who has a soft spot for the Professor. Perhaps ShIK's intimidation tactics just became too much.

I am sad that I have not had a chance to say goodbye. And sorry that he didn't try to. He has made up a good part of my life here, and he has been a friend. He is a good man – full of fire and decent intentions. But demons hold him back I suppose and they will stop him being what he might have been. I wonder how exile will suit him. He loves this place, at least as much as he fears it, and the hold it has over him. I do not expect to see him again. Just as I will not see Sanda, Roma or John.

Maurice rings me at the Ministry. God knows how he got through. I picture him in his office in the City, in some granite-coloured pad with flashy, black windows and the brown Thames running below. He sounds tired, fragile almost, and he is cross that I know so little about the whereabouts of the Professor.

"I know he's in Washington, just can't track him down. You of all people, Alexi! Thought you'd have been chatting to him. Want to know if he's alright, that's all. The bugger's not returning my calls. Good mind to fly out there and see him for myself."

"I'll see what I can do, Maurice. I'll call some of his friends. One of them must know how to get hold of him."

"Eternally grateful, Alexi."

"Talking of getting hold of people, Maurice. I'm desperate to get the General to the Conference. Can you help?"

There was a pause.

"To be honest Alexi, I can't. We're not exactly friends, the General and I. I'm trying to get hold of him too. The bugger owes me quite a lot of money."

"How do you think I can get him to the Conference? You couldn't..."

"I'm afraid I can't afford to ask favours of the General at the moment – it would queer my pitch. Spoil a moment of carefully tuned tension." He pauses, and I can hear him pulling on a cigar. When he speaks again his voice is a warm hush, honeyed with trickling smoke.

"Between you and me, Alexi, I'm about to break the fucker's balls."

FRIDAY 26TH APRIL
MANOEUVRES

I give the General one last try. At last I get through to his secretary.

"Hello, I am calling from the Ministry of Finance. The Minister would like to invite the General to attend the Investment Conference."

"The General has already been asked to the Conference. By the President. He is unable to attend."

"Is it possible to arrange an appointment to see him? To pay him my compliments."

"I am afraid it is impossible to see the General without an appointment."

"But that's what I want, an appointment."

"You cannot speak to the General without an appointment," she repeats, shrilly. I put the phone down, giggling nervously.

"Do you think I'll ever get to talk to the General?" I ask Popoli, later that afternoon. He is sitting behind his desk in his tatty office, wearing a parker jacket with a fur hood.

"The General! Everybody wants to speak to him. The bloody President wants to speak to him. But people can only see the General when he wants to see them. He's the most powerful man in this country. He is paying the wages."

"Is he paying yours?"

He smiles. "Always questions, Alexi. No, he's not paying my wages, but one day… who knows. Sometimes I think that Conference or no Conference, one day my country falls down. The schemes will run out of money, everyone will blame President, there will be chaos. I do not want this to happen but sometimes... I lose hope. See this fax (he takes a piece of paper off his desk), listen and you will understand. We received it this morning:

> *Dear sirs,... I am international businessman in tourist industry... I like to develop Ambassador Club casinos on coast of Albania... situated on floating vessel... drinking and dancing girls... international clientele... near Saranda... I make one million dollars (American) investment... please assist me with licence and tax credits... etc.*

Popoli reads it out to me, until he loses his way.

"When did we last get fax from IBM or Daimler Benz. Never. Just faxes like this. It's not funny is it?"

"No," I reply, thinking about Richard, "it isn't."

SATURDAY 27ᵀᴴ APRIL
TAKING IT EASY

I spend most of the day sunbathing on Dritan's flat roof, listening to the radio, reading a novel and generally pretending I'm not in Albania. It isn't very easy. After lunch I am spotted by the gypsies. The young girl sees me first, prostrate on the flat roof, stripped to the waist and shiny with suncream. She begins to scream and her mother runs out and stares and soon they are all there, standing in the corridor of the derelict bus with a good view of me on the roof. It's impossible for someone under the constant, silent scrutiny of an entire family to relax. After a bit, father starts shouting abuse and I call it a day.

It's a difficult climb down from the roof. Dritan has an old iron ladder, missing a few rungs but otherwise fine. The tricky bit is manoeuvring onto the ladder, whose feet tend to skid alarmingly as you shift your weight onto it. This time the ladder falls sideways at a critical moment and I am left dangling off the side of the roof, my hands greasy with sun-cream. Looking down I have an untried view of the lemon tree before my hands give way. An imprecise parachute roll saves the day but the shouts of joy from the bus ring in my ears.

MONDAY 29TH APRIL
MISADVENTURE

Lunch with Anetsi and a blond Finn who has asked to see us. He has one blue and one brown eye. He is about my age and works for a Finnish cosmetics manufacturer. He wants to ask our advice.

'Open up the Albanian market' he has been told by his bosses in Helsinki. He arrived last night and is terrifically cheerful. He has no doubt that Albanian women will buy his make-up.

"They want the real thing. And more and more Albanian women can afford it." He carries an enormous briefcase full of samples. Out of it he produces a brochure with all the panache of magician and rabbit. His line is eyeshadow.

"You'd be a quiet green – avocado. Or a hazel," he tells me in spotless English.

"Do you sell a lot of it to men?"

"We do in Finland. It cheers them up during the winter months."

"Do you think that men in Albania will buy it?"

"I've still got to explore the market. We've got high hopes for Romania. But Albania – your guess is as good as mine. I'm optimistic."

"How are you going to sell it here?"

"Well, there's a company called Vari that has a chain of supermarkets." He is like a retriever puppy.

Walking home from the Ministry, it is a warm afternoon. The bulbs that have not been stolen from the communal beds around the pyramid are in flower. There is a trace of gaiety in the faces of the people I pass in the street. High up one slippery side of Hoxha's pyramid sit five urchins, bracing themselves with their sticky palms. The marble sides are steep and smooth. One-by-one, they let themselves slide down the slope, their palms and bare feet beating on the marble like brakes. Below a crowd of older boys howl them on. The last braces himself like a downhill skier and pushes off. Half way down his palm misses a brake and he gathers speed. His flailing arms cannot slow him, nor can his feet, now rapping down on the marble like steam hammers. Below him, his friends watch fascinated as he slides towards them. He hits the horizontal with a dramatic bump. His face moves from concentrated terror to sheer misery and he screams and screams. It looks (just) like he hasn't broken anything. His friends fall about and try to console him with a cigarette.

MAY

Richard arrived yesterday, ready for the final push. I meet him early for breakfast at the Dajti.

In the lobby we bump into Spartac, who waves us into his office and produces raki. In a corner sits a dapper man in a moustache. He is a DP Deputy. He is also Minister for Sport and well remembers Dritan's cycling triumphs.

"I too was a cyclist. I am still so strong," he smiles, flexing his biceps "I could be in the wrestling team!"

Spartac tells the Minister that I am a descendant of Winston Churchill. The Minister looks impressed.

Making the most of my elevation, I ask the Minister whether he would give me a tour of the parliament building.

"No," he says, with a twinkle in his eye, "even to a member of Churchill's *fis*. Anyway, it is shutting up for the summer. And I will tell you a little secret – it is a great relief. Parliament is not the same these days. There are not enough Socialists anymore. Sure they are arseholes but they make good arguments. And the fights we used to have – it was like being back in the army!"

"Come on," says Richard, who is impatient to see Popoli, and I drain my glass of raki and follow him out of the door.

Durres is also an important holiday centre for the masses of the people. It has three beaches, Durres, Currila and Golem. The main beach in Durres has 6 big tourist hotels where tourists from various countries of the world spend

245

their holidays, 1,200 rooms for hire and a number of hostels
for workers and pioneers. (AGO, p.69)

There is a heatwave and Suzana wants to go to the beach. The Durres road is slow with holiday traffic, full of families enjoying the beginning of summer. We are in Dylber's car which heats up like an oven. Out in the country we pick up speed and the breeze cools us down. Soft patches of tar stick to the tyres. We cross the Erzen river. From the bridge I can see children swimming in the river.

A couple of miles outside Durres, where the marshes have been drained to provide arable land, we run up against a traffic jam. It curls away around the side of a hill in front of us. Families have left their cars and are squatting by the side of the road, boys are playing football with their fathers.

The sun beats down. It is almost intolerable, but the jam is accepted – like every other delay and hardship met daily by the holiday makers. Dylber and Dritan are the same, grinning and shaking their heads. So we resign ourselves to the heat of the afternoon sun, sitting in our steel boxes. Dylber takes his shirt off to display Pop Hemingway body hair. Only Suzana, with her childlike enthusiasm for the beach, is impatient.

And then, quite suddenly, the queue responds as one to some deeply-propelled need for movement. Cars are backed up and turned all at once, there is hooting and minor collisions and all the time the sun throws off its temper. Dylber steers us down a dusty side road and through scruffy farmland and rural poverty into the outskirts of Durres. It is a roundabout route and poor farm children stand at the side of the road staring at this convoy of aspirational city dwellers with Queen blaring through their open car windows and bathing towels wrapped around their necks. The dust settles in their hair and that is how we

246

leave them, sucking their fingers and shyly watching our mechanised column.

The beach is crowded. Suzana is in a swim suit and Dritan rubs oil into her back. Dylber is impervious to the sun as he seems impervious to most things and lies on his elbows, watching the bathers trying to make something of the waves that drawl over the dark sand. His wife is still in Germany. Does he miss her? Does she take a lover in Munich and live the life of a bohemian? Perhaps he is just content to see her art prosper. There he sits, staring into the sea, and I ponder on still waters running deep and all that.

Around us Albanian families mill like actors playing holiday makers on a tourist beach. Only the costume department has a cheap line in men's swimwear, which tends towards the worn speedo look. Women wear flowery, shapeless costumes which stretch, barrel-tight, across fat bellies. The costume department is also out of the other everyday props of Mediterranean beach existence – sunglasses, beach balls, windbreaks, suncream, umbrellas and pedalos. Instead there are pink bodies toasting and a solitary game of football among aggressive, young men. Most men sit like Dylber, looking at the sea and smoking cigarettes. They don't really appear to be enjoying themselves. Are they just doing this for the show – because 'THE BEACH!' is where 'Voice of America' tells its Balkan listeners to head on the weekend. No, that is a silly thought. Heat and the cooling sea are not the preserve of California but, nonetheless, there is a self-consciousness about the whole event, as if everyone is a little worried that somehow they're not doing it right. Or that mother might suddenly appear through the pine trees and give them a thick ear.

We lunch off fried fish and chips cooked in a large bunker standing among a group of pines. Once it would have contained young men in uniform, sweating over a machine gun pointed out to sea. Now it is painted in pink and yellow flowers and the young men sweat over a stove, and dip small fish in a china bowl full of batter.

Dear Dritan insists on paying. Afterwards, we swim, which is disappointing. The water is too warm and very salty. I have the unpleasant sensation of leaving it feeling a little dirtier than when I entered. By the time we get home my hair is thick with salt and Dritan is the colour of boiled lobster. For the rest of the week his movements are exquisitely slow, as if he is performing an agonised form of ballet, or walking underwater.

MONDAY 6TH MAY
ACFIP

Popoli's busy so I wait outside in the hall, eating an ice cream. Ten minutes later two men, both carrying enormous briefcases emerge and walk smartly downstairs. "Russian mafia," he grins.

"What on earth are they doing here?" I ask him.

He shakes his head.

"They wanted to sell me some jet fighters. They think Albania might need them one day – Kosovo, Milosevic... Go to the Defence Ministry, I tell them, I have a Conference to prepare!"

Back outside Popoli's office I come across the Finn. He sits on one of the dusty chairs in the waiting room. I know that look. It is a look that the ACFIP engenders in a lot of energetic, hopeful people. His head is in his hands. His puppy eyes are bloodshot. A pile of cigarette butts lie between his feet. Beside him stands his briefcase.

"How's it going?" I ask him.

"OK. I'm a bit tired," he says, sheepishly.

"You look tired. You could do with some of your make-up."

Mrs Ademi is sick again. Her lawyer's earlier confidence has proved ill-placed. After much enquiring and petition-writing he has advised her to give the whole thing up and handed her a big bill. Dritan is still away down the corridor when I go to bed.

THURSDAY 9TH MAY
BREAKING THE BANK

A week to go. Tomorrow the first wave of Vito's invasion force lands in Tirana, to erect giant signs outside the Hotel advertising the Conference.

Richard wants some data on interest rates from the Central Bank for a speech he is writing.

"Would you pop over to the Bank, Alex? American on loan from the US Treasury, fellow called Glister, he's got the figures I need."

I cross busy Skanderberg Square, dodging the hooting cars and the black clouds of exhaust that squirt from the old buses. In front of the bank is 'Wall Street', the name given to the corner of the Square where the black market money changers congregate every day, a soukh's worth of bored men holding great cakes of cash and grubby calculators.

"Yes, sir", "change sir", "dollars" they shout as I walk past them.

But I have official business at the bank and I am sweating in my heavy wool suit. Messrs. Anderson & Sheppard of Saville Row could not possibly have imagined that twenty odd years on from the day that my father's winter-weight, navy herringbone walked out of the fitting room it would crop up in the thick of the Balkans. Neither could they have guessed quite how hot Tirana can get during May.

I climb the steps up to the large iron door of the Bank. The sun beats down on my back, the black metal throbs with heat. I press the buzzer on the intercom by the door. There is no answer. I push it again, and the wait intensifies the heat. It is three o'clock. I buzz again and this time an angry voice shouts back.

"Stop!"

"I have an appointment with Mr Glister."

"Ehhh?"

"I have an appointment with Mr Glister. The American."

"No."

"I have spoken to him on the telephone. I have an appointment."

"No!" screams the voice.

I lose my temper. I am in a hurry. I have an appointment. The sun crackles overhead, sweat runs down my back, face, legs. I try the door. It gives way.

"Thank you" I shout into the intercom and begin to push open the door.

"No. No!" screams the voice. But it is too late. I am going in.

The great black door gives slowly but with a shudder. From somewhere inside the door comes a low whine and there is a clicking sound, as if cogs are being disturbed. I keep pushing and step inside, into an oblong of bright yellow light, and on into a delicious cool. As my eyes adjust to the darkness I see a small reception desk. Behind it sits a small, furious-looking man. He is staring at me. His mouth is open. He looks from me to his desk, where he is pushing a button, again and again, jamming it down hard. There is silence. Then he looks up at the door and at a black box fastened above it, attached to the door by a strong looking metal arm. The box houses an engine for opening and closing the door. The engine has stopped working. Someone has broken his door. Me.

The man lets out the most enormous yell of rage – something between a werewolf and an angry baby. Leaving his desk he lunges towards me, grabbing the lapels of my suit. Looking into my eyes, he screams and screams. I am about a foot taller than him. Otherwise I might worry about being head-butted. Nonetheless it is irritating to be shaken and shouted at and I am about to shove him away when two soldiers with Kalashnikovs over their shoulders race around the corner. One draws his gun and covers me, and I find myself raising my arms as the other shouts for help.

Luckily, the next man on the scene is Glister, on his way to meet me. "What the hell's going on!" he says.

"I'm afraid I've broken your front door." I reply, my hands raised above my head.

"Goddam! Well, sure looks like you won't be invited back. Hey buddy, come on! Take your hands off him."

I push the receptionist's trembling hands away from me and give what I hope is a diplomatic smile. More Albanians appear and I am terribly apologetic and talk in long sentences to confuse them.

"Prime Minister," I repeat ominously, catching the receptionist's eye.

It takes five minutes with Glister to get the information I need. He is anxious to get rid of me. On the way out I wave to the receptionist who is hunched over his control panel, muttering to himself. Seeing me his face curls in menace and he points at me, as if to say 'I'll have you, boyo'. The door is stuck fast, frozen in my image. The two soldiers have put down their automatic rifles and are trying to push it shut, straining and puffing.

FRIDAY 10TH MAY
LOW PROFILE

They are still fixing the door when I walk home past the bank. A soldier stands guard outside to compensate for the compromised security arrangements. Behind him a group of men in overalls are preparing to take the door off its hinges. I imagine the white hot wrath of the receptionist, his peace interfered with, his importance muted for a day

251

or two. Perhaps he is this minute planning some reckless act of revenge. Shuddering at the thought I hurry past, looking the other way.

Dylber is asleep on Dritan's sofa. Snoring under a pile of blankets, like some hibernating bear. The flickering television in the corner is showing Albania's national singing championships. The guests of honour are the President and the General, who hands over the winner's cheque to a blushing young girl from Elbasan.

SUNDAY 12TH MAY
LAST MINUTE PREPARATIONS

A busy weekend, spent finishing off briefing papers for the Conference. Richard running at an impressive speed. He has worked until two or three am for the last few nights, but is there every morning at seven thirty, eating breakfast in the Dajti, bright-eyed and stubbornly good-humoured.

MONDAY 13TH MAY
THE URCHINS

Vito has arrived with a coven of beauties from Bari. He is surrounded by them in the downstairs bar of the Tirana. Blondes, brunettes and a redhead sip cocktails around him. One of them (the redhead) is his fiancée. Vito is drinking an Americano, a bitter drink favoured by James Bond. Leaning back in his chair, he shakes the ice cubes against the glass.

"Ahh, Alex. We have been expecting you," he drawls like Bloefeld.

Vito is hungry and takes us all out to supper. On the way to the restaurant we are spotted by the urchins who run up, palms upheld. The girls are prettily disturbed and I play the old hand, swearing at them in Albanian.

"Now they'll go away," I murmur reassuringly. They don't and I end up giving them money and whispering "now piss off" under my breath. In the restaurant a violinist plays a frantic gypsy waltz. This place is plush and polished, with good service, and a long wine list. It is easy to forget that we are sitting no more than fifty metres from the urchins who are at this moment probably searching for fag ends in the gutter.

On our way home the urchins throw a firecracker at us. They stand back with satisfied faces to watch the result. It lands between the girls, its blue fuse fizzing. Carefully I stand on it, grinding it under my heel like a Gestapo officer crushing a suspect's fingers. This followed by a cold stare at the urchins. As we walk on they rush to inspect it. I feel rather pleased with myself. Seconds later a stone hits Vito's fiancee on the back of the head. Mike's advice rings in my ears: 'You want to watch that lot. Never take them on. They're dangerous.'

TUESDAY 14TH MAY
CONFERENCE EVE

Outside the Tirana an enormous wooden hoarding advertising the Conference has been mounted on stilts. Last night the urchins set fire to it but the doorman saw them off before they could do too much damage. One stilt is a little charred.

Vito is too busy to indulge his impressive temper. The lobby of the Tirana has been transformed. Four check-in counters have been constructed in one cool marbled corner, where the delegates will sign in on arrival. Each will be manned by a smiling member of the coven dressed in a red uniform like an upmarket air hostess. An 'information point' is being set up opposite the main doors and the walls jostle with signposts and agendas to direct the confused executive. Upstairs, finishes are being made to the Conference room, which now has booths running down one wall where the simultaneous translators will sit. But there is still the PA system to check and the TV crew to brief and the catering manager to meet. So Vito is busy, sweating in a sky blue silk shirt and, but for an hour over lunch, rushing about like a madman.

It is my birthday and Suzana has baked a cake. Dritan, Dylber and I drink too much raki out on the terrace. Dylber takes one of his wife's paintings off the wall and hands it to me. Dritan promises me a graft from the lemon tree. He wants me to plant it in England.

WEDNESDAY 15TH MAY
UNDESIRABLES

A fat Greek arrives from Brussels called Potopoulos. He is a G24 'Officer' and 'Task Manager' for the Conference. Potopoulos is easily placed in Brussels' menagerie – a bird of reasonable plumage, halfway up a tall tree, able to whistle tunes to order. So far his contribution to the Conference has been nil. Now he descends, like some metropolitan grandee, to stick his nose in and shout at the natives. He sweats a great deal and seems ill at ease outside the broad city walls.

Potopoulos' principal concern is that the Conference pleases his boss, the Spanish Co- Chairman of the G24. He has to be reassured that all the right people have been asked and that we have been sycophantic to those that deserve it. The EU Ambassador is summoned and together they check tomorrow night's menu, try the Spaniard's Conference chair for comfort, even check out the Spaniard's hotel room.

"Please leave us while we inspect the bed," Potopoulos squeaks at Vito.

Potopoulos' other priority is that the Conference be inundated with Greeks – as committee chairmen, as floor speakers, on top table, lined up to meet the President…

In the lobby of the Tirana delegates are standing in line, waiting to check in with one of Vito's smiling girls. Talking to a few is Richard, who is wearing a pinstripe suit. He stands there, tall and smiling, with his hands clasped behind his back like an ambassador. Richard would make a very good ambassador.

The delegates look fed up. A red-faced German in a fragile pair of spectacles and a checked jacket is muttering to himself as he grinds a cigarette out on the marble floor. Despite Vito's efforts to get them VIP treatment the delegates have had a bruising experience at Rinas airport. It warms my heart a little – the picture of a pampered financier wrestling his Louis Vuitton luggage from one of the airport urchin. But now the delegates are in Vito's sanctum, in the soft hands of his girls who sign them in and hand them their room keys and colourful satchels filled with conference bumph. Vito emerges to stand beside Richard. He is wearing a navy, silk suit and a yellow Hermes tie. His hair is damp and slick, fresh from the shower. He smells deliciously of citrus.

But smelling deliciously of citrus won't make the queues of delegates disappear, or persuade the clock to stand still. It is ten to five. Many of the delegates have re-emerged from their rooms and are now taking up their seats in the conference room. But there are still twenty to thirty people queuing to check in. They are blocking up the lobby with their suitcases and briefcases and soft-eared copies of the International Herald Tribune. The President and Prime Minister are due to arrive in ten minutes.

Richard has got through to the President's office. They have agreed to stall his departure by ten minutes, but no more. Major disaster averted. But Richard has not been able to stop the Prime Minister, who is this very minute approaching in a black Mercedes flying a flag and paced by outriders, sirens singing his way through the rush hour traffic. I can hear them now, approaching across Skanderberg Square as I look down on the Hotel lobby from my vantage point up the stairs. Now the sirens have stopped, doors clunk, doormen salute and in through the glass doors of the hotel walks the Prime Minister, a small, bald man with a moustache and quick feet which rush him up to Vito and Richard, hand outstretched, mouth turned in a not insincere smile.

Vito has prepared a VIP suite near the conference room. Where speakers can gargle and pull their thoughts together and check that their flies are not undone, and premature Prime Ministers can preserve their dignity. Richard and Vito confer quickly. Richard escorts the Prime Minister up the stairs, stooping to talk quietly to the low-down Albanian, explaining the problem. The Prime Minister nods. It looks like a beautiful little piece of crisis management, until they get to door of the suite and discover that it is locked.

"Key. Key!" hisses Richard, looking at Vito, me and then the lurking hotel manager, who turns neatly on his Swiss heel and canters back down the stairs. Various ministers arrive, looking about them self-consciously. The Deputy Prime Minister (a.k.a Minister for Tourism and the Environment) waves over the hotel manager, who is on his way to his office to get a key for the VIP suite. The Deputy Prime Minister presumes the manager is graciously coming to greet him. He pumps the Swiss' hand and hands him his coat. Upstairs, the Prime Minister is getting impatient, standing outside the locked door like a bellboy.

The President arrives in a black Mercedes. White flashlight bounces off its buffed sides. TV cameramen race past the glass doors of the hotel and behind them walks the President, grinning. Vito, who has just taken his eye off the Prime Minister (as Richard leads him up another flight of stairs, bound for the privacy of the Terraza Bar) greets the

President warmly, all the time smelling deliciously of citrus. Richard is with the Prime Minister in the Terraza Bar, making small talk and apologising. The Prime Minister is taking it pretty well.

Vito leads the President up the stairs, out of the camera-clicking lobby, towards the conference room which is on the first floor. Behind him Vito's girls giggle by their check-in desks. The queue has gone. The last delegate was checked in five minutes ago. On the stairs, Vito and the President are ringed by heavy security men. By the time the presidential entourage has reached the first floor the delegates have taken their seats in the conference room. The late arrivals have sat down next door where they can see an empty podium on the screen.

In one corner of the conference room, not far from the podium, a TV camera aims at the door. Just in time to catch the Prime Minister waddling up the aisle besides Richard (they have scurried back down the stairs and nipped in front of the presidential guns, cameras, escort and person just in the nick of time). And, after an appropriate pause, enter the President, on his own (the guns, cameras and escort have peeled off and returned quietly to port). His shiny black hair flapping slightly, his shoulders filling out a nicely cut suit, the President strides up to the podium. He grips it with two hairy hands.

"Ladies and Gentlemen..." The Conference has begun.

Afterwards there is an evening reception on the hotel terrace. Richard introduces me to the President, dapper and smiling. Blue shirt, bright red tie, matching handkerchief. Just like John.

"Congratulations on your great efforts," he tells me, squeezing my hand.

"Thank you, Excellency." (I have always wanted to say 'Thank you, Excellency'. Much more than plain old 'Mr Mayor'.)

"You are a friend of the Professor's I believe."

"Yes. I'm sorry he's had to leave."

"A great shame."

Below, Tirana hoots and skids by. It is a balmy evening. I talk to the Minister of Finance, awkwardly balancing his plate of chicken and a glass of wine. I ask him what happened to the old Director for Public Policy Administration, whose office I now occupy. He smiles sadly.

"He drowned in Lake Ohrid. It was after a romantic lunch. His wife was in Tirana."

Shortly, two merchant bankers from London muscle in. The terrace is noisy and crowded. After everyone has gone to bed I sit up with Vito. The terrace is calm again and the air cooler. Vito is jubilant. Day one has gone well. I drink several martini cocktails and stumble home, indifferent to the threat of dogs.

FRIDAY 17TH MAY
CONFERENCE DAY TWO

Laco chairs the morning's session. He is looking groomed and healthy and full of chutzpah, fresh from a work out and freshly squeezed orange juice. I have already seen the Doctor, shuffling about on his flat feet. He winked at me as we passed each other in the lobby.

During the morning coffee break I chat to the Professor's cousin, the former Minister whose fate I listened to with bated breath on the radio, that gloomy January afternoon in the Professor's sitting room.

"What's happened to the Professor?"

"He is in USA – teaching economics at university in Washington."

"Is he alright?"

"He says he is OK but I do not believe. He should be here in Albania. In America he drinks too much."

Richard speaks just before lunch. 'Creating an investment-friendly environment.' It is well attended, the Prime Minister comes along especially. In the afternoon, the Spanish Co-Chairman of the G24 chairs a session on 'Joint Ventures and Privatisations'. The Finance Minister follows, looking lean and cross in his grey suit, describing the government's mass privatisation programme.

"Courageous, realistic... just what the doctor ordered" translates the young man in the interpreter's booth.

To dinner at the Palace of Brigades. Outside the hotel, buses wait to take us to Zog's palace. As the international businessmen shuffle out to the bus the urchins move in. Sleeves are pulled, hands offered up as if in prayer. Dirty little fingers point to empty little mouths while doe eyes look sad and hungry. Hooray for the urchins.

Inside the Palace, ministers and bureaucrats rub shoulders with Australian mining tycoons and Dutchmen from Siemens. It is insufferably hot. I chat to Mr Skenderi, head of KESH, who is my favourite utility chairman. He has the requisite glossy silver hair and heavy jowls and the manner of a kindly uncle. How fine he would look in a pinstripe suit. Rama, head of AlbTelecom is too small and technical. Xasher of AlbPetrol is an ex-communist dud. But Skenderi is the genuine article. He is just back from a fact-finding mission to the UK.

"How is it?" I ask.

"Very well," he smiles. "The tube is what I cannot believe. It is so confusing. Like the maze at Hampton Court." He is fascinated by Henry VIII and all his wives.

Across the banqueting hall run long rows of tables, set for dinner. Despite the chandeliers, the great room is gloomy. Across the walls great tapestries describe mountain ranges and the heroic silhouette of Skanderberg. A castle stands on a bluff above a river and the dark mass of trees. Below the hideous figure of a wolf sits the Prime Minister, looking like a don presiding over top table. Richard is nearby. I am sitting next to the Finn. He's back to his terrifically cheerful self.

"How did it go at the ACFIP?" I ask.

"OK. There are a few problems. But I'm not concerned."

"How come?"

"I met this girl last night at Vari's night club. She's really something."

"Albanian?"

"Yeah. We're going to Saranda together for the weekend."

He is beaming in two colours.

Opposite, a couple of Albanians get very drunk and fall about, telling jokes to each other. In fact everyone seems to be getting very drunk and the temper of the room is shrill and it is terrifically hot. All the food seems to be covered in dill. I will never be able to eat dill again without thinking about Albania and Zog's hot banqueting hall.

Through the shouting comes the ring of a glass being tapped with a knife. The Prime Minister and all the other ministers and diplomats fall quiet but the rest of the room haven't heard. The ringing of the glass rises to a crescendo and then the glass breaks. Peals of laughter. Someone calls for quiet.

The Prime Minister is on his feet, talking, but around me no one is paying attention. His pate is shiny under the television lights. I can see his lips moving but all I hear is my rowdy neighbours and the clatter of people eating. The two English merchant bankers look sternly in our direction and shake their heads. Their emotional home is the Mansion House, not the southern Balkans.

Suddenly the Prime Minister is seated and I have heard not a word of his speech. There is great clapping, the loudest from my end of the room, where faces are greasy with drink.

Outside we queue for the buses. I sit next to the Chargé. We are good-humoured after the supper. As the bus labours back through Tirana we chat about the Professor.

"I don't think he's coming back."

The Chargé shrugs.

"Heard anything from Maurice?"

SATURDAY 18TH MAY
CONFERENCE DAY THREE

Just before lunch the Prime Minister and the Spaniard from Brussels hold a press conference. 'Encouraging progress', 'genuine interest from the international delegates gathered here', 'of course there is a long way to go, but government has all the right policies in place, etc, etc'. The Conference is over. But it has been a great success. Richard has triumphed. Vito, still smelling deliciously of citrus looks on, delighted, from the shadows. No one has mentioned the pyramid schemes.

In the lobby, Godo is at my shoulder, bouncing up and down like Tigger.

"Alexi, how do you do!" he bounces and shakes me warmly by the hand. He is very excited.

"I have new job, Alex, in the private sector. With Deutsche transport company. I am now the Albanian manager. On good money. Substantial package. Paid in dollars. US dollars. Oh yes!" He looks fit to burst into song as he bounces off into Skanderberg Square.

Richard is on an evening flight to London. I say goodbye, sadly because it has been so much fun. He is a fine man, with so many virtues – gentleness, curiosity, determination, enthusiasm, energy, a sense of the ridiculous. He has done such a good job here. I shall miss him very much.

"It's been fun, hasn't it," he says with a grin. "What on earth are you going to do now?"

When I was young, soon after my father died, I had a recurring dream. Into sunny, cine-camera footage of our street in London walked a man. He was tall and he wore a pale suit and a panama hat. In the dream I am playing in the street but, when I see the man approaching, I break away from my friends to stand and watch, fascinated. I recognise his build, and the pace of his feet. His hat is one I have worn myself many times, its straw insides itching my scalp.

"Daddy," I shout. He has come home, as I always knew he would. I run towards him, shouting his name. He pauses in front of our house and I am catching him up.

"Daddy, daddy!" I am almost there, my hands reaching out to him when he turns to look at me. I peer into the shade of his face and he smiles at me and waves, and turns away.

In every dream he turns away, and I would wake in floods of tears. Last night I had the same dream. The same figure, the same sense of relief and excitement at recognising him. But this time I cannot reach him. I run and run and he gets no closer. I shout his name but this time he doesn't hear. Then he turns and walks away, a small figure in the distance, walking away down the road.

I hear my feet clicking down the cold corridor of the Ministry for the last time. The place is deserted. There is no crowd outside the front door, no policeman inside, no echoes of laughter or slamming doors. I clear out my office, and go to leave the bronze key on Anetsi's desk. Next door sits Katrina, his pretty assistant. We stare at each other surprised, like two apocalypse survivors who had thought they were all that was left of mankind.

Skanderberg is empty. I cross it towards Dritan's house, a

cardboard box in my hand. Suddenly there is a sharp nudge at my shoulder. It is Gaz. His grey face is smiling, he looks older and uglier. It is Gaz.

"I saw you on the Square. I couldn't believe it. I followed you here."

"Just like old times."

"I said to myself 'God is generous, it is my old friend Alex!' How are you?" Premature crows feet hold up the bright eyes. The magic is still there. Who am I speaking to – is it the PLO or the PhD?

"You are leaving?"

"Yes."

"Without telling me."

I am too exasperated to answer.

"I am desperate. I had good job working as security for Swiss Embassy. Very good job. But the budget was cut and... no money left."

"Didn't you manage to save any?" He hasn't. And he expects me to do something about it.

"I haven't enough to eat. What am I going to do?"

"Go away Gaz. Go away and help yourself."

"But Alex, you promised…"

I am already walking away. He runs after me. Grabbing the back of my jacket.

I spin around. "Fuck off Gaz. I can't help you. I've got nothing to give you. I am going home." My voice booms across the empty plain of Skanderberg Square. A flock of pigeons lift into the air while the two of us confront one another like angry lovers.

MONDAY 20TH MAY
THE GENERAL

I am back in the Terraza Bar – this place has had a womb-like quality

263

for me ever since I retreated here after my mugging. This is where I drank with Vito. This is where I was spooked by Eda. This is where Richard brought the stranded Prime Minister the evening of the Conference. I have played much of my Albanian life out on this small stage. Today the bar is empty – it is mid-afternoon. Tomorrow I am going home.

Out of the lift walks the General, under a shock of frizzy, grey white hair. He wears an open raincoat over a shiny blue suit. The trousers are too short and they show off white socks and a fussy pair of slip-ons. He wears several rings on his fingers. He is short and plump with stubby hands and the face of a dishonest squaddy. The General's slip-ons tap across the floor of the bar as he drifts past. Either side of him walk two black-suited heavies. The General looks me in the eye, swanky and cool, and takes a drag on his cigarette. There goes the man of the moment.

The Swiss hotel manager appears, full of 'I heard that you were here sir and just thought I'd come and make sure that you were being looked after'. He has dropped his customary dourness and doesn't recognise me. Moments later a couple of men trickle in and enter the booth, under the impassive eye of the hoods. One of them is a DP politician I recognise from the Conference.

There is low-key muttering and a little laughter. I do my best to eavesdrop but all that I can hear is in Albanian. Coffee is brought by a gawping waiter. No doubt he is a Vari share-holder. After forty minutes the men leave and I seize my chance. Journalist's notebook in one hand I smile up to one of the bodyguards and look past him into the booth. The General is combing his hair.

"General" I say. Already the man is pushing me away.

"Alex Hickman of the uhhh… Economist magazine," I clatter into the booth, "the Economist of London? Could I possibly have two minutes... I've come all the way from London just to talk to you." Our eyes meet again, comb is put carefully back in inside pocket of his jacket, a gentle nod and the muscle retracts and there is space enough for me to slip through into the booth.

On the table strays the offspring of Balkan commerce – plastic wallets, a filofax, Marlboro, a full ashtray, a mobile phone. Opposite me sits Albania's richest man, the President's friend, the ruling party's banker, the subject of a thousand conversations in cafés and kitchens up and down the country. I am looking at a scoop – I am looking straight into the horse's mouth.

"Can I get you anything to drink?"

He raises a plump right hand. No, he is fine..."Thank you," he says after a pause, watching me carefully. I put my notebook on the table and place my pen on top of it.

"Do you mind if I ask you a few questions?"

"It depends on the questions."

"Well..." The mobile phone bleeps and almost immediately it is at his ear.

"Yes. Ahh Maurice... I have been expecting your call. One moment please." He looks frightened.

"Excuse me, Mr Hickman. I have business to attend to." He leaves me with a shrug and a goodbye. He taps off in his slip-ons. The bodyguards snap to attention and wipe their gun hands down the sides of their trousers. Maurice.

On my way out I spot the Finn, sitting in a corner of the lobby with a statuesque young woman and three large men. The girl is wiping her eyes with a white handkerchief. It is Eda. The Finn holds his head in his hands. In front of him on the table climbs a mountain of spent cigarettes. Three more are being smoked by the three Ghegs who sit implacably facing the Finn.

The chickens, as they say in Tropoja, are coming home to roost.

Skanderberg's fountains clatter into their chipped pools. Around them splash the urchins, who seem to have taken the day off. They fight over a small rubber dinghy. The winner lies back in it, bobbing around the fountain with a cigarette between his teeth.

Nearby, the Chargé is giving a party in his offices. Like me, he's leaving Albania – off to a hotel room in some recently independent capital of Eurasia where he will hang his Union Flag out of the window like a distress signal. I chat to the new commercial consul, a former economics lecturer at Tirana University.

"You British! Always asking questions," she sighs as I peer at the label on an enormous cardboard box fresh from London. It is a new ping-pong table for Paul.

Gzim is waiting in the road. My favourite taxi driver in Tirana, polishing his Volvo and smiling like a genie. This morning I love that car – it has 'escape' and 'freedom' written all over it. I pat its roof as I climb in.

"Good car," I say, as if it was a favourite dog. Gzim pounds the dashboard with his fist and shouts 'Wolvo. *Very* good car, *very* good car. Wolvo!" And we smile at one another like proud parents. We drive away towards the airport, the fan whirring like a lawnmower.

Above Rinas airport dark clouds are gathering. Warm rain falls. The airport is in chaos. A policeman slaps a young man trying to worm his way through the crowd, leaving the imprint of his hand on the man's cheek. Waiting for me are Dylber, Dritan and Suzana. They have come in the Chargé's Discovery.

Dylber helps me haul my bags out of the back of the Volvo. Then he grips my hand in his, iron hard.

"Good trip," he says and then turns, embarrassed.

"Goodbye Gzim, thank you for all the driving" and I pat the bonnet of the Volvo. Gzim stands to attention, his tweed jacket straining over his round stomach. I walk towards the check-in queue with Dritan and Suzana. She is crying. I am embarrassed. I kiss her. She hands me a bunch of plastic flowers, done up in a red ribbon.

Dritan smiles awkwardly.

"Farewell, Alexi." Farewell. How often do those words bear their true meaning. He has been my greatest friend here – kind, gentle, fun. Without him things would have been very different. I remember my rescue from Loti, our evening chats, our shared suppers and morning coffee, our trip to the beach. How we tried to give up smoking together and both failed. I realise, suddenly, that all my cares for this country, all my interest in its success are focused on him. I want it to be a better place for Dritan. As I board the plane my image of Albania is of Dritan's smiling, patient face as he stands by Suzana, juggling his keys in his hand.

The propellers take us up over Rinas and into cloud. Over the intercom the first officer tells us that the going is good, although 'we do expect a bit of chop, yes a little bit of chop'. I picture his moustache. Next to me sits a woman, plump and dark and dressed in a seventies khaki leather suit. The woman is called Pranvera, like Hoxha's daughter. It means 'Spring'. Pranvera is a lawyer working in the Ministry of Labour. She is off to Athens to stay with her sister who is married to a Greek.

"How long will you be in Greece?"

"I do not know. Perhaps I don't go back," she says archly. Xhaja, Leda, the Professor. Now Spring is leaving Albania. It seems ominous in some silly way. The plane bobs about in thermals. Behind me, Albania settles into memory. It is getting dark and there is a storm on the way.

EPILOGUE

When it hits, the storm ravages the country. Before long the pyramid schemes crash. The General and his bodyguard disappear. He's probably sunning himself somewhere in Mauritius or the Cayman Islands at this very moment. Or did Maurice nab him in time to lock him up in a Sofia safe-house, and extract Swiss bank account numbers out of him with those antifreeze eyes and a pair of pliers?

Whatever the General's whereabouts, he was well away from Albania, where tens of thousands are ruined and blaming the government. They vent their anger in violent anti-government demonstrations unseen since the fall of communism.

The President admits that the government was too slow to act against the schemes and wrong not to warn the people of their frailty. Pyramid schemes are declared illegal. But it is too late. The people want compensation but the government is broke.

"We cannot eat your words," shout the crowds in Skanderberg Square.

The President orders Laco down to Lushnja in an attempt to placate the demonstrators there. He is a well-chosen emissary: the Dardha Investment Company is bust, the Argentine coach is packing his bags and Lushnja has become enemy territory. Diplomacy is badly needed. But within moments of climbing out of his helicopter, poor Laco is seized by the angry mob, a turnip is forced into his mouth and he is dragged along the ground by his silk tie. Diplomacy doesn't get a look in. Laco and his ShIK bodyguards eventually barricade themselves inside Lushnja's football club. Rescue comes several hours later: Mr Skenderi switches off Lushnja's electricity supply and special forces are sent in after dark to extract the beleaguered minister and his terrified guards. This is no ordinary crisis.

Protest turns to rebellion. Much of the country becomes lawless.

Wild Vlora, whose prosperous local mafia has lost millions, becomes the centre of a rebel uprising, who demand the resignation of the President and his government. Anarchy spreads through the south, from town to town – Tepelena, Saranda, Fier, Gjirokaster... Army and police stores are looted for weapons. Soon the centre and then the north of the country are also heavily armed. The sympathetic military (plenty of soldiers and policemen have lost money in the schemes) stand aside. Unopposed, the 'rebels' divide into violent gangs, which take to vandalism and robbery; and ordinary citizens, who become their victims. Death from accidental shootings becomes commonplace. From Vlora and the south the rebellion spreads to Elbasan and then Tirana. The terrified President sends his family to Italy as expatriates are lifted off the Durres beaches by the Italian navy. Britain sends in the SAS to rescue isolated nationals.

Behind them, Albania boils over. At the beginning of March the President sacks his little Prime Minister and the rest of his government in an attempt to placate the rebels. A government of national reconciliation is formed and a young socialist and former mayor of Gjirokaster becomes Prime Minister. The new man disbands the hated ShIK, declares a week-long arms amnesty and appeals to members of the police and armed forces to return to their posts. He also appeals for international assistance. The Italians, who are once more receiving refugees by the boat load, offer to lead an international relief force into the country. The force waits only for a mandate from a grateful UN before setting sail from Italy. Hours later, Italy's greatest battleship runs aground off Durres.

Closely behind the Italians comes 'King' Leka, flying in from Johannesburg, a tall malcontent stalking the streets with pearl-handled pistols on his hips. He fancies himself the saviour of his people, ready to deliver them out of chaos. In fact they don't trust him or the ultranationalist crowd he hangs around with. An emergency referendum on the re-establishment of the monarchy is defeated and the final adventure of the Zog dynasty seems to be over.

Elections are also held, with the help of the Italian-led force, and are judged to be as free and fair as could be hoped for in the circumstances. The SP win and the President swaps State House for Parliament, where he is now leader of the DP opposition.

In just five years Albania is back where it started – socialists with links to the communist regime are in power, the country is broke and propped up by foreign aid, the country torn apart by anarchy. Its people are exhausted, impoverished, wary of the state, reluctant to risk hope. And the country is awash with guns – every family has an AK47 – just right for the next tit-for-tat revenge killing. Crate loads are being smuggled over the mountains to Kosovo, arming the angry KLA, now threatening rebellion against Belgrade.

The AK47s are the ideal work tool for the mafia, who now control towns like Vlora and Saranda. The mafia men remain at least capitalists. There is a danger that many of their countrymen will by now have written it off as a bad job. After all, the mafia are the only clear winners at this new game, with its bitter rules that go up and down, taking out the unprotected and the foolhardy. Creating losers. Albania has become a nation of losers. The people have lost their money. The President, the pro-democracy warrior, is disgraced. His economic miracle shafted by the peculiar mathematics of the pyramid schemes.

I can best try to comprehend the country's chaos in human terms. Tragic terms. Dritan fortifying his compound, locking in the lemon tree. The Dajti being sprayed with bullets, Spartac's cellar raided by thugs who down the last of the good reisling from the bottle. I know that Fidel's café, a well-known opposition haunt, was torched, probably by ShIK. Did Genc convert his Fiat into an armoured car and drive down the gate of the fish farm to duff up the man in waders? Or did he make a tidy sum ferrying Greek journalists about the battlefield. Poor Gergj, who cares so much for his country, watching it splinter about him, but busy at least with the ECMM, on red alert in spotless white, pointing their Land Rovers towards new shifting borders as the rebels park their tanks in sight of Tirana. Gzim putting the Wolvo under canvas in some Tirana backstreet, praying that an armed posse doesn't snatch it for a runabout. Eda padding dreamily about some tented brothel near the front lines, servicing the ShIK thugs. Safet screaming '*inshallah*' as he guns the bullet-splattered Opel at another road block.

And Anetsi, Ibrahim, John, Baba, the fat woman, Katrina... Leda well out of it by now perhaps, like Konda watching the pictures on late night cable in the middle fortune of the States. Not far from the Professor, who is in Washington and doesn't come home in his country's darkest hour. Why not? Why not? This was his chance to play white knight, a Balkan de Gaulle, forming his cabinet in some nearby foreign capital. I watched the Professor one night on the BBC. He looked tired and depressed. The stuffing has been kicked out of him – boof, boof. By his wise guy students? By the memories of home? By the cheap bourbon? The intellectual, the idealist, the great dreamer – pray to the booze like too many handsome boys with a turn of phrase before him. The hero of the revolution, the Professor of the silver brain, who had been born to greatness. And now greatness was thrust upon him. So why didn't he come home – this was his time. It was a flight away, a rattle of helicopter blades and he would be stabbing the tarmac at Rinas, TV crews at his shoulder. But he funked it.

And Gaz. What happened to Gaz? Did he profit from the anarchy that bombed about? He had little to lose. Strangely I cannot picture him with a gun or in the forefront of looters, despite his stone thrower looks. But Gaz was born out of the tortured Albanian soul. He carried anger and self-doubt and arrogance and passion about with him. It clung to him, masking his natural smell. If Hoxha had a son it was Gaz. He would have made a quick lawyer with a good nose for wine in the west. But in his homeland Gaz is just another gaunt nobody, trawling the streets, marking time on the pavements. Ruined by his father, a redundant piece of flesh, saved perhaps for eternity on an anthropologist's tape recorder.

Can I think of any winners? Maurice of course. Albania's collapse was good news for him – there are rumours that he made a packet out of the crisis, buying up looted guns at \$5 a head and shipping them out to Rwanda and the Sudan. I heard him speak the other day, at a press conference held in London on behalf the new SP government. He sat up on stage, in swanky pinstripes as the Albanian Ambassador introduced him as a 'valued adviser' to the government. Maurice had just lead a 'business taskforce' to Tirana and sipped water during a searching question about plans to rescue the ailing chrome industry.

And what about me? By the time Albania blew up I was working in the City, and doing a bit of part-time writing on Albania. Enough to be billed 'country expert' on satellite tv programmes, sweating nervously into camera. I never thought much of my analysis, and not one of my predictions ever came true, but no one seemed to mind and the receptionists at work got used to the car from Bloomberg or European Business News turning up at lunchtime to take me to the studio. Sitting in make-up one morning, while a woman dusted my cheeks with some of the poor Finn's blusher, I realised that Albania's transition mirrored the story of my father's family. Poverty rescued by the forcing pull of history and a bit of fortune. Nouveau riche confidence, the chimera of settled prosperity, then tragedy which may, or may not, have been self inflicted. Well – self inflicted in Albania's case, with my father I will never know. But, if the moment that he injected a radioactive potion into his veins was fatal or not, the gambling desire for achievement, for progress, was one he shared with the President and his men. In Albania I have not come face to face with my father, but I have come closer to his soul.

Descendants of the Illyrians, who settled in the western Balkans around 1000 BC, Albanians have been kicked about for most of their unhappy history. Subjugation and persecution is a legacy of Albania's small size as well as the lack of any strong political cohesion before the 1940s. It is also the result of the country's geographic position on the borderline between east and west, between Islam and Christianity. As history has blown itself out across the Balkans, and the armies of east and west have in turn billowed their flags across its pieces, Albania has swapped political masters.

After being absorbed into the Holy Roman Empire, conquered by the Bulgarians and then the Serbs, Albania was invaded by the Ottomans in the fifteenth century. Resistance to Muslim conquest was led by Gjergj Skanderberg, whom modern Albanians regard as a national hero. A soldier and a Christian, Skanderberg was dubbed the 'Champion of Christendom' by Pope Nicholas V. He died in 1467 of a fever and Albania was left, undefended, to the Turks. The Ottoman policy of dishing out favoured treatment (such low taxation) to its Muslim subjects persuaded the majority of Albanians to convert. And those that remained Christian (Catholic or Orthodox) paid for it (mainly through higher taxation). By 1912, when Ottoman rule was overthrown, around 70% of Albanians were Muslim, 20% were Orthodox and 10% Roman Catholic. Despite the fact that the religious attitude of the elite and even many ordinary people was pragmatic, religious identity had become an important part of the country's political language. And the Ottomans' religious heritage left Albania isolated – a Muslim enclave surrounded by Orthodox Greece, Macedonia and Serbia.

The Turks left behind them a feudal and impoverished country. Political power was dispersed among rival clans, dominated by a few land-owning families; banditry was rife. With the rest of Europe on the edge of mechanised slaughter, pastoral Albania was an echo of the Middle Ages. The absence of unifying government was important because it made the country vulnerable to two threats: invasion and communism. The former came almost immediately, as the First World War gave Albania's neighbours an excuse to occupy chunks of its territory. At the post-war (1919) Paris Peace Conference Serbia, Greece and Italy all laid claim to parts of Albania but were beaten off by an Albanian delegation led by Aubrey Herbert MP. However, it was not until June 1920, when a popular uprising forced out occupying Italian forces, that Albania became properly independent. In the same year she was made a member of the League of Nations and in 1921 the country was recognised as an independent nation. But attempts to establish parliamentary democracy failed and the country quickly reverted to its traditional pleasures of feuding and thieving.

Some are better at feuding and thieving than others and in 1926 Zog, a powerful clan leader from the north, declared himself Zog I, King of the Albanians. Zog's rule, bankrolled by Italy, brought about a period of stability and economic and social modernisation. But Italy's influence was remorseless and Zog was increasingly seen as a puppet of Rome. Then came the Second World War and Mussolini, anxious to emulate his expansionist ally in Berlin, ordered Italian troops back into Albania.

Communism was taken in fearful doses under a vicious war hero called Enver Hoxha. Hoxha was a first class shit. One of history's criminals. The same height as Hitler. And just as spiteful. Like Tito, Hoxha used war-time resistance leadership to springboard himself into post-war power. Albanian resistance to Italian and then German occupation was split between the pro-monarchy nationalists (mainly made up of northerners) and the communist Partisans, mainly recruited from the south. Both movements were assisted by the Allies, particularly the British, who sent members of the Cairo-based Special Operations Executive (men like Patrick Leigh Fermor, Leo Amery and David Smiley) up into the mountains to lend a hand.

Hoxha's partisans forces were more effective than the nationalists and they were soon receiving the bulk of allied assistance and making the running in the war against the Axis troops. In November 1944 Hoxha's partisans re-occupied Tirana. He had already turned on the nationalists and chased the likes of Smiley out of the country. Now Hoxha set about establishing a one-party state. In 1948 Albania became a People's Socialist Republic, ruled over by Hoxha's Albanian Workers Party (AWP). Hoxha shut the gate and the free world lost sight of Albania for almost half a century.

Behind closed doors, Hoxha settled down to construct a modern, socialist state. This was no easy matter. In 1945 he inherited Zog's Albania: tribal and feudal, the size of Wales, with a population of about 3 million. Much of it mountainous and wild, with little experience of government and a concept of community that spread as far as the outskirts of the village or the hills on the horizon. Down in the southern plains, malaria lingered in pockets along the coast. Most of his people were illiterate. There were few roads. Mules were ridden, harvests were reaped, fish were caught, religious festivals were celebrated with dancing and music. Albania was a long way away from steam hammers and a space programme.

Nonetheless, Hoxha set about pummelling Albania towards his version of progress. By 1950 he had exterminated all opposition within the AWP and broken with his old friend Tito, who wanted to absorb Albania into the Yugoslav Federation. Instead Hoxha moved Albania alongside Stalin, who was willing to finance two Soviet-style Five Year Plans, developing hydroelectric power schemes, kick-starting the engineering industry, collectivising agriculture, organising the mining industry and expanding education. So the economy grew and the population was drilled into action.

Hoxha declared Albania an atheist state. Beards, a badge of muslim faith, were banned. Attempts were made to bring Albania's peripheries – especially the stubborn northern clansmen – to heel. Young people were marshalled into conscript regiments wearing hand-me-down uniforms. They spent much of their unisex training, under canvas or each other. They had little else to do and not much to look forward to. Back at school, they were taught to cherish Enver, who had made Albania the greatest country on earth.

Everywhere Hoxha's face looked down upon his people and his party, the AWP, lay at the centre of political, economic and social activity. The Sigurimi, Hoxha's ruthless secret police, began to patrol the lives of his people. Even dreams, it is said, were not safe. Albania became a kind of open prison, its sealed borders patrolled by armed men with bayonets. Naval launches and searchlights patrolled Saranda's waterfront looking for swimmers drawn by the tantalising lights of Corfu. Hoxha would shoot those who were captured, or put them down mines in the frozen north along with political dissidents and errant members of the Party. 'Dissident villages' were established, where life was made deliberately hard.

Aided by Soviet know-how, Albania underwent impressive socio-economic change during the fifties. It became more urban. Its industry diversified. There were tractors, radios, copper wire, fertilisers, even televisions, though none of them were terribly good. And its schooling improved. Illiteracy began to disappear. But by 1960 Hoxha's ideological differences with Kruschev (Stalin died in 1953) had transformed Moscow into an enemy – 'At this time when the whole country was engaged in the work to accomplish the work of the economic plans...' explains the AGO '...the Soviet revisionists came out openly with their hostile activity intended to keep Albania simply a source of raw materials for the Russian metropolis. In order to make Albania submit to their will they organised the twofold imperialist-revisionist blockade and encirclement'. So Albania split angrily with Moscow and, without its aid, the economy soon stalled. The stagnation, poverty, boring food, queues and blunt razors that constituted Albanian life from then onwards was blamed by Hoxha on 'imperialist blockade and encirclement'. Imperialist blockade and encirclement never really went away.

Albania was once more alone. Until, that is, the Chinese came along during the seventies, after Albanian chrome and a toehold in Europe. They provided more cash and expertise and persuaded Hoxha to terrace Albania's hillsides. But before long the Chinese turned out to be hostile revisionists too and in 1976 Hoxha sent them packing. Albania, built by Stalinists, betrayed by revisionists, encircled by imperialists, pilloried by the west, was on its own again.

By the beginning of the eighties, with modernisation onhold, the communist dream became farce and Hoxha's propaganda ludicrous. The tiny political elite, now old and crusty, pampered itself with cars and villas on the Albanian riviera, recycled tired myths about the Party and its socialist victories and turned out the honour guard for Hoxha, whose health was now failing. Meanwhile the people atrophied in poor, oppressed communities.

Hoxha's death in 1985 was the beginning of the end for the communist one-party state. His appointed successor, Ramiz Alia, was weak enough to make tentative reforms and for the first time the regime began to show its age. Dissenting sections of the population, especially intellectuals and young people, whose communist training had been muddied by the enticing messages of Italian television, the BBC's Albanian service and western music and writing, began to press for more reform.

It was the anti-communist upheavals, which began to sweep across eastern Europe in 1989, that triggered outright rebellion. The AWP had lost its mandate to govern. Now it began to lose the will. Against a backdrop of general strikes, widespread vandalism and mass emigration, the economy went into free fall, leaving the country dependent upon food aid from Italy. In the face of this sustained protest the communists were forced to hold elections and in April 1992 they were all but wiped out. A handsome cardiologist and leader of the recently formed Democratic Party (DP) was elected President and a former archaeologist became Prime Minister. Thousands celebrated in Skanderberg Square, where Hoxha's gilded statue lay clumsily in a corner, his face obliterated, his body spattered with paint. Not far away, in one of the grey government buildings, the new DP government was announcing plans to privatise, to join NATO and to send Mr Alia and his prime minister to prison.

APPENDIX II

TRIBES AND CUSTOMS - A CRUDE ANTHOLOGY

Albania is divided by the Shkumbini River, which rises in Lake Ohrid on the Macedonian border and runs in a wavy horizontal line across Albania and into the sea above Fier. Below the Shkumbini live the Tosqs, above it live the Ghegs. The Ghegs are mountain men, known for their hardship, their inflexible will and their strong sense of personal and clan honour. It was the Ghegs that Edith Durham, a doughty, early twentieth century explorer of Albania, loved best. The President is a Gheg from Tropoja, one of the poorest northern districts. Many of the key posts in his administration, especially those connected with security (the chief of ShIK for example) have gone to fellow Tropoja Ghegs.

Poor pastoralists and keen blood feuders, it is the Ghegs who cherish the *Kanun* (or law) of *Lek Dukagjini*. The *Kanun* is a complex etiquette employed by tribal elders since Ottoman times to regulate the behaviour of prickly communities. Revenge and killing are inherent to northern Albanian culture. The *Kanun* codifies these murders and counter murders into good and bad, legal and illegal. It also makes available an antidote to the revenge cycle – the sworn truce or *besa*. By obeying the *Kanun*, Albanian men ensure that they protect the honour of themselves, their womenfolk and their clan or *fis*.

Hoxha tried to abolish the practice but his grip on the minds of Albania's isolated mountain communities was weak. Revenge cycles have continued among small, isolated villages for generations, as score settled score settled score. Since 1991 revenge killings have been on the increase and not just in northern districts like Tropoja, Kukes and Puka. In February 1992 a man was beheaded with an axe in the lobby of the Dajti. The culprit was the son of a man the victim had murdered in a Puka village over twenty years before. In 1994 a blood feud reconciliation agency was established in Shkodra in an attempt to monitor and deter feuding. But it has yet to make much of an impact – anthropologists estimate that there are currently around 2000 blood feuds in progress involving up to 60,000 people.

If the Ghegs are a granite people, the Tosqs belong to the limestone. The Tosq is more of a plainsman, more cosmopolitan, easy going and sociable. The Tosqs are also more numerous that the Ghegs. But I have less to say about them. If I liken them to the English, and the Ghegs to the Scots, it is only to illustrate the fact that the Ghegs are a proud northern minority, with general characteristics that are perhaps more immediately striking than those of their southern cousins. The Tosqs are a more Mediterranean people. They fish and they sow, quite a few live in cities, they are mainly Muslim. Those that aren't Muslim are orthodox Christians. Hoxha was a Tosq as were most of the communist nomenclature.

Other Titles from TravellersEye

Desert Governess

Author: Phyllis Ellis
Editor: Gordon Medcalf

ISBN: 1903070015
R.R.P: £7.99

In 1997 badly in need of a new start in life, Phyllis answered an advertisement: *English Governess wanted for Prince and Princesses of Saudi Arabian Royal Family.* She soon found herself whisked off to the desert to look after the children of HRH Prince Muqrin bin Abdul Aziz al Saud, the King's brother. In this frank personal memoir Phyllis describes her sometimes risky reactions to her secluded, alien lifestyle in a heavily guarded marble palace, allowed out only when chaperoned, veiled and clad from head to foot in black.

Both as a Governess and as a modern western woman she constantly ran up against frustrating prohibitions and unexpected moral codes, only a few of which she could work her way around – usually in the interests of her young royal charges.

Discovery Road

Authors: Tim Garratt & Andy Brown
Editor: Dan Hiscocks

ISBN: 0953057534
R.R.P: £7.99

Their mission and dream was to cycle around the southern hemisphere of the planet, with just two conditions. Firstly the journey must be completed within 12 months, and secondly, the cycling duo would have no support team or backup vehicle, just their determination, friendship and pedal power.

"Readers will surely find themselves reassessing their lives and be inspired to reach out and follow their own dreams."

Sir Ranulph Fiennes, Explorer

Fever Trees of Borneo

Author: Mark Eveleigh   ISBN: 095357569
Editor: Gordon Medcalf   R.R.P: £7.99

This is the story of how two Englishmen crossed the remotest heights of central Borneo, using trails no western eye had seen before, in search of the legendary 'Wild Men of Borneo'. On the way they encounter shipwreck, malaria, amoebic dysentery, near starvation, leeches, exhaustion, enforced alcohol abuse and barbecued mouse-deer foetus.

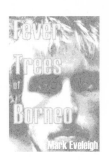

"Mark has the kind of itchy feet which will take more than a bucket of Johnson's baby talc to cure...he has not only stared death in the face, he has poked him in the ribs and insulted his mother."   Observer

Frigid Women

Authors: Sue & Victoria Riches   ISBN: 0953057526
Editor: Gordon Medcalf   R.R.P: £7.99

In 1997 a group of twenty women set out to become the world's first all female expedition to the North Pole. Mother and daughter, Sue and Victoria Riches were amongst them. Follow the expedition's adventures in this true life epic of their struggle to reach one of Earth's most inhospitable places, suffering both physical and mental hardships in order to reach their goal, to make their dream come true.

"This story is a fantastic celebration of adventure, friendship, courage and love. Enjoy it all you would be adventurers and dream on."   Dawn French

Riding with Ghosts

Author: Gwen Maka   ISBN: 1903070007
Editor: Gordon Medcalf   R.R.P: £7.99

This is the frank, often outrageous account of a forty-something Englishwoman's epic 4,000 mile cycle ride from Seattle to Mexico, via the snow covered Rocky Mountains. She travels the length and breadth of the American West, mostly alone and camping in the wild. She runs appalling risks and copes in a gutsy, hilarious way with exhaustion, climatic extremes, dangerous animals, eccentrics, lechers and a permanently saddle-sore bum. We share too her deep involvement with the West's pioneering past, and with the strong, often tragic traces history has left lingering on the land.

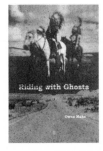

Tea for Two...with no cups

Author: Polly Benge
Editor: Dan Hiscocks

ISBN: 0953057593
R.R.P: £7.99

Four months before her 30th birthday Polly finds herself in
a quandary. Fed up with dancing a swan or woodland
nymph every night, failing to impress Barry Manilow with
her singing abilities and falling in love with a New
Zealander with a rapidly expiring visa she needs to come
up with some answers quickly. She decides the only way
to do this is by embarking on a 'love test'. With a yet
uncalloused bottom she joins Tim and Lee on a bicycle
ride from Kathmandu to Assam in the hope of finding some
answers.

The Jungle Beat – fighting terrorists in Malaya

Author: Roy Follows
Editor: Dan Hiscocks

ISBN: 0953057577
R.R.P: £7.99

This book describes, in his own words, the experiences of
a British officer in the Malayan Police during the extended
Emergency of the 1950's. It is the story of a ruthless battle
for survival against an environment and an enemy which
were equally deadly. It ranks with the toughest and
grimmest of the latter-day SAS adventures.

*" It tells the story with no holds barred: war as war is. A
compelling reminder of deep jungle operations."*
                              General Sir Peter de la Billière

Touching Tibet

Author: Niema Ash
Editor: Dan Hiscocks

ISBN: 0953057550
R.R.P: £7.99

After the Chinese invasion of 1950, Tibet remained closed
to travellers until 1984. When the borders were briefly re-
opened, Niema Ash was one of the few people fortunate
enough to visit the country before the Chinese re-imposed
their restrictions in 1987. *Touching Tibet* is a vivid,
compassionate, poignant but often amusing account of a
little known ancient civilisation and a unique and
threatened culture.

*"Excellent - Niema Ash really understands the situation
facing Tibet and conveys it with remarkable perception."*
                    Tenzin Choegyal (brother of The Dalai Lama)

Heaven & Hell

An eclectic collection of anecdotal travel stories – the best from thousands of competition entries.

"...an inspirational experience. I couldn't wait to leave the country and encounter the next inevitable disaster."
The Independent

Travellers' Tales from Heaven & Hell

Author: Various
Editor: Dan Hiscocks
ISBN: 0953057518
R.R.P: £6.99

More Travellers' Tales from Heaven & Hell

Author: Various
Editor: Dan Hiscocks
ISBN: 1903070023
R.R.P: £6.99

A Trail of Visions

Guide books tell you where to go, what to do and how to do it. A Trail of Visions shows and tells you how it feels.

"A Trail of Visions tells with clarity what it is like to follow a trail, both the places you see and the people you meet." Independent on Sunday

Route 1: India, Sri Lanka, Thailand, Sumatra

Photographer/Author: Vicki Couchman
Editor: Dan Hiscocks
ISBN: 1871349338
R.R.P: £14.99

Route 2: Peru, Bolivia, Ecuador, Columbia

Photographer/Author: Vicki Couchman
Editor: Dan Hiscocks
ISBN: 093505750X
R.R.P: £16.99

What is TravellersEye?

TravellersEye was set up in August 1996 by Dan Hiscocks. His vision was to publish books which showed that great things can be achieved by ordinary people.

Dan lived, worked and travelled in over forty different countries in his early twenties. During this time he met many people who had achieved things against the odds, and with little recognition.

He saw that the value of the achievements was not only for the achiever, but the receiver (in this case himself) as they motivated and inspired him to have belief and desire to stretch himself in order to achieve. As he says: "Don't ever let anyone tell you the world is small ... it is absolutely huge and out there for the taking. The world has never had more opportunities and been more exciting. We no longer need fantasy for dreams, we can achieve this aspiration with reality – we just need to push ourselves as individuals to our own limits."

TravellersEye has a list of books which show that 'ordinary people can achieve extraordinary things'.

TravellersEye Club Membership

We receive hundreds of enquiries from people who've read our books or entered our competitions. All of these people have one thing in common: an aching to achieve something extraordinary, outside the bounds of our everyday lives. Not everyone can undertake the more extreme challenges, but we all value learning about other people's experiences.

Membership is free because we want to unite people of similar interests. Via our website, members will be able to liase with each other about everything from the kit they've taken, to the places they've been to and the things they've done. As well as regularly up-dating members with news about our forthcoming titles, we will also offer you the following benefits: Free entry to author talks / signings, direct author correspondence, discounts off new and past titles, free entry to TravellersEye events, discounts on a variety of travel products and services.

To register your membership, simply write/email us telling us your name and address (postal and email). See address at the front of this book.